UNTIL THE WH[...]

"Life and Times in a 70's California Motorcycle Club"

By

Robert Clay Norman

Published by Brighton Publishing LLC

501 W. Ray Road,

Suite 4

Chandler, AZ 85225

UNTIL THE WHEELS FALL OFF

"Life and Times in a 70's California Motorcycle Club"

By

Robert Clay Norman

Published by Brighton Publishing LLC

501 W. Ray Road,

Suite 4

Chandler, AZ 85225

Printed in the United States of America

First Edition

Copyright © 2011

ISBN 13: 978-1-936587-27-8

ISBN 10: 1-936587-27-0

Cover Design by Tom Rodriguez

UNTIL THE WHEELS FALL OFF

"Life and Times in a 70's California Motorcycle Club"

ᘓᕀ *Author's Note* ᕀᘒ

This narrative occurs in the 1970's. It is the story of a motorcycle club in Northern California, told from the viewpoint of one member. This is a look into the counterculture of street choppers and what it was like for a small group of young men to exist in that time and place.

It is not a cops and criminals caper. There are no gang wars, drive-by shootings, meth labs, drug deals, or undercover narcs and snitches. This is the story of young people, trying their best to grow up and become a part of the world of bikes and brotherhood.

To protect current identities, the names of many individuals have been changed for this story. However, there are no "composite" characters in this book. Each person in this narrative is real.

Until The Wheels Fall Off

❧ *Chapter One* ❧

"Spark"

The Harley Davidson chopper motored smoothly into the nearly empty parking lot. The lunch rush was over, and the middle-aged ladies who worked part-time from eleven to one had clocked out. That meant I had to help cover the counter, if needed . . . bad duty. However, that didn't happen much, since we had the least sales of any McDonald's in the San Jose area, so the regular front window guys would usually be enough until late afternoon. There were no drive-thru windows in 1970, so everybody had to walk up to the counter.

This spring day had been quiet so far. That is until the Harley drove in. Sometimes a fight or two—occasionally even a minor car crash—would punctuate the lunch rush. We had the fights because our store was about halfway between two San Jose high schools that were bitter rivals: Willow Glen and Pioneer. Willow Glen had the earlier lunch, and a lot of the guys who had cars would show up to profile and attract the dollies . . . the usual stuff. Then, the Pioneer crowd would hit just after they left and repeat the process. The kids from both schools were okay; in fact, a number of them worked at the store.

Sometimes the testosterone and the strutting would combine to set something off between the two groups. I only remember one real free for all. That was pretty cool. Of course, none of the employees got in the middle of it . . . we were only spectators. Our store manager called the cops, though. Bad for business, you know.

Generally, the mid-afternoon was my time to solo on the grill. During the lunch rush, I was the Number 2 man, cooking the buns and dressing the burgers with condiments. However, after the noontime crush was over (with a mix of business people and high school kids) the Number 1 grill man, Roy Givens the assistant manager, did paperwork, hung out, and smoked, so I got the grill to myself. It was a chance to improve my speed and clean up the total mess he made during the rush. Givens was fast—he and Marc Boyd were the fastest we had—they were always bragging how each was faster than the other was, as if anyone cared. Nevertheless, Givens was somewhat sloppy—although not as bad as Boyd, who was terrible. This, of course, drove the manager, Gary Carlisle, crazy. Gary was clean cut, trimmed out and ship-shape all the time, and wanted his unit (that's what the management and owner types called the restaurant—a unit) the same way.

Anyway, the slow afternoon was my time to be the only grill man. At McDonald's' "units" in the 1970's, being the grill man was the top. I'd been at it for a month or so, having moved up from fry man. That's what I was hired on as the previous September—a seventeen-year-old fry man. I wasn't complaining though. I got a forty-hour a week job (I guess Carlisle liked my demeanor during the job interview) in an environment where most people were part-time employees. I could use the cash, all $1.60 an hour of it, minus ten cents an hour for the food I ate, of course. Hey, no problem, I figured. We all ate just before we went on shift, then again on break, and once more after clocking out. All the guys got their ten cents worth each day and every hour. Of course, I had to go and get a salad occasionally . . . just to counter the entire fast food intake.

See, in those days there were no salads at Mickey D's. Also, there were no sundaes, McRibs, chicken sandwiches, or any of the other menu stuff Ronald and friends have added in the ensuing four decades. They just had burgers, Big Macs, and those awful fish fillets with the crappy tartar sauce on the menu. Hell, no breakfasts either. We would have loved munching those egg biscuits for a dime. It didn't matter how limited our menu was, there was always some Gomer coming in and asking for something that no McDonald's had *ever* offered; hot dogs, chili, fried chicken . . . stupid shit all the time, man. The most memorable time for me was when I worked a shift with the night manager, Jeremy Garcia. Once in a while, if some lame-ass called in sick, the manager, Gary Carlisle—we called him Carpile behind his back (me too, even though I liked him . . . hey, we were teenagers . . . of course we had a nickname for the boss). Besides, it was his second in command, Givens, who gave him that handle, not any of us. Anyhow, Carpile would put one of us on night shift to help out if they were short. We were such a slow store that, after the dinner rush, there would only be three guys working, including Garcia. Jeremy was without a doubt the laziest worker on the whole crew, with the possible exception of his buddy, Dean Sanchez, who usually worked with him. Naturally, this meant, whichever unlucky stiff was assigned as the third man would end up doing all the work. Sanchez was such a screw-off that sometimes he would take off his shirt and be bare-chested during work hours, with just his grill apron half covering his torso. He and Garcia thought that was quite funny . . . and actually, it was.

One night, a woman came in and asked Garcia if we had any doughnuts. Jeremy looked at her sympathetically and said somberly, "Only on Thursdays, ma'am." I'm sure she came back on Thursday and pitched a fit when Carpile had to give her the bad news.

Now, I was on my own grill during the slow afternoon, looking forward to end of shift. 4:30 was it for my day. I started at 8:00 a.m., doing set-up. That's when you do all the BS to get the grill and other equipment ready for the 11:00 opening. Assemble the milk shake machine, get the food ready, prep the grill surface, and get the puke fish fillets ready. (Who went to McD's to order fish, anyway)? Grill sure beat being the fry man. As fry man, you had to haul up 100-pound sacks of potatoes from the basement. At least four or five sacks each morning. In those days, McDonald's french fries were homemade, not frozen. Each day, hundreds of pounds of potatoes were peeled, washed, rinsed, blanched, racked, cooked, salted, and bagged.

The good news was that, after a time, I was able to make a damn good-tasting french fry. Just ask my family, I make terrific homemade waffle cut fries to this day. The secret is the wash. Cut the fries, and then agitate them in a bowl of cold water. Drain. Repeat until they are firm and will snap apart in your hand. Then dry the fries before you pop them in the fryer. Liberal use of salt and chili powder helps even more.

The bad news was, I had to lift 100-pound sacks of potatoes (usually with a few rotten ones on the bottom) when I barely outweighed them. Did I mention that I was skinny? I was so skinny, that when I hired on at Mac's, I weighed about 110 pounds. So me and the spuds had a fine tussle four or five times every morning; as I tried hauling that 100-pounder up the metal stairs from the basement. That was the first part of the job that Givens trained me on that first day—hauling the bloated burlaps up the stairs. Then I had to peel the sons-of-bitches.

Speaking of potato hauling, the number one guy from our crew in that regard was Martin Gerdwagen. Martin was an ox, built like a beer truck—not overly tall, but solid. One afternoon, he decided to cut his trips up the stairs by half. Martin loaded a 100-pound sack of taters on each shoulder and somehow squeezed his fire hydrant frame and the two burlaps up the narrow staircase. Givens, the assistant manager, couldn't let that slide, and tried to carry two sacks up at once also. He made it, too. A couple of other guys had to prove themselves also. I loved it of course. With the burly boys trying to out macho each other, by the end of the day, there were so many taters stacked up by the peeler that I had my next morning's quota already covered.

That was all behind me, though, since I made it to the grill. Yep, the slow afternoon with the bit of independence that accompanied it was my *second* favorite part of the day. The *most* favorite part was doing the store set up. Because then I got to work with Miles. Miles Van Meter was the store's maintenance man. In at six . . . out at eleven. Miles was a couple of years older than I was, but way ahead of me on grow-up. Plus, he was the acknowledged coolest guy on the crew. Miles was a drummer in a local rock band. Not just a garage band, they got real gigs as an opening act for name bands that would appear in the area. They covered a lot of songs by *The Who, Cream,* and *Nazz*, plus some original tunes. Miles's hero was . . . Keith Moon, of course. Double bass drum and all . . . just like Keith. Miles had long hair, the only longhaired worker at any McDonald's there was at the time. Maybe *ever*, I don't know. The owner was always trying to get Carpile to make Miles cut his hair, or just to get rid of him altogether, but Carpile liked him, and he did a damn fine job of getting the outside of the store in shape. Gary always made sure that Miles and his long hair, however, were off the premises when the doors officially opened. Miles and I got along great; but I was just a kid, and couldn't party with him and keep up. I remember more than a few mornings when Miles looked like shit and was hung-over as hell from partying and playing the night before, but he would be out in the cold using a squeegee on the windows when I got in to work at eight . . . with a joint dangling from his mouth.

Within a year, Miles left and went to work as a stage hand at the San Francisco Opera House, which paid real well because it was a union job. I don't know if he kept his music going or not. Later on, I did get his old job, for a time anyway; although I didn't continue his weed-on-the-job tradition. Not my style and I never liked that stuff anyway.

On this day, when that chopper pulled into the lot, however, it led to a change in my world. Back in those days there was a full glass front to McDonald's stores. You could easily see all the vehicles drive in. This was especially true in our case, since it was our slow time. I watched the bike pull in to a close-in parking space, and the rider dismount. He was tall, slender, and dark-haired. He moved with a casual purpose about his gait. He had leather pants with silver Conchos on the outside edge of each leg spaced from knee to ankle. I looked closer at the bike. A real Harley chopper, shiny with chrome . . . I hadn't actually seen a real chopper before. I mean live, not like in those grade B biker movies of the day.

4

The guy came in to the empty lobby and ordered only a Coke. To drink it, he went outside and sat on one of the tables. Yes, he sat *on* the table, not on the bench *at* the table. Even *more cool*. When he turned to leave the lobby was when I'd seen it. In bold red letters across his back . . . HELLS ANGELS CALIFORNIA. My first thought was "You mean to tell me that *Hells Angels* hang out at McDonald's?" No matter, though. I had seen my first real *Angel* . . . not a big, ugly, biker *looking* dude, mind you. Not a wannabe who people *thought* was a biker, but who had never actually *owned* a motorcycle. No, he was a real, in the flesh, verifiable, *genuine Hells Angel.*

At that moment, the seed had been planted, and the spark was lit. I wanted to become a biker. Not a *Hells Angel* naturally . . . I knew they didn't take in guys who were 110-pound rotten-tater-toters . . . but a biker, nonetheless. A real, longhaired, it's time to hide your daughters, who-does-he-think-he-is, *Biker*. I didn't know the first thing about becoming a biker, of course. In fact, I barely knew anything about *anything* at that point . . . (except french fries). I just knew that I wanted to be one. Hey, so did a lot of people, I supposed.

I'm not saying I set my mind to it and pursued that goal with a single-minded purpose from that day forward. A lot of stuff would happen, good and bad, before I got myself focused. I had a powerful lot to learn and quite a bit of grow-up to get through.

But three and a half years later, I was in a motorcycle club, riding a chopped Harley, and spending a little time with the San Jose *Hells Angels.*

Oh, and I never did find out who the *Angel* with the Conchos was that day.

5

ᴄ✐ *Chapter Two* ✑ᴅ
"Backstory"

M y parents met in downtown St. Louis in 1949. They were living at a boarding house, as many young people did in those days, having moved to a big city for the job opportunities there. My dad had been at the boarding house for a few months, along with a buddy of his, Charlie Swift. My mom showed up in late summer, paired with one of her friends, Julie Lakin.

My father, Bob Norman, was a World War II veteran. He was 33 years old and worked as a shoe-cutter. Bob was the sixth of eight children, born in western Kentucky. He was raised in a small town in southeast Missouri. A wide age gap existed among the eight kids. My dad was an uncle at age two, his oldest sister having been born in the 1890's. She had six kids of her own. Consequently, I had many cousins who were the ages of typical aunts and uncles. That is pretty much how my siblings and I looked upon them, too.

Dad's parents, who were both deceased by the time he met my mom, were pretty much the typical poor white, subsistence farmer type, from what I have learned. By the way, all this info comes from either my mom, or my dad's brother Paul and his wife Beulah, who were kind of the family historians, or my cousin Janice, who seems to know everyone in the family. Dad rarely mentioned anything about his past. I guess his wasn't a pleasant childhood. Dad was born with one eye closed. I think he had some surgery as a youngster, and it somewhat improved, but from what I've heard, he was teased often and spent a lot of time alone. He was also quite skinny, which didn't help.

When I was about eleven, I asked Dad about his childhood . . . who his friends were, that sort of thing. All he said was that he had a friend named Ed, but he and his family drowned when their car rolled off a ferryboat during a river crossing. *Oo-kay fine . . . nice talking with you,* I thought. I do know that he started smoking and drinking at age fifteen, not *that* unusual for poor country boys growing up during the Great Depression. Dad quit school after ninth grade and started working in local shoe factories, in the Charleston, Missouri area. By the time he hit his twenties he had grown to six feet and had filled out pretty well. Bob and his brothers, Sam and Allen, got quite a reputation as hell-raisers and brawlers during this time. They would fight other sets of brothers, or a

6

group of black guys, or other white country boys from the next county—that sort of thing.

When World War II came along, Bob, Allen, and younger brother, Maurice each joined the service. All three served in the European Theatre, and each survived the War. Maurice was the youngest of the three and was quite short. He became a ball-turret gunner in a B-17 Flying Fortress. I think of Maurice whenever I see a World War II movie with the heavy bombers. Allen was in an artillery battery. He received a battlefield promotion to lieutenant while fighting in France, so somebody must have thought he performed pretty well. My dad was in the motor pool of a medical unit. He served all his time in England and never saw any fighting.

Dad's military career was a kind of up and down affair. He told me how he benefited from his time in the Army, and indicated that he liked being a soldier. Information I received from others didn't quite confirm that outlook, however. My Aunt Beulah saved wartime mail that she received from all the brothers, and once showed them to me. These were called "Victory Mail." They were cool little letters from service men that were sent to the home front by the millions. The ones that Bob sent to Paul and Beulah were constantly complaining about Army life, and how he couldn't wait to be discharged. Added to that was my mom's story, told to her from my dad years before, about how he had been busted from staff sergeant back down to private. It seems that, while he was attending a dance in England, my dad took exception to a black man dancing with a white English woman. Bob was demoted for knocking the guy down. Mom said Dad never would admit he was wrong in this incident because, in the time and place in which he was raised, races never mixed. I was never told directly, but I'm sure alcohol was involved. At any rate, Bob made it back to buck sergeant by war's end.

A positive occurrence during the war was that the U.S. Army performed another eye operation on Dad, improving his droopy lid to where it was nearly back to normal. Another plus for the family was that Dad picked up a lot of medical knowledge. He was adept at fixing the cuts, sprains, and bruises that all of us kids would get.

What seemed to resonate with my dad and his siblings was the one story about how their father died. I heard a little about this when I was young, but I got the full story only after I was fully-grown. My Uncle Paul told it to me. He would know, being as he was there.

One day in 1936, Paul was driving a truck to his home in the little town of Diehlstadt in southeastern Missouri. Paul ran a small

7

trucking company in the area. I guess Paul was about twenty-five, and was married to Aunt Beulah. Their house was kind of like a hangout for the brothers who were still living at their parents' house a few blocks away. As Paul was heading home, he noticed his dad walking along the road. Paul gave him a lift and, Granddad stood on the running board ready to jump off as they neared the house. Paul warned him to wait until the truck came to a complete stop. Granddad hopped off the running board as the truck was rolling at two or three miles an hour. Somehow, he tripped, fell, and the back tires ran over him. End of Granddad . . . right in his own yard. When Paul told me the story, nearly fifty years later, he still seemed affected by the event.

In an ironic twist, Granddad's only brother, named John Norman, had been killed almost *exactly* ten years earlier, in 1926, when he had been run over by a city-owned truck in Detroit. Like many people in those days, John carried no identification. He ended up in the city morgue as a John Doe, about to be buried in an unmarked grave. By chance, some local government workers from back home in Missouri were visiting Detroit in an official capacity. While touring the morgue, someone in the coroner's office remarked on the large volume of John Does that the city had every year. As an example, he turned the sheet back from one of the bodies, and the Missouri people all said, "That's John Norman!"

I don't know much about the post-war years for my dad, except that the biggest event in his family was his mother's death in 1948. All of my aunts and uncles would always talk in reverential tones about their mother. She must have been truly special. My dad was at her bedside when she passed, and all the relatives would say that Bob always was her favorite. In fact, my dad was the role model in his family to all of his seven brothers and sisters. Even as kids, we could see that. All of the aunts, uncles, and cousins would always defer to Bob and seek his approval. I'm not sure why that was the case; but, there it was.

Bob wasn't the oldest. He wasn't the wealthiest. (Later in life, my Uncle Maurice would become wealthy. He owned many businesses, including the largest dealership of Barbie Doll collectibles in the world— called Diamonds and Dolls). He wasn't the best educated. However, he did seem to have personal integrity and character traits that were admired by all of the extended family.

Dad always dressed well. I don't mean fancy or flashy, just well dressed. He never wore old T-shirts, never owned sneakers, and almost never wore shorts. His clothes were always crisply ironed. I have a photo of Dad with his Army platoon in World War II. He is by far the sharpest looking GI there. When Dad wore casual shirts, they were always fully buttoned. When he wore dress shirts, he would sometimes sport cufflinks. He didn't wear three-piece suits, but always had a sport coat and tie. In addition, his shoes were shined to the max, of course. Dad even had his trousers (he always referred to pants as trousers) modified. Near a belt loop at his hip, he added a little place to hold toothpicks. Dental care was a big deal to Dad, and he was always cleaning his teeth. The only facet of Bob's appearance that was out of place with his zeal for neatness was his smoking. Dad smoked *all* the time. First, he smoked Camels and then later on Winstons. At least *those* were filtered. Smoking wasn't so bad (especially back in the 50's and 60's, when it was more common than it is today). The problem was Dad would never pay attention to his cigarette ash. There would always be about an inch of ash dangling from the end of the cigarette, which would then fall off and plop on the carpet or furniture. We kids would follow him around the house with ashtrays, trying to catch some of the ash before it dropped off.

My mom, Anne Buchanan, was born in San Jose, Calif. She had a decidedly different childhood than my dad. Her father was a stockbroker in downtown San Jose, and the family was financially well off. My grandfather got a new Buick every few years, owned a vacation cabin in the Santa Cruz Mountains, and just before World War II, bought a hilltop home on five acres in Los Gatos, an upscale suburb of San Jose. The next-door neighbor was Admiral Charles Lockwood, who was in charge of the Pacific Fleet submarines during the War, and a famous author, too. It was not a bad lifestyle for a one-income family during the Depression. My grandmother never worked and never learned to drive a car. All she had to do was raise my mom and my Aunt Helene. They even had a housekeeper, a Japanese woman named Elise Fuchida. Unfortunately, Elise and her family were interned in the Tule Lake "camp" by Federal authorities for the War years, along with most of the other Japanese living on the West Coast.

Mom's family would go on vacations, picnics, concerts, and the like. They also had two or three horses to ride, which were stabled on their property. Both of my mom's grandmothers lived fairly close, so there would be train trips over the mountains to Santa Cruz, the beach resort town in Northern California, to see them. Mom had a car of her own to drive to high school, a rarity back then. She didn't even live in the family home but in her own little caretaker's house on the property. Mom got out of high school in 1945, just as the War was ending. She worked in a few local businesses for a couple of years, and then spent a little time in the Sandia facility for atomic research in New Mexico before heading off to St. Louis with her friend Julie, who also came from a wealthy family.

Unlike my dad's folks, I did get to know my maternal grandparents a bit. Of course, by the time I met them they were around sixty, so I only knew them as old and gray. Some people seem to quickly age to a certain point and then just stay there. That's how my grandparents were. My grandmother lived until age eighty-five. To me, however, she always looked the same as when I first saw her nearly thirty years before . . . old. She didn't look ancient or decrepit—just old and gray.

My grandmother was born Pauline Granger in Ventura, in Southern California. The house still stands and is registered as some sort of historical landmark. My mom is active in family trees and the Grangers date back to 1654 in Massachusetts. The oldest known ancestor is Launcelot Granger. (You just don't hear of kids being named Launcelot any more). Another Granger ancestor from Connecticut, Thaddeus, fought in the American Army during the Revolution, so I guess Pauline could have joined the Daughters of the American Revolution, but I don't know if she did. Some of the Grangers moved west, along with many Americans. In 1846, Lewis Cass Granger took his family and joined a small wagon train heading to California. Upon reaching present-day Nevada, unsure how to proceed since there was no trail, the party split into two groups. Granger's group safely reached Southern California, near San Fernando, but the other party stumbled into Death Valley, the name of that place being earned by the terrible experiences of this wagon train.

Pauline was a highly dignified and austere person, at least as far as the grandkids thought. There was no hugging or touching with Grandmother, which was fine by me. When we were little kids and would go to Grandmother's house, our parents would stress to us not to roughhouse around and break anything. That seemed to be the main thing about my grandparents—don't break any of their stuff. My mom has always told me that Pauline didn't like her much and that she favored Mom's sister Helene instead. I suppose that is true. Helene and Grandmother seemed to be tight . . . Anne and Grandmother, well, not as much. In regard to the grandkids, my cousin Alison was clearly

Grandmother's favorite; but, that was to be expected. Helene's family lived near Pauline, and we didn't. Plus, Alison was the only granddaughter on that side. (Helene had four kids too . . . just like my mom). Ali was, and still is, a cute redhead. She is cool and funny to boot. I reckon my sisters never much liked the favoritism shown by Grandmother though. Then again, every family has this situation I suppose. As for me, Pauline was okay. Not knowing any different, I figured that's how Grandmas were—aloof and proper. Later, when I was going to junior college, I found out that Pauline was sending money to all the grandkids that were attending college. Well . . . all but one, I guess. Hey, maybe she just didn't like me. After I was grown, I found out that Pauline bought Kessler whiskey by the case, so maybe she wasn't always quite so prim and proper. Regardless, I always thought well of my grandmother.

I didn't know my grandfather for long. He died when I was about fourteen. His name was Herbert, but only Grandmother called him that. To everyone else he was Buck, like most guys with the last name of Buchanan. Mom adored him, and he seemed smart and funny. Buck was a Doughboy in World War I. I saw his helmet and blanket once in his old Army trunk, but I have no idea what happened to his old military stuff after Grandmother died. Buck grew up near Fresno, I think. As a youth, he was a telegrapher for the railroad. After the Great War, Buck became a stockbroker and, like I said, did well financially. He also partnered in some small businesses around the area. He seemed to have a knack for making money. Buck would invest in large corporations like ATT and Standard Oil (now Chevron). He was able to retire early and leave his widow a sizeable estate.

One mistake Buck did make, however, was that he never felt real estate was an excellent long-term investment . . . in *California*, no less. Not long after their younger daughter Helene left home, my grandparents sold their five-acre spread outside Los Gatos. Today, that particular parcel has been split and is worth millions. Buck sold all the real estate he owned and he and Pauline settled in an upscale mobile home park in Santa Cruz. It was a custom place on two lots, but it was still a mobile home. I can only imagine how wealthy he would have been had he kept the real estate investments to go along with his stock portfolio.

Buck seemed okay, but he treated his grandsons as if they were dopes. Even as I reached junior high, Granddad acted as if I was about six years old. All of us—my brother, my three cousins, and me—were born within about four years of each other. Maybe having five boys of relatively the same age horsing around his environment was upsetting to him. Or, perhaps, having no sons of his own, Buck forgot what being a boy was like. I don't know. At any rate, he always talked down to all of us, like we were morons. He was especially harsh, I thought, on my cousins. Of course, he knew them better, since they lived near Granddad for many years and my brother and I had not. They were wilder than my brother and me, so maybe there was some history there. Even so, Buck would always be giving us some curt lecture on something. All the while we would be thinking, "I got it already, Gramps. Move on, will ya?" Maybe Buck thought he was the kindergarten cop.

Mom and Dad were married after only three months of dating, which surprised and disappointed other family members on each side. My mom's folks were certainly upset that their elder daughter was marrying some southern boy whom they never met, and who was poor to boot. My dad's family was mostly Baptist, and didn't much take to the California girl who listened to classical music and traveled across the country on her own. Anne didn't even know how to cook, which was basic to the women on my dad's side. For instance, my Aunt Alvera (I *know*—Alvera—what a handle for a girl) would routinely cook up homemade chicken and dumplings without ever consulting a recipe. She was always cooking fabulous meals for loads of people at the drop of a hat. Dad taught Mom how to cook after they were married.

It still shows, too. Mom just doesn't have the culinary flair. Her method of cooking a large meal is to apply heat to food in some manner—oven or stove, set the timer, then engage in conversation until the timer goes off. Some elapsed time later, depending on the status of said conversation (it could be from two to fifteen minutes) transfer food from heat source to plates. There. Dinner is served. Now resume conversation. I didn't realize until I moved away from home that many others eschew this process model for food preparation. Thank goodness.

Bob and Anne soon settled in the San Jose area. I guess they chose there to be nearer to my mom's folks, and probably because there were more work opportunities for Dad. My older sister Embry was born in 1950, nine months and three weeks after the wedding.

(*You bet* she and I did all the requisite arithmetic once we were teenagers)! I followed a year later.

Dad got a job as Sales Manager for Chase Candy Company, which was a step up from the factory jobs he had been working in San Jose. The drawbacks were that Dad would have to travel a lot and the family had to move to Fresno. The move from San Jose didn't make the

Grandparents too happy, but that was okay because it got worse. A few months later Dad was told that Chase was going to shut down operations, and he would be out of a job. Then, Dad's brothers in Missouri—Allen and Maurice—said they wanted Dad to join them in a new business which they were about to start. The family packed up again and in late 1952 moved to Springfield, Missouri, Queen City of the Ozarks, where Dad became part owner of a cookie business. Now Buck and Pauline's daughter and grandkids were 2000 miles away. Bob soon convinced the brothers that candy was more lucrative than cookies, and shortly after we arrived, Dad's youngest brother John joined the others to form Norman's Budget Pak Candies.

Budget Pak became the all-consuming constant in our life for the next ten years. The brothers would buy candy in bulk from eastern distributors, then re-package and use their own distribution resources to put product on grocery store shelves throughout the area. After a while, the business started to grow beyond the Springfield area. In those days, in the South—and Springfield was one half south and one-half Midwest—people bought a lot of packaged candy. It was quite common to see grocery shoppers with two or three bags of candy in their shopping cart. By *bags,* I mean clear cellophane ones with about half a pound of candy in them. The modern supermarkets, big-box stores, were not yet prevalent, and most people bought foodstuffs at their locally owned neighborhood grocer. These weren't always Mom and Pop shops, but most folks knew their checkers and bag boys on a first-name basis and had allegiances to their local markets.

The brothers divided the duties among themselves, each to his area of expertise. Bob knew the candy business a little and headed up sales. Maurice, who was always scheming ways to make a buck, did the finances. Allen ran the operations at the small factory. He received the in-bulk candy and supplies, and then bagged them under the Budget Pak labels. John was a skilled carpenter, and he ran the shop where the display racks were made. These were wooden or pressboard freestanding shelves to display the bags of candy. The shelves were a significant selling point to the grocers. They only had to allocate floor space, not their own shelving, for the candy. In those days, most grocers set up a market per their individual taste, not like the cookie-cutter, mega stores you see today.

After about five or six years, Budget Pak was pretty busy. The brothers had accounts all over Missouri and into Arkansas, Kansas, and

Oklahoma, as well. This coincided nicely with me growing up, as I was beginning to understand a little of the real world, and so starting around seven years old, I tried to hang around the "plant" as the brothers called it, as much as my parents would allow.

The business was a six-day a week operation with their big day being Saturday. The trucks were loaded that day. Then they were ready to head out on the road early Monday morning. The route drivers would turn in their new order sheets on Friday. These sheets would call out for cases of candy, usually twelve bags per case, of the nearly 100 varieties of candy Budget Pak sold. Every kind of candy—Kraft Caramels, cinnamon red hots, mint pillows, lemon drops, orange peanuts, malted milk balls, candy corn, butterscotch, candy canes, peanut clusters, chicken bones, and on and on. Workers would stack up the cases by type in the warehouse and would load the trucks by the use of the old conveyor roller system. These conveyors were portable linking tracks with metal rollers that would be mounted on a stanchion-like support. They were quite heavy; at least, I thought so. The linked track was like a giant railroad set with some straight pieces and some pieces curved either right or left. The track was probably waist high for an adult. The workers would stack six or seven cases on the roller at a time and then push the stack down the line, picking up further stacks of different candy varieties on the way to the loading dock. The trick was to be able to navigate the stacks through the curves without dropping any cases. Whenever I was allowed, I would try to help with the loading. My stacks were only two or three high but sad to say, my sojourns down the conveyor tracks ended with more than a few train wrecks.

Helping to load up each of the cases was cool, but by far the coolest part was getting to climb around inside the trucks. These were box vans, mostly Fords, with perhaps sixteen-foot beds. There would be eight or ten vans to be loaded on any given Saturday, but to a little kid there seemed to be dozens of them. The paint scheme was a red cab with red on the bottom half of the box, and yellow on the top. Separating the halves was a blue band. Blue letters on the upper half spelled out Norman's Budget Pak Candies. Painted on the back doors that swung-open was the slogan "When your sweet tooth says candy, let your wisdom tooth say Budget Pak." I never knew who made that one up. The most important thing to me was to be able to clamber about the trucks. I'd play inside the box, with the built-in racks that held the cases of candy. I'd get in the cab, and pretend I was driving. I would fool around with all of the paperwork that the drivers stuffed on the dash and played with the long stick shift, which had all those gear numbers printed on the knob. These were my favorite activities. Even more, there were also a couple of local delivery trucks in the lot. These were small step-vans, kind of like mini-sized Fed Ex trucks today. They were "one-seaters" with sliding side doors and were loads of fun to play in. I don't know what the official names of these trucks were, but we all called them "Metros."

There were other exciting places to play within the candy plant. I would play on the bagging machines, which fed bulk candy through a large hopper, the top of which was accessible from an attached metal ladder and platform. There was also a cool, old soda machine. The kind that was built like a chest where you would open the heavy metal top and slide the bottles along a double metal lip to a lever-like release mechanism, then lift the bottle up and through the release. The chest was full of sodas like Orange Crush, RC Cola, Nehis, and 7-Up—all the brands that are not seen much these days. Plus, the bottle caps (no cans) had the cork underneath the top—also a thing of the past. Of course, just playing around the stacked cases of candy was fun. We would play hide and seek, and make small forts among the cardboard cases . . . the normal stuff that kids do.

However, to clear one thing up, my siblings and I weren't allowed to eat much candy. Our parents were pretty strict with our upbringing. When it came to the candy at Dad's plant, we could only eat from bags that were already opened. We would scour the plant looking for cases that had a bag sticking out that was already opened for some reason. More often, we would find open bags in the bagging area where the machines were. I guess it never occurred to us just to open a bag and claim it was already opened.

As for owning a candy factory, my parents didn't keep much of it around the house. Our sweets were pretty well rationed to us by our mom. Our big night of treats at the house was Saturday. We would watch *Gunsmoke* and *Have Gun Will Travel* on television, and Mom would make up a batch of popcorn. Each of us would get a small bowl of the popcorn, except for Dad. He liked to put his popcorn in a glass of milk. I tried it once . . . it was awful. But then, Dad liked a lot of foods that we thought were strange. One of his favorites was milk toast. This was a concoction of two poached eggs on toast, which was then placed in a large bowl. Warm milk was then poured over everything. Dad would then proceed to put about a pound of black pepper on the delicacy. I tried that too . . . awful. Dad also liked fried bologna . . . again, awful. He also liked those little Vienna sausages that came in a can. I tried that too and

. . . yeah . . . you guessed it. I guess these foods were something he was raised with, being poor and all. Kind of like the folks who ate potted meat, to which we were *never* exposed . . . thank goodness.

Along with the Saturday night popcorn, we would get to have a glass of Coca-Cola. Mom would open one large, 26-ounce bottle, and then divvy it up five ways. (Dad didn't drink the Coke—maybe it clashed with the popcorn milk). So, the four kids' big, weekly treat, was five ounces of Coke and one small bowl of popcorn. Can you see why we liked to hunt through the candy plant for open bags?

Two other avenues were available for us to receive candy treats, however. One was the homemade peanut brittle that the brothers had made in one of the back rooms of the Budget Pak candy plant. I'm not certain, but I think the man who made the brittle was named Charlie Widmer. He and his wife would cook up the mixture in a big kettle, and then spread that on a large marble slab table to cool. Then they would break up the brittle with a small hammer and bag it by hand. And . . . it was fantastic. They would always hand out some of the candy to any kids who were present. Needless to say, I endeavored to be present as often as possible.

Our parents' insurance agent provided our other infrequent candy treat. His name was Lowell Snider, and he was a tall fellow who had a moustache—which was an immense curiosity to us kids. Very few men had facial hair in Missouri, circa 1960. Whenever Lowell would visit the house, he would bring all of us candy cigarettes; packs of them—and not the little hollow ones either. There would be about ten solid candy sticks in a replica pack of Camels or Pall Malls and such. Lowell smoked about as heavily as my dad did, so the two of them got along well.

Another fun thing I liked to do was to hang around at the candy plant on Saturdays while the Norman brothers and the route drivers would chat with one another. The drivers were mostly guys in their twenties or early thirties—a younger group than my dad and his brothers. These were all good ol' southern boys, just hanging around and bullshitting on their time off. I never figured out why the drivers would be gone from home all week long, only to come back to the plant to load up on Saturday morning (without pay) and then stick around even longer just to shoot the shit with their bosses. I'll bet their wives didn't appreciate it much either.

But I loved it. There would be six to eight men, each in turn telling some tale—the taller the better. All these guys would refer to any

16

other guy who wasn't there as "that ol' boy." It didn't matter the age, race, or economic status of the person about whom they were talking. Everybody was always "that ol' boy." Also, they would always pronounce the word "no" as "new." They would draw out the *"new."* As they would all be laughing in agreement after one man's story, somebody would say, "Hell, that ol' boy didn't know what to say then . . . *neeewww,* new sir!" Then the rest of the guys would laugh and echo *"neeewww."*

Some of my favorite drivers that I can remember were two brothers named Calvin and Marion. My dad and uncles liked them a lot, too. It was unusual around 1960 for a rough and tumble truck driver with a name like Marion *not* to have a nickname, like Buddy or Butch or something. However, my *most* favorite driver was a guy named Elbert. I didn't know his last name. Elbert was a happy-go-lucky guy who had his hair slicked back, creating "wings" on the side. He looked like your typical late-fifties "hood." He always had a pack of smokes rolled in the sleeve of his white T-shirt and looked as if he were from the touring troupe of *West Side Story.* I don't know what my dad and uncles thought about Elbert, but he was the *coolest* guy to me. Now that I think of it, he was another candidate for a nickname, *Elbert* . . . jeez.

There's one more thing to mention regarding the truck drivers for Budget Pak Candies. They received a per diem for their week on the road of seven dollars per day; *seven* dollars . . . *per day.* Even in 1960 that was nothing. Dad told me my Uncle Maurice figured it out this way: one dollar for lunch, two dollars for dinner, and four dollars for a motel room. Breakfast was on your own. That was typical of Maurice. He was exceedingly reluctant to part with any money that didn't directly benefit him. I found out later that, indeed, there were four-dollar-a-night motel rooms in the region, but I don't think I would have necessarily wanted to stay in them.

Hanging around and watching my dad and uncles interact with the drivers showed me how men form bonds with one another, although I was too young at the time to have thought along those lines. I also came to realize that my dad didn't spend any time with people outside the business or who weren't from his extended family. Dad worked six days a week. He got up at five in the morning on Monday, had a cup of coffee, stopped by the plant for a short while, then hit the road to make sales. He wouldn't come home until after dark on Friday nights. Then Saturday was back at the plant, catching up on the details he missed while on sales calls all week. Mom actually raised all four of us kids. Dad was never around, except for Sundays, when he would maybe do a little yard work and barbecue.

The only thing our dad did with us was to take the family out for drives. Even though he drove all week long, Dad frequently packed the family into Mom's station wagon for a Sunday drive. Sometimes we would just drive around and look at rural areas outside of town, or view neighborhoods where my parents would like to live. I always liked these drives—just the feeling of being on the road—more than my brother and sisters liked them it seemed. They would sometimes get cranky and complain about driving around with no real destination. To me, however, being on the road was terrific fun. I guess I figured that since I was too young to be a Budget Pak route driver at least I could be on the road most Sundays, albeit in a different form.

Sometimes my parents would take us to a nursing home outside of town where my Uncle Sam lived. A few years before my memory, Sam had fallen asleep at the wheel of a car that he just bought from my parents. It was a five-hour drive from Springfield to where Sam lived in southeast Missouri, and he was one turn of the highway short of his house when he fell asleep. Sam was paralyzed in the accident, and since he didn't have a wife or family, my dad and his brothers put him in Sunshine Acres near Springfield; at their expense, I'm sure. None of us kids liked going to the nursing home where Sam lived. The place smelled like old people and medicine to all of us. All the residents at the home always stared at the four of us kids; and I mean *stared*. It kind of gave us the creeps. We figured it was because those folks probably didn't get many visitors, especially children. Added to that was the fact that the four of us were well-behaved children (because if we were not, our parents would take a belt to us) and we showed proper manners and respect to adults. Like most parents, Bob and Anne beamed when other adults would remark on how well behaved their children were. We could tell that we showed well in public, and our parents thoroughly enjoyed that. I always wanted to add my own postscript to those commenting adults, about what would befall us should we misbehave, but I never did. Hey, I was somewhat of a rebel intellectually, but I wasn't *entirely* stupid.

Even though the kids didn't like the outings to the rest home, seeing Uncle Sam was always fascinating to me. He seemed different from all the other adults in my dad's family. Sam was unmarried, had no children, and other than an occasional carpentry job with my Uncle Paul,

18

had no steady source of income, even before his car wreck. Dad and his four other brothers were all hard-working, straight-laced middle class family types. On the other hand, Sam seemed to be a free spirit, even though by this time he was in his sixties. In fact, his name wasn't even Sam; it was Walter Ray—Sam was just a nickname. No one ever explained that one to me either. My dad and his brothers would sometimes tease Sam about things from the old days when they were growing up. All the Normans are big on teasing, by the way, but Sam would shrug it off. I got the feeling that Sam, who was by far the biggest of the brothers physically, was the butt of many jokes back in the day. It also seemed that either Sam kicked the crap out of each brother at some point in the past or else he defended each in some brawl—or both.

Sam was paralyzed from the waist down, so he could use his arms. His hobby was CB radio. He had cards made up with his name and a figure in a wheelchair with the words "No Walkie . . . Just Talkie." Even talkie was difficult for Sam, though. He was one of those people with a lazy mouth. You know the kind of people who slur a bunch of their words together. It was difficult to understand Sam when he was talking right in front of you. I couldn't imagine chatting with him over a CB radio. However, my dad understood everything and he would translate for the rest of us. After a while, I got to be fluent at understanding Sam, too. Sometimes, though, I still had no idea what he was saying, although Sam always seemed to be happy about whatever it was. Sam eventually had to have one leg amputated. He lived to be about seventy-five and spent about twenty years in the wheelchair. After my parents divorced, my mom moved us to California, so I only saw Sam once or twice. He was an easygoing guy and fun to be around, from what I could tell. I do have to admit that I didn't miss smelly old *Sunshine Acres* with all the staring old folks.

My family lived in a small two-bedroom, one-bath house on the south side of Springfield. It might have been perhaps twelve hundred square feet. My sister Embry and I would walk to Holland Elementary, a little less than a mile away. If it was snowing or raining, Mom would give us a ride. Ninety percent of the time, however, we'd walk. Back then, most kids did. I don't remember many school buses at Holland. There were no sidewalks in that part of town, but I don't remember my parents making a huge deal about safety, so we didn't either. They just said don't accept rides from strangers and stay out of the way of cars, and so we did. Besides, walking was fun, especially when we got to tromp through the snow.

My Uncle Allen and his family lived just a few blocks away from us, but he had only one daughter, Barbara Ann, who was quite a bit older than we were. Uncle Maurice and his family lived in the Holland district also, so we would see our cousins Rick and Greg at school, although we all were in different grade levels. There was no public kindergarten in Missouri in those days. Since my parents couldn't afford private school, none of the four kids ever went to kindergarten. The only pre-first grade training I had was one quick lesson from my dad. He sat me down at a tray table, the day before I started school, and on a piece of paper slowly printed the letters B O B. "That's your name," he said. End of training session.

Elementary school was okay. I did pretty well at Reading, Arithmetic, and Social Studies; fair at English; and not so well at Science. That would pretty much be the pattern for the rest of elementary school. Another quickly established pattern was being compared to the accomplishments of my older sister. Invariably over the next twelve years, at some point early in the school year, the following classroom conversation would occur during roll call:

Teacher: "Robert Norman . . . Oh, are you related to Embry?"

Me: "Yes."

Teacher: "Then we're expecting great things from you this school year!"

Me: (under my breath for a few years, but later as an aside to nearby students) "Well, if life teaches us anything, it is to prepare for disappointment."

See, Embry was real smart. Always got all A's. On the rare occasions when she got an A minus, fits of depression would follow. Embry would later finish seventh out of 400 in her high school graduating class. Business Manager of the school yearbook, scholarship to University of California at Davis, etc . . . you get the idea. Embry has always been smart, driven, good-looking, and bossy. So naturally we didn't get along too well as the years progressed.

Dad wasn't on the road all the time, though. He made it home often enough that the Norman family added two new offspring, Bill and Nancy. Bill is four years younger than I am; and, if I understand mathematical progressions correctly, will always remain so. Bill was pretty much an average-size kid, perhaps a little stocky. Given that I was always super skinny, though, we looked to be about a year or two apart in age. We always got along well, but generally went separate ways at playtime. I liked sports (although I was never any good at them) building forts and playing Army with toy guns, and playing with toy soldiers. Bill enjoyed digging in the dirt. He and his buddies were always playing in some new tunnel they had dug, or building some sort of construction project. Nancy came along two years after Bill, and our parents promptly began calling Embry and me, the "big kids", since we were a year apart, and Bill and Nancy, the "little kids."

The four of us were officially named Embry Lou and Nancy Sue, Robert Clay and William Ray, cute, huh? I hated being a "junior." Bob was too common a name for my taste. Being called Bobby or Bob Jr. got old for me. I would have to make do with Bob, however, until something else came along.

Our folks added a bedroom onto our little house, along with an eating area; but, it was still cramped accommodations with six people sharing one bathroom. Fortunately, Budget Pak Candies was doing well, and Dad was starting to make decent money. He bought my mom a brand new family car: a 1960 Ford station wagon. It was the first new car my parents ever owned. Mom's favorite color was red, and this car was all red with red and white interior. I was becoming enthusiastic about cars at this time, and I thought ours was hideous. 1960 was a terrible year for Ford, design-wise; I don't like solid red and station wagons aren't two-door coupes, which were what all boys growing up in the fifties, longed for. Oh well, I knew the wagon was practical, and it did fit the family needs.

The bigger news was that, by 1961, Dad had saved enough money to move us to a nice subdivision on the outskirts of town. This was a three-bedroom, three-bath house roughly *twice* the size of our old place. We had a two-car garage, fireplace, and unusually large front and back yards. The subdivision, called Park Crest Village, was only about half built, so there were open fields and home construction sites all around us. My younger brother Bill was in puppy-heaven with large dirt piles everywhere. Behind the houses across the street from us was a field where the farmer would rotate crops of corn and wheat. There was plenty of space for my friends and me to build forts and play Army. It was never called playing Cowboys and Indians—it was always *Army*. The television series *Combat!* was our favorite show.

Our schools were miles away, via a highway, so walking was out. We became bus riders, the "big kids" Embry and I going to South Kickapoo Junior High, and the "little kids"—Bill and Nancy—to North Kickapoo Elementary. Embry and I weren't actually in Junior High.

Because of space considerations, fifth and sixth grades were collocated at the Junior High site, with first through fourth grades only at the elementary school some miles away. As for the name Kickapoo, naturally, as kids, we hated it. Kids from other schools were always making fun of us "Kick-a–shitters" or some such other permutation. Later on, though, I rather liked the name. It's just that when you think about Indian tribes and the names Mohawk, Comanche, Cheyenne, and Apache come to mind . . . *Kickapoo* doesn't easily slide into the listing . . . you know?

Growing up in Park Crest was really fun. There was a vacant lot behind our house, at least for a while, where we would play baseball and football. It was pretty typical Norman Rockwell stuff—a bunch of neighborhood kids with taped-up, cracked bats, old gloves for bases, and a chain link fence in the backyard for our automatic catcher. We could usually get around eight or ten kids together for sandlot games, sometimes more when the older guys would show up. These kids were a few years older than our group and were all top-notch athletes. One of them, John Bittner, was the starting quarterback on Kickapoo's football team. John lived two doors down from us and had a cute sister named Cathy, who was my age. Of course, I had no confidence around girls, and wouldn't for years, so it didn't matter.

See, the junior highs in Springfield played a full schedule of tackle football, just as the high schools did. On Saturday mornings, Kickapoo would play Pershing, Pipkin, Study, Jarrett, or Reed at the Parkview High stadium in town. We'd go and watch Bittner, Jackie Redding, Jimmy Reddick, Greg Mann, and all the older neighborhood kids play. Sports were prominent in Springfield in the early 60's. The Yankees were always in the World Series, and Mickey Mantle, every kid's idol, grew up in nearby Oklahoma. In addition, the American Football League was new, and Kansas City had a team on weekly television. I even had a real major league baseball player as my Sunday school teacher, for a little while.

Jerry Lumpe was an infielder for the A's and Yankees. He lived right behind our church, Southminster Presbyterian. I guess he must have had a child in our age group in church. Speaking of the church, I came to realize years later that Mom and Dad didn't make it to Southminster as often as all the kids would. We'd be in various Sunday school classes and our parents were MIA. I think Sunday mornings tended to be frolic time at the Norman household.

For some unknown reason, during my sixth grade year at Kickapoo, I became close friends with many of the more skilled boy athletes. It's never happened since, at any level. They even talked me into trying out for the Little League team they were all on . . . called Bob's Yanks. They were one of the best teams in the county. However, in those days—unlike now—not everybody who wanted to be in Little League made the team. Besides, I was lousy, never having played organized ball before, and didn't make the roster. I did remain friends with the players who did, though.

My buddies in the neighborhood during these years were Denny Corrigan, Jim Herre, and Tim Senner. We would play sports all the time, unless we were building forts in the nearby fields or woods, or playing Army. Denny was a Catholic. That made him a rarity in the Ozarks . . . and he was adopted. He was also left-handed, so he was unusual just about all the way around. Denny's parents were older—at least they looked older to us—and were members of Twin Oaks Country Club. Denny would caddy out there and play some, too. Denny's family were Kansas City A's fans, when almost everyone else we knew was a fan of the St. Louis Cardinals. I'm telling you, Corrigan was *just different*, man. Tim was maybe two years younger than I was and had twin sisters named Kay and Gay who were in my class. The Senners just moved to Springfield from Wisconsin. They were intense Green Bay Packer braggers. Nice enough people, but enough already with the Wiskahhnnson accents and how terrific Jim Taylor is. I still can't root for the Pack. My best friend was Jim Herre (pronounced hurry). Jim was a droopy-lidded, slow-talking, good-natured kid. His family was from the D.C. area and Redskins fans, but not the in-your-face type like the Senners. Jim and I got along splendidly, and his mom was very kind to me.

It was about this time that I went to my first, big-time sporting event. Denny's family took me with them to Kansas City for an Athletics' game. It was a doubleheader against Baltimore, I think. Of course, the A's were terrible back then. They probably lost both games that day, but I was hooked. I've followed the A's ever since.

It had to be somebody like the Corrigans who took me to a ball game because my dad was not into sports at all. He never took any of us to *any* sporting event that I can recall. My mom liked baseball, and we would talk about it after I read the newspaper standings and so on. Dad, however, never taught me anything about sports. Whatever I picked up along the way was on my own or from the neighborhood kids. Except for hitting fungos, that is. That's when you toss a baseball to yourself, and practice your batting. My grandfather taught me how to do that one time when he and my grandmother came to Missouri for a visit from their home in California.

My dad wasn't a hands-on type parent; at least, not toward me. We never hunted, we never fished, and we never camped . . . okay, except once in Big Basin, Redwoods State Park in California, when we were visiting Mom's family nearby. The only real, hands-on experience I got from my dad was when we would wrestle. Sometimes, on the rare nights when Dad was home, he would wrestle with Embry, Bill, and me. I almost always seemed to end up crying, though. Guess I just wasn't as tough as my siblings were. However, that rather fit the pattern for the dynamic among the children in our family.

As sometimes happens in larger families, two of the kids tended to take after one parent, and the other two children tended to have personalities more aligned to the other parent. For us, Embry and Bill were more outgoing, like Mom. Or, as Mom would say about similar people, "they have a good personality," which meant they liked to talk a lot. On the other hand, Nancy and I were more introverted, like Dad. Not that one type is better or worse than the other . . . they're just different.

In our family, Bill received quite a bit more attention from adult men than I did. They would call him "sport" or "tiger" or some such nickname because he was more outgoing and sociable than I was. I couldn't blame them for that. Just the natural way of things, I guess.

The activities we did have as a family were based largely upon auto travel. These consisted of the previously mentioned Sunday drives; trips to visit my dad's extended family, going to the movies at the Hi M Drive-In (which was just beyond our neighborhood); and about every three years, a vacation journey to California.

The trips to California were special to me. We went out in 1959 and again in 1962, if memory serves. My mom was a highly organized person. She would pack the station wagon with a cooler, a picnic basket, and all the other gear to keep a family on the road and self-sufficient. We always took the southern route along Route 66 through the Mojave Desert and into California's San Joaquin Valley, then over to San Jose. We would start out early, stop to eat the lunch that Mom packed, and then continue until late afternoon when we would check into a motel. No Holiday Inns for us, though. We stayed in those horseshoe-shaped motels that were prevalent at that time. Route 66 wasn't all an interstate freeway back then, so the all-day drives were never a bore, at least to me. There were impressive sights everywhere: the farmlands and oilrigs of Oklahoma and Texas, the high-desert mesas of New Mexico and Arizona, the vast expanse of California's Mojave. Throughout the journey, we would see the old Burma Shave signs. Sprinkled along the way were the roadside eateries with names such as Wagon Wheel Café, Roadrunner Diner, or Trail Boss Burgers, with nary a McDonald's or a Waffle House within echo-shouting distance.

On the trip in '62, we stopped at most of the tourist attractions along the way. Grand Canyon, Petrified Forest, Painted Desert, Meteor Crater, man . . . we hit them all. To make all the detours from the direct route, Mom must have worked hard to get Dad to agree. One day, when we were westbound on 66 through the Navajo Reservation, we saw a solitary Indian youth in the distance, mounted on a pony. He looked to be about fourteen. The boy was sitting atop his horse, watching the cars go by. There were no structures, or other signs of life in any direction; at least none that we could see. The dichotomy of this scene could have been straight from a movie; two different worlds meeting at a brief point of contact. The white, middle class travelers are speeding along their way west, while the native youth, at one with the land, watches their progress from a hilltop. My parents remarked that the boy, to be at that spot, could have ridden for hours. He could as easily have come from his home just beyond the hill, for all we knew. This was my parents at their best, I thought. They planted a seed for their children to reflect on, as I have done with the scene of that Navajo youth on that distant hilltop so many years ago, even now.

The other standout memory from these vacations along the old, "Lincoln Highway", was the seemingly endless array of trading posts and souvenir stands along the route. These were especially prevalent in New Mexico and Arizona. Signs would announce, many miles in advance, that "Indian Curios" were straight ahead. I had no idea at first what "curios" were, but the roadside signs sure looked fabulous, so I was quite eager to check them out. We would track our progress toward the next curio shop by the miles listed on the billboards, then sink back into our seats, crestfallen, when our dad would pass by the stand without stopping. Finally, our parents would acquiesce and pull into one of the trading posts. All of us kids would scour the aisles for that perfect "authentic" Indian or Cowboy artifact that we just had to have. These places sold all kinds of articles. Some of them were high quality, like expensive Navajo rugs, for instance. Most of the items, however, were just inexpensive throwaway type stuff, which suited us kids perfectly. My brother and I would get a couple of those rubber tomahawks, say, and bonk each other with them for miles to pass the time. Eventually we'd end up smacking our sisters with them, and our parents would take them from us, or maybe just threaten us with the belt, which always got our full attention.

Those were wonderful trips, chasing the lowering sun every afternoon on the way west, while marveling at the purple and crimson sunsets. On the return leg, we'd track our progress on the map towards the towns that we had seen on the way out, expectantly awaiting our old friends . . . Winslow, Gallup, Albuquerque, Amarillo, Tulsa. I had many keepsake memories from those road trips. Not to mention a slightly used rubber tomahawk to show to my Army buddies back in the neighborhood.

As for our parents spending what people nowadays call "quality time" with us kids, well, there didn't seem to be too much of that for any of us. Mom had her hands full raising four kids and doing all the work around the house. Dad was hardly ever home; not that my folks were terrible parents, however. Mom was probably just overwhelmed, alone, and a long way from home. Dad just wasn't around to have too much of an impact, except for disciplinary purposes. The only time I remember, what I suppose one would call "bonding" with my dad, was when he would take me on the road with him on one of his business trips while I was on summer break from school. We would visit the small towns where he made his sales calls, and I would watch as he talked with the grocers. The daily highlight, aside from driving from one town to another, was lunch. Invariably, we would hit some small café, which was usually situated right on the town square. We would have the Blue Plate Special, something like meatloaf, mashed potatoes, and green beans, for instance. I would get milk in those little bottles with the cardboard pull-off tops. I'll bet the tariff wasn't much more than a dollar per Blue Plate, drink included.

However, while I was enjoying being on the road, the highway hadn't been quite so kind to Dad. He began to wreck company vehicles at a fairly steady clip. First, he flipped a box van somewhere. He wasn't hurt, but the truck was totaled. The brothers set the burnt out hulk behind the candy plant in downtown Springfield, perhaps as a reminder to the route drivers as to what could happen if they weren't careful. Then a few years later, Dad was driving home on a Friday night in his company panel wagon (a station wagon with no windows down the sides, popular as a work car in the days before mini-vans) when he rear-ended a car on the highway. The man he hit was a minister who stopped to pick up two hitchhikers who were from Iran. Dad was thrown from his car as it burst into flames. The only items salvaged were his eyeglasses and cigarette lighter. I guess the other people were okay, and they later sued Dad, although, I don't think they collected anything. The kids found out about the wreck the next day when Dad was sporting a large bandage on his forehead. I don't know if alcohol was involved in either of these wrecks. However, I wouldn't bet against it.

Surprisingly, for a man who spent so much of his time around trucks and automobiles, Bob Sr. imparted remarkably little knowledge to his children about the subject—even though I was nuts about trucks, cars, and highways. Dad did teach me how to mow lawns, though. He had me using the power mower from about age eight. My other big job was to burn the trash. In those days, everybody had a fifty-five gallon drum in the backyard, and folks burned up most of their household trash. Pollution concerns later put an end to that practice. As for my siblings, I don't know how much they learned from Dad. It couldn't have been a lot. Most everything we knew, our Mom taught us.

As a matter of fact, Dad wasn't teaching too much of anything to any of his children by this time. Bob Sr. developed into a big drinker, or more accurately, an alcoholic. I always remembered my dad as a casual drinker when I was small, sharing some Falstaff beer with my grandfather and such, but he had gone way beyond that. Dad became the type of drinker who couldn't stop until he was falling down drunk. Then my mom would get upset, and there would be loud fights between them. Mom did most of the yelling while Dad just slurred out some words now and then.

Being stuck with four kids some two thousand miles away from home with the family breadwinner in a stupor much of the time was not quite the life Anne envisioned when she married. I think she was terribly hurt, and scared, by my dad's downward spiraling behavior, and she let her emotions pour out onto him with, shall we say, vigor? I had no idea that Mommy knew those kinds of words. The bedroom my brother Bill and I shared was right next to the kitchen, where many of my parents' late night fights occurred, and since Bill was younger, and went to sleep earlier than I did, I alone, among the four kids, heard those arguments.

Our dad's drinking came to dominate the family dynamic in our new household. Dad didn't drink much in front of the children. He would come home in a stupor, sometimes being led into the house by one or more of his brothers. Other times, Dad would be sequestered in our parents' bedroom for days at a time, completely out of touch with the world except for contact with my mom. Dad was not a social drinker. He was one of those people who drank hard, straight, and fast on the expressway to total oblivion.

Arguments between Mom and Dad became more frequent, and not all of them occurred late at night. During these dustups, each parent would try to enlist the children to take sides against the other parent. All of this daily drama took its toll on the kids, of course, but it was especially hard on my older sister, Embry. She was one of those kids who always tried to grow up fast anyway. Since girls mature emotionally more quickly than boys, it was only natural for Embry to step up and defend Mom, especially when Dad would knock Mom around, which happened sometimes. The rest of us kids tended to be spectators, except for those times when Mom would send me out on a bottle hunting expedition.

For some reason, Dad would stash empty whiskey bottles around the household. I never quite figured out this process. I thought a person with an obvious drinking problem would hide *full* bottles, and dispose of the empties, but Dad made a specific point of hiding the empties in all kinds of off-the-wall places. I found bottles (usually pints of Jim Beam or Hill & Hill) under the seat of his car; in the stack of firewood; behind the lawn tools. Mom once found some under the hood of Dad's car, stashed around the battery. The biggest haul was when Mom went up the pull-down ladder to our attic one day and found *twenty-nine* empty bottles. They were hidden within the insulation among the rafters.

A turning point occurred about this time, 1963 I think. One day when I came home from school, Dad was at home. That never happened. After I made my obligatory snack of a P B & J, my parents sat me down and said they had something serious to tell me. My dad sold out his interest in the candy business. There would be no more Budget Pak road trips, no more Saturdays at the plant, no more route drivers, no more loading of trucks. I was *crushed*. My parents frequently told me that part of the business would go to my brother and me, but that wasn't important at all to me at that time. What mattered, however, was that our family would no longer be a part of the plant's activities. Later I found out that two of Dad's brothers in the business, Allen and Maurice, forced Bob out due to his drinking. I got the impression that, besides wrecking a sizeable chunk of the company vehicles, Bob torqued off some customers with his behavior while under the influence. At any rate, our time at the Budget Pak plant was over.

There was a little good news. Dad took his buyout money and bought a brand new GMC cab-over semi with a forty-foot Fruehauf trailer. It was beautiful. The idea was for Dad to be an independent trucker, with the largest share of his work coming from Budget Pak. He would bring in the bulk candy with his rig for Budget Pak, and contract other work on his way east, so as not to run empty—the usual routine for truckers. While we didn't have Budget Pak route trucks to play on any longer, we did have a shiny, red and silver big rig in front of our house . . . always a plus.

The problem was that Dad kept getting into wrecks on the highway. First he and another driver named Jack crested a hill on the Pennsylvania Turnpike in the middle of the night and plowed right into a stopped car, reportedly killing four people. It must have been one horrific scene. The story I got was that two drunken dentists, with two women who weren't their wives, just stopped in the middle of the lane. They didn't pull over onto the shoulder of the highway. It was Jack's semi, and he was off the road for a time until his truck was repaired. I never heard of any legal repercussions for Dad or Jack, nor do I know who was driving the truck at the time of the crash.

Then, a few months later, Dad jackknifed his own rig one night in a rainstorm near the Arkansas border. He was unhurt, but his trailer was on its side and pretty badly damaged. Unknown to Dad, under the trailer, a Ford Falcon station wagon had been flattened. Rescue workers had to get an industrial crane from the nearby School of the Ozarks to lift the trailer, packed full of frozen chickens, off the Falcon. I don't think anybody died in *that* crash, thankfully.

After Dad left the candy business, relations between my parents deteriorated even more. Arguments and fights were more frequent, and the family environment was very bad, especially for my sisters. Embry, who continued to stand up for Mom, received Dad's enmity for her actions. Nancy, however, had always clearly been Dad's favorite. It must have been tough on her as she watched while her father lost stature in her young eyes. Family acrimony is always hardest on the youngest child, and Nancy was only six or seven years old at the time.

Dad ended up in jail a few times, I'm not sure exactly why. He also spent a lot of time in various mental hospitals; the ones I remember were in Nevada, Missouri, and another was the VA hospital in St. Louis. Mom would take all four of us to visit. Dad also received electric shock treatments for his drinking problem, which seemed to be standard procedure for the times. One place Dad *never* went to was an Alcoholics Anonymous meeting. Mom would go to the Al Anon support group for help, but Bob Sr. admitting to others that he had a problem? *No way* would *that* happen. During some of these bad times, all of us kids would stay a day or two at our neighbors' house, the Senners. Herb and Adele Senner were generous to take all four of us in, even though we had to sit through some Green Bay Packer hurrahs along the way.

There were periods of time when Dad would try to stop drinking. That never lasted for long, though. When Dad would fall off the wagon, he would drink our household supply of vanilla extract or Old Spice aftershave, common occurrences, we found out, for alcoholics. Once, Dad got the DTs, which scared us all pretty badly. He was acting crazy and saying weird stuff. The ambulance had to haul him away for yet another stay in the hospital.

Events came to a head one day when Dad, in a drunken rage, came after Mom. She kabonged him in the head with a seven-pound iron skillet . . . three times on the forehead . . . left, right, and center. Knocked him right out, too. Chalk up another hospital visit for Dad. Fortunately, none of us children were around the house at the time. She told us about the incident and then showed us the kitchen floor, with blood all over it. I guess that was when Mom decided it was time for divorce court.

In June of 1964, she filed the papers, called her father back in California to find us a place to live, packed four kids in the red, Ford station wagon, and set off toward the sunset. This time we would be going via the northern route—through Colorado and Utah. The first stop in Kansas City would be to see our friends, the Cline family. I have no idea how the finances worked for our family; but Mom, always an outstanding organizer, must have been on top of her game for this venture. We always had a warm place to sleep and plenty of vittles. I gave my baseball card collection to my friend Jim Herre, and the Herres took in our family dog, a cocker spaniel named Blackie. All of us kids hated to leave Springfield. It had been the only place we'd known as home. There was some good news. There would be no more fights between Mom and Dad (at least for a while) . . . and just as significant from my perspective . . . road trip.

30

☙ *Chapter Three* ❧
"Golden State"

We stayed with the Clines in Kansas City for a few days. Bob and Irene had five kids and used to live a few houses down from us in Springfield. Their oldest child, Rob, had been one of my neighborhood buddies. Rob was a fun kid to be around, always coming up with a quip or a prank. I wasn't crazy about Bob Cline. He was always pushing his sons into sports, although none of them appeared to have any extraordinary talent or inclination for it. Bob was one of those guys who never seemed to know when to back off and just be a spectator parent. Irene, though, was a real joy. She was one of my all-time favorite grownups. Irene would talk religion, politics, sociology, and culture, practically anything at any time—with eleven and twelve-year-old kids. I can only imagine how fascinating the conversations were among other adults. Irene had the knack of treating kids as if they had valuable opinions, and might even have insights that she had not considered. She would drive us to a ballgame, or to the Community Center, while she would moderate a lively discussion on some topic of the day. Usually I felt a little more grown-up and a lot more positive about my own self-worth after spending time with Irene.

We left KC and headed west through Denver and Salt Lake City. The trip was fine, but it wasn't my old amigo, Route 66. I discovered I much preferred the Southwest and the Mojave to the Rockies and the Basin and Range of Nevada. Not many Indian curios, either. Since Mom was doing all the driving, a new duty for her, we didn't make a lot of miles each day. It took us quite a few days to make our next resting point, my Aunt's place in Incline Village, Nevada.

Mom's sister Helene divorced her husband Jack Sanders a few years earlier. She got custody of her three boys and a short time later married a guy named Bill Wiggers. With Bill, Helene had her last child, Alison. Bill was in construction as some kind of heavy equipment operator, and he found work near Lake Tahoe. My family stayed with Helene and her clan for about a week, I guess. We were in no real hurry since the house my grandfather found for us in California was not quite ready for us to move in. We didn't mind. Bill and Helene's house was a fun place for kids. It was a split-level home, which was a style we had never seen. It had beam ceilings and a large back deck. It was summertime at Lake Tahoe, with terrific weather and fresh mountain air. After only a few days of being there, Bill Wiggers replaced my dad as the baddest dude I had come across. Bill was tall, trim, and prematurely gray. With his work boots on, he looked even taller. Bill had been a Marine in the Korean War and was at the famous winter Battle of Chosin Reservoir. Nevada seemed to fit Bill to a tee, as he liked to smoke, drink, and gamble . . . as did Helene.

My brother Bill and I got along great with our cousins, for the most part, and that would continue over the ensuing years. Steve was the oldest, a year younger than me. He was super smart and constantly read books. Steve was the type who would concentrate so hard on his reading that he would be thoroughly oblivious to anything around him . . . train wrecks, nuclear explosions, and the like. Jeff was next in age. He was quite funny and the best athletically of all the boy cousins; although in our family, as Major Winchester said in *M*A*S*H*, that was roughly equivalent to being the "finest ballerina in Topeka." Jeff and brother William were close pals, and they both had the knack of being able to talk as Donald Duck did, which I didn't think was all that funny, but the rest of the family would always quack up (sorry). Jon was the youngest boy, and was a real friendly and open kid who was fun to be around.

The Sanders boys had one good thing going for them, and one bad. The good was, they had three sets of grandparents (counting their stepfather's folks) and received loads of Christmas presents from them every year. Their haul of toys would invariably dwarf our haul, and *not* by a little. Of course, since they were so rough on their playthings, ninety percent of those toys would be broken or lost by the next Holiday Season, so their joy was only temporary.

Their bad news was medical. Steve was born with a serious heart condition. He had heart surgery as a child; even more operations as an adult. Steve still had a full childhood; it's not as if he were quarantined or anything. He just didn't get to participate on a regular basis in all the activities the rest of the kids did. Jeff was born with missing and deformed fingers. He had numerous surgeries that helped somewhat, but he had only the pinky and thumb on his left hand, and perhaps three half fingers on his right. This adversity never slowed Jeff down a bit. Like I said, he was the best athlete among us. He can even throw a football and swing a golf club—no problem. I have to wonder how good Jeff might have become if he had been given ten full digits, like most people.

No explanation was given to me as to why my cousins had these birth defects. However, I have to believe that Helene's drinking and smoking during pregnancy contributed. Nothing against Helene, that was commonplace in the early fifties. I'm just glad my mom didn't have that lifestyle.

I developed my own set of defects over the previous five years or so. First, I had surgery for "lazy eye" when I was eight. It was a pretty standard procedure for that affliction back then, I was told. They pop your eyeballs out and clip a muscle or something like that. Two memories linger from that hospital stay. One was the feeling of lying in the hospital room with bandaged eyes for two or three days. The experience wasn't as foreboding as I thought it was going to be. My parents hung around the hospital room when they could, but for most of the time, I was alone. I didn't mind too much, though. It was plenty quiet in that room and I always could handle solitude.

The other memory was the transistor radio my Uncle Maurice gave me. It was my first experience listening to music. I spent a substantial portion of my stay fooling around with the little dial, trying to get decent reception on that low-budget radio.

After the surgery, the eye doctor, a guy named Dr. Ivy (yeah, he was poison to me) fitted me with a black eye patch over my good eye. The idea was to make the weaker eye stronger by forcing it to work harder. Nice theory, but the practical application left much to be desired, from my viewpoint. I was the lucky kid who got to hear about a million pirate jokes over the next few months.

Then, after the eye surgery, I was fitted for braces. I had buck teeth. I guess the lowers must have been crooked too, for I got a full set of braces. I then received the full sampling of tin-grin and metal-mouth teases, too. During this same time period, and to complete the dental display, a bad-hop grounder from a softball hit me in the mouth. One of my upper front teeth was broken. They gave me a silver crown, which was particularly noticeable. Now, besides being one of the shortest and skinniest kids in my grade, I also sported braces, a silver tooth, and an occasional eye patch . . . what a handsome devil.

After we left Lake Tahoe, the family moved into a house my grandfather found for us in Los Gatos, a suburb of San Jose. Mom was quite happy that we would be going to Los Gatos schools, which had an excellent reputation, and where she graduated high school two decades earlier. Our new place was a three-bedroom, two-bath tract home that was in one of the few middle class areas of town. Most areas were upper middle-class, or just downright rich. Los Gatos was a wealthy place then, and is much more so now, I'm sure. The people in Los Gatos don't call it a city . . . it is the *Town* of Los Gatos. The schools were first-class, and the weather was pleasant, but it was a tough adjustment for me. California was way ahead of Missouri as far as pop culture and the like. This was the time of surfers and skateboarders, and I was neither. All the boys I met seemed to have long blond hair and rode those stingray bicycles with the long, white "banana" seats and the high handlebars. Everything seemed foreign to me. I was the hick kid from the Ozarks with short hair and braces; poor, skinny, short, and lacking the sophistication of the other kids my age. I suppose my brother and sisters felt the same. However, we adapted, learned, grew . . . as children will.

After some months, Dad made his appearance in California, as we all knew he would. He tried to get my mother to take him back for the next year or two, but to no avail. There were more fights off and on during this time, but at least Dad wasn't living with us, which was an improvement over conditions in Missouri. Dad convinced the Veterans Administration that his alcoholism was service related, so he received disability payments from the VA for the remainder of his life, I think. Dad also worked at a rental car place, as a salesman, and other brief stints elsewhere. However, he kept losing all those jobs because of his drinking. Dad sold the Missouri house and lost his big rig, too, before he showed up in California. In those days, a divorce took one year to finalize. It was a long twelve months for us. The three older kids, Embry, Bill, and myself, grew to dislike Bob Sr. being around at all. He would disparage and browbeat us on a regular basis, although there was no physical abuse to speak of. He still showed clear favoritism for Nancy, the youngest, which didn't exactly endear him to us, either. Eventually, he moved back to Missouri when the divorce became final.

I'm not certain if there was a "final straw" between Mom and Dad, which led to his exit. During this same general time period, however, my Aunt Helene and her four kids moved in with us. That may have contributed to his decision. Helene's marriage to Bill Wiggers had broken up, and so we now had eight kids and two single-parent moms in a thirteen hundred square foot house. There were some arguments, of course, but overall everybody got along pretty well with one another. I will say that when Helene got back on her feet financially some months later and moved her clan into their own place in San Jose, everyone in both families was happy to be parting ways.

Mom got work as a bank teller and gradually we all became California-ized. About a year after our arrival, I got my braces removed.

I still had to wear a retainer, though. I was even allowed to grow my hair out (a little) so I began to fit in a bit. It wasn't all forward steps, though. Sometime during this same general time frame, I was diagnosed with a heart murmur. The doctor said it was slight, and would have been nearly undetectable if I weren't so skinny; but, I thought back to all the trouble my cousin Steve experienced with his heart problems, so I was somewhat upset with the news. Of course, my condition was nothing compared to Steve's, but that didn't stop me from whining a bit that all of the family medical problems seemed to land on me.

My self-pity soon got its comeuppance with a quick little one-two punch. First, besides the dental braces I mentioned earlier, my orthodontist fitted me with one of those wire harness contraptions that strapped around the neck . . . what an ugly and embarrassing piece of crap *that* was . . . painful to wear, too. My neck is fucked up to this day because of it (there is no scientific evidence for this, I admit, but that's my story, counselor . . . I was there).

Then, to cap off the whole puberty process, I was prescribed eyeglasses. Everybody in the family had glasses already except me, so Mom was always taking us to the eye doctor. I guess weak eyes must run in the family. I know it does on my mom's side. She and my sister Embry are especially Mr. Magoo-like. I was told the glasses weren't needed full-time, just for reading, television, and the like. However, that didn't matter to me. The eyeglasses were my tipping point. After a few weeks of intermittent usage, I took the glasses and shoved them into the back recesses of our homework desk, and there they stayed . . . for years. Surprisingly, I didn't get into trouble with Mom over this. Perhaps she was simply too busy trying to make a living and keep four kids in school to care too much. At any rate, it was one of the first times I can remember making a firm stand on something. I felt pretty good about it, too. Of course, I was still an eighty-pound fourteen-year-old with suspect eyes, a heart murmur, a dental harness, no money, no athletic ability, no girlfriend, and no father . . . so, feeling *pretty good* might be a relative term.

Then, out of nowhere, a father figure appeared. After two years in California, my mom started dating. Next thing we knew, she was going out with the man who lived right next door. Clay Anderson was a forty-year-old divorced father who had custody of his five kids. We actually didn't know the Anderson kids well, even though we were all close in ages and went to the same schools. About all we knew was that

Clay's mother, who lived in their house and took care of things, would always get into funny arguments with Steve, the second oldest child. Steve was rebellious and quick to become angry. He and his "Gramps"— as the Andersons called their Grandma—would get into hilarious yelling and shoving matches. All the neighbor kids would come and watch.

Soon, Clay and Anne got quite serious, and the two families began to spend a lot of time together. There was a continuous stream of kids going back and forth between the two houses. Shortly thereafter, Clay and Anne got married. They got a loan, added rooms on to our house, and sold Clay's house. "Gramps" was able to move back to her own little place, and the rest of us began to figure out how eleven people could live together under one roof.

After some adjustments, it got to be a fairly stable environment. All five boys lived in a thirty by twenty foot upstairs bedroom. There was plenty of room for beds, and a good-sized area to roughhouse, too. We built World War II era model airplanes, mounted them from the ceiling with string, and positioned them into dogfights. My oldest stepbrother, Dave, was especially skilled at assembling a quality model. He had the patience, and artistic flair, to make them look authentic. I was the type of kid who usually ended up with too much glue on the model, or smudged paint, or other mistakes and blemishes. My contribution was to be the set decorator. I would come up with the aerial scenarios, such as a Hellcat chasing a Zero, or a Spitfire angling toward a Messerschmitt, or a Focke Wulf attacking a Liberator . . . that sort of thing.

My brother Bill and I sometimes talked about what it would be like if we had a lot of brothers, and suddenly, we did. Our stepbrothers were all quite different from one another. Dave was a year ahead of me in school, in the same grade as my sister Embry, although he was older, having been held back a year somewhere along the line. All the kids from both families looked up to Dave. He was a muscular guy with a powerful chest and arms. Dave looked like the stereotypical older brother of the 1960's with pompadour hair and a white T-shirt. He was car crazy, especially Mopars. Dave got a job at a local fancy restaurant, and soon bought his own car, a 1959 Chrysler with the giant fins that were so stylish then. It got terrible gas mileage, but then gasoline was only about thirty cents a gallon. Once in a while, he would give me a ride to or from school, if his girlfriend wasn't around. When she was around, stepbrothers and other family members were history, as in "go away kid, you bother me," which was fine.

Steve was next oldest, and in my grade at school. Steve was a big kid too, but just not terribly bright, to my mind. Steve was constantly getting himself into trouble—at school, around the house, in the neighborhood—everywhere. Steve got into trouble enough on his own, but the rest of us (me included) would tease and trick him into losing his cool, and then he would do something foolish and get into even more trouble. Steve wasn't mean or anything; he was just a kind of goober kid who was like the bull in a china shop.

The third brother, Greg, was the opposite. He was a small kid, like me, and maybe two years younger. Greg was the consummate shrewd operator. He was always looking to pull scams and pranks. Greg was all for quick and easy money and, if he had it, he always shared. Dave applied hard work to everything, Steve attacked every opportunity with sheer force, and Greg would always work the angles.

My two stepsisters were next in age. Judy was about my brother William's age. She desperately wanted to be grown up, and I mean, right now. Not having her own mother around, she kind of looked up to my sister Embry, who was about four years older than Judy was. She and Greg were close in age and close as siblings. They would always stick up for one another and would pal around a lot. Joanna was the youngest, about my sister Nancy's age. She was a sweet kid and never did anything wrong, just like Nancy. Everyone got along with one another pretty well. You would think that, with eleven folks in the house, there would have been some others to share my affinity with sports, but alas, I was still the only sports crazy person in the household.

Clay and Anne quickly set a routine for the Anderson/Norman crew. My mom was the chief organizer, as I have said, and she set up the weekly schedule. Laundry was done on certain days, grocery shopping on another, house cleaning on another, etc. Added to that was breakfast for eleven daily, eleven brown bag lunches, and dinner at six o'clock, at which attendance was mandatory. I discovered I had some of the organizational knack too, and I made up a weekly dish washing and drying schedule for all nine kids. That doesn't sound too hard, but juggling everyone's nightly and weekend activities while being equitable was a little tough. The best part was your nights off. That was when you would look condescendingly at the forlorn stiffs who had KP that night, only to receive the same treatment a day or so later when it was your turn to clean up after eleven trough feeders.

If Anne set the solid framework for the active household, Clay provided the bedrock foundation. My sisters, brother, and I never experienced a man like Clay before, at least not up close. He was unlike our own father in almost every way.

Clay was born in Apache, Oklahoma in 1926. That made him and my mom about the same age. Clay and both of his brothers enlisted in the Marines in World War II as quickly as they became age eligible to do so. Dale and Clay made it back to the States—Buster wasn't as lucky. His landing craft took a direct hit, at Iwo Jima, I think, and he was killed instantly. After mustering out, Clay took one look around California and added his name to the list of transplanted Okies residing in the Golden State. Clay was a welder and, with the building boom in post-war California, there was plenty of work to be had. He was hired at Westinghouse in Sunnyvale, making large turbines for power plants.

Clay never missed a day of work . . . *ever*. He was one of those Great Depression Era guys who believed that you always show up for your job, lest you should lose it. Clay always arrived home from work happy and optimistic, ready to relax and interact with the family. He didn't make much money, especially for upscale Los Gatos, but he was calm and content, living in a stable household with a family experiencing the pains and elations of growing up.

Clay was always the first one to arise in the morning, and he would be playing solitaire and smoking a cigarette when we got up. He would make breakfast for anyone who wanted it. This is where the two families differed. The Normans usually had cereal and toast, with perhaps a bigger meal on weekends. The Andersons preferred pancakes, covered with peanut butter, nearly every day . . . no thanks.

Another routine was Friday night dinner. Clay would take my mom out for a nice meal, while the kids would get take-out pizza from Magoo's Pizza in downtown Los Gatos. On the way home with the pizzas, we would stop at the A & W Root Beer stand down the street for a gallon of their finest. The food and drink were tasty, the camaraderie with the nine of us was super, but the cherry on top was . . . no dishes!

Once a month, Clay and Anne would take one of the nine kids with them on their Friday night dinner. The child got to choose the restaurant, within reason. The monthly dinner was a big hit with all the kids. It was an affordable way to make each kid feel special. Everyone looked forward to his or her individual month.

Not everything went easy for the parents, though. A key issue was smoking. Even though Clay smoked, he was dead set against any of us taking up the habit. Dave smoked, but as he was already eighteen,

Clay couldn't do much about it. However, when Greg and Judy started up, Clay became upset. He sat Judy down and made her smoke the whole pack, or at least as much as she could until she got sick. It did cure her of the urge, for a while anyway. Bill and I started smoking a little about that same time, just trying to be cool, I suppose. It seemed that we had all kinds of kids sneaking cigarettes for a time.

The other significant problem was run-ins with the local authorities. During one summer, 1967 I think, it seemed as if the Los Gatos Police were delivering one of us to the house every week for some minor offense. Bill and Judy were adept at getting caught for petty theft, shoplifting or stupid pranks. One time, Bill was setting off the streamer type popper fireworks on cars in the local grocery parking lot. When he exploded one on an unmarked police car, the cop, who was right there, grabbed him and told him to get in the car. Bill said, "My parents won't let me accept rides with strangers."

Steve got into trouble, seemingly all the time. It was always dumb stuff, too. One time he accidentally burned up an entire field while setting off firecrackers. He tried to put the fire out, but with the dry California summers, it quickly got out of control. Steve took off, leaving his yearbook (they had just been distributed that day) behind, with his name inside the cover. When the cops came to the house, Steve denied everything, as he always did when he was in trouble.

Denied everything with cinders and ashes on his clothes, no less.

Denied everything with his hair singed, too.

When the cops produced the yearbook, he still denied.

With all this denying, I thought the rooster was going to crow anytime. Steve had to clean fire hoses at the local fire station for the rest of the summer for that one.

However, the best petty criminal in the family, hands down, was Greg. He was inventive and clever. Greg never got into trouble for foolish or fun things. His primary motive was one reason only—financial gain. Greg had schemes going on all the time. Soda machines and newspaper machines were his favorites. He made up his own skeleton key to open newspaper racks all over town. Greg was generous with his newly found wealth. He would frequently take lots of his friends and brothers to breakfast or lunch. Greg's biggest piece of thievery came when he managed to steal the keys to all the used cars on the local Dodge dealer's lot. Every key, to every car, was in the hands of a fourteen-year-old. The dealer ran an ad in the local paper begging for the return of the keys, no questions asked. Things were getting kind of hot, so late one night Greg slipped out of the house and threw the keys, on one large ring, back on their property. That caper kind of cured Greg of his little adventures, I think.

I only found myself in trouble once. One night, Steve, Bill, and I threw water balloons at passing cars from a hidden spot in some trees. We nailed quite a few, too. Any activity of this nature, which was associated with Steve, just had to have a high dumb quotient, however. Our frolic was no exception. We were too stupid to change positions, and enough tagged motorists called the police to make scooping us up an easy affair.

Steve, naturally, denied everything.

Denied all with full water balloons in our possession.

Denied all with pieces of our exploded missiles yards away from us.

Denied all with water from the balloons soaking all of our clothing.

Does this sound familiar? Do I hear a rooster?

We did a lot of weekend activities as a family during this time. We would go to the beach, to an occasional baseball game, or camping in the Sierras. Clay took all five boys on a camping trip in the high country early one spring. We fished a little, built a homemade toboggan course in the snow, and constructed an alarm line around our campsite. We made it from tin cans and wire to warn us of any approaching bears during the night.

During the summers, the family signed up for a membership at Club Almaden, which was a day use picnic, sports, and swim facility about a dozen miles away in south San Jose. We would pile in two cars with all of our gear and spend the day working on our sunburns and hamburger munching skills.

The Vietnam War was the leading headline in the news during this time, as was the growing anti-war movement. Even though he was a former Marine, Clay was dead set against the war in Vietnam from the outset. He saw no compelling reason to send young Americans to a far-off land to "protect our interests." Clay was one of the first adults I ever heard speak out against our involvement in Vietnam. He was a classic candidate for the so-called "silent majority"—a Middle American, blue-collar worker, military veteran—but Clay was the type who made up his own mind concerning weighty matters.

The family status quo changed a little when my stepbrother Steve went to live with his mother, and her husband and children in Montana. Steve had a lot of problems getting along with everyone, and he and our parents thought a temporary change to finish out high school somewhere else might benefit him.

The status quo changed a lot in March of 1968 when Clay suddenly became sick. One day at work, he was found asleep inside a turbine under construction. The company sent him home because he seemed disoriented. The next day Clay called in sick, which never happened. That evening, while walking down a hallway in our house, Clay stopped, walked backwards a few steps, and then collapsed. An ambulance rushed him to a hospital. They started running tests right away. The next day Mom went to see Clay, and he seemed stable. However, that night Mom received a call from the Doctor. Clay had suddenly passed away.

Everyone was dumbstruck. We had a houseful of crying people. I had to get away, and went outside to shoot baskets at a neighbor's house. At that point, I needed to do something physical, I guess. It turned out that Clay had thrombotic thrombocytopenic purpura, or TTP, a rare blood disease. TTP causes reduced blood flow to the cells, resulting in organ damage. I don't know anything about the disease, but in Clay's case, from first outward symptom to death, was only a matter of a few days.

Needless to say, everything changed in our family. Within a few months, my stepbrother Dave and sister Embry graduated high school. Dave moved out and married his girlfriend, and Embry went away to college. Steve stayed with his real mother in Montana, and Greg, Judy, and Joanna soon joined them. There were hurt feelings, and some harsh words exchanged among many of the family members. Eventually, the Andersons and Normans pretty much lost touch with one another. I did see Dave a few times after my high school days, but he didn't want to have any contact with our side and, from what I have heard, with his own brothers or sisters either. He moved to Oregon a few years later. He had some kids, was divorced, then he later remarried. Steve stopped by my mom's place three or four years after Clay's death. I came over to say hello. Steve didn't much like my long hair. I guess he became the conservative, silent majority type in place of his dad. I never saw Greg again. I heard he moved to Texas. I'll bet he still has some wheeling and dealing going on. He probably still shares his gains with others, too. Joanna is married and lives with her family in Idaho and still keeps in contact with my mom. Judy married her childhood sweetheart and had some up and down times. I saw her a few times during my early days in the biker world, and we shared some laughs. Sadly, Judy died in 1994 from the same blood disease as Clay, TTP. I think doctors, because of the genetic link in such a rare disease, studied her death closely.

Our family had recently been eleven—now we were four; Mom, Bill, Nancy, and me. Our dad made an occasional appearance over the next few years, now that Mom was single again. However, it was just more of the same. The only differences were the hospitals he would be in and out of, and the jobs that would come and go. Finally, when he realized Mom wasn't coming back to him, he left for Missouri once again.

As for Clay, where do I begin? He died far too young, nine days past his forty-second birthday. I wish I had questioned him about his wartime experiences, but I wasn't wise enough as a teenager to do so. I do know that he was a surrogate . . . no, a *real* father, to the four of us . . . if only for a few years. Selfishly, I could have used his know-how and guidance as I grew up and moved out on my own. However, more importantly, all of the nine kids lost his presence forever, changing each life in so many ways. Life became one hell of a lot harder for a bunch of people on March 29, 1968. Still, Clay's legacy lives on. At least three boys in the family have been named after him.

I firmly believe that people need heroes in their lives, both the historical type, and the up close kind. For me, the latter category is headed by Clay Leroy Anderson of Apache, Oklahoma.

My high school days were mostly uneventful. I wasn't in the social or jock crowd, and I was not a good student. That is not to say that I hated school or almost flunked out. I was one of those kids who seemed more-or-less, invisible. I wasn't into many extra activities, either school related or party related. I had no career plan, as some kids did. It was the time of hippies, social unrest, and the counterculture, so there was a lot going on. I did try to pay fairly close attention to things, but as far as participation . . . no, not me. I was an observer only. Scholastically, I earned a few A's in History and Civics, and a few D's in Biology and Geometry. I probably finished in the middle of the pack of our graduating class with a "B-" average.

My friends at school were comparatively few and far between. Russell Moulds was a good friend for a few years. Russ was very smart. Because of his black, horn-rimmed glasses and quiet demeanor, there were some who thought he was a geek. Nevertheless, Russ was unquestionably, funny. He was a big fan of Johnny Carson, as was I, and we would stay up late to watch part of *The Tonight Show* as often as we could. We would compare notes the next day at lunch to see what each of us liked the best from the previous night's show. Russ also was a ham radio operator, and had funny stories about the conversations he would have with people from all over the world. Russ hated being in high school. He considered the shallow students and the boring class work a waste of his time. He proved it, too. Russ graduated halfway through our senior year and took a job. I was stunned. I didn't know a person *could* graduate early. It just wasn't done back then. I wouldn't be surprised if Russ was one of those genius types who founded a Microsoft kind of company and is a mega millionaire now.

Another friend was Jim Burger. He was a real friendly guy whom everyone liked. Jim was really into film and music. His dream job would be as the director of musical documentaries, like *The Last Waltz* or *Woodstock*. In fact, after high school Jim worked as an usher (when there still were ushers) at an artsy movie theater in San Jose called the "Towne", in the Rose Garden area. When *Woodstock* played there, Jim got me in free every night. His manager didn't mind. He was a cool older guy named Mr. Babbitt. He was quite a philosopher, and was the first person to tell us that the Romans said, "In taste, there is no dispute." Mr. Babbitt may have thought differently when, shortly thereafter, the Towne was sold. It became a porno theatre, and Mr. Babbitt was out of work.

Jim also taught me a lot about music, especially about being open to unfamiliar types of music. Jim was a fan of rock and roll, sure, but he also loved the blues, especially the old guys like Sonny Boy Williamson, Leadbelly, and Sonny Terry and Brownie McGhee. Jim was always playing some new music for me that he had come across . . . *Pentangle* or some obscure folk group or something. Sometimes we traveled to Tower Records in San Francisco. Back then, it was the most popular record store in The City. As we would walk through, Jim would point out to me what I should buy. I never heard of the groups, but Jim would say "Don't worry, you will. This is only their first album. They're going to be big." The groups were bands like *Santana, It's A Beautiful Day,* and *Led Zeppelin.* Yeah . . . Jim knew music.

The other close friend from high school was Rick Wilson. Rick was a different dude. He transferred to our school as a junior from Blackford High in west San Jose. Rick's parents were rich and lived in their new place in the hills behind downtown Los Gatos. I think we met in gym class, and we hit it off right away, although I'm not sure why. Rick was everything I was not: a good athlete, smooth with the girls, wealthy, and philosophical. Rick loved to question teachers and tweak their sensibilities. The tough guys in school didn't scare him a bit, even though he was but medium-sized himself. Rick oozed confidence, and nothing seemed to disturb him. He seemed as if he were a college guy trapped in high school. Rick had a Triumph motorcycle, a 250cc I think. Once in a while, he gave me a ride home from school, which was my first experience on a motorcycle.

By our senior year, Rick, Jim, and I hung out together on a pretty regular basis. We were all in Drama class and worked on the Senior Play. Jim had a part-time job, and Rick *always* had a girlfriend, so it wasn't as if we were welded at the hip or anything. However, sometimes we would gather at The Wine Cellar, a darkly lit, bohemian type restaurant in a re-developed shopping center near school, called Old Town. There, we would hold extensive discussions on every subject, with Jim providing a lot of background info and Rick questioning and challenging everything.

After graduation, though, Jim was concentrating on getting into a film school, preferably USC. Meanwhile, Rick was in the process of becoming involved with the study of eastern religions. That didn't interest me much. My focus was gaining some sort of employment. I finally found a full-time job in September at McDonald's. My mom liked that, too. She definitely wanted all her kids to move out right after high school.

I enrolled part-time at the local community college, West Valley, in nearby Campbell. As it happened, my first day on the job at Mickey D's was also the first night of class at West Valley. So I became a working class hero and Joe College on the same day. I rushed from work, back to the house to change clothes and try to get the grease and Big Mac smell off me (to little avail) and made it to school for class. It was time to concentrate on being a real live college student, and to put the potato hauling behind me for the evening.

Class started, and a student arrived late. He walked to the next row over from me and sat down directly next to my seat. He was a tall, somewhat geeky looking guy with a fake-leather black safari jacket, milkman white pants, and Beatles boots. Something about him seemed familiar. I looked again. It was Roy Givens, the assistant manager who trained me that day at McDonald's.

Words to describe the situation failed me. No . . . come to think of it, there were words . . . *three* words, in fact.

What . . . The . . . Fuck.

ᴄ✍ Chapter Four ✑ᴅ
"St. Joe"

A full-time job, coupled with even a part-time attempt at college, proved too difficult for this skinny boy. I dropped my classes by midterm; or, so I thought. It turned out I didn't officially drop one class, California History. The instructor gave me a D for the term, which was fair since I had an A for the first two months, but an F for the last two. That was too bad for me, as it took a long time to get my GPA to any kind of respectable level. One life lesson learned—complete the paperwork.

In the meantime, I got my first car, and started to put some money aside to move out and away from home. A few months into the McDonald's job, my friend Rick from high school called and said he needed a roommate for an apartment he and another guy rented in west San Jose. Since my mom and I were in "argument mode" on a frequent basis, that worked for me. It was always over the usual teenager/adult topics—hair length, bills, chores, etc.

Rick and his friend Nate Collins rented a three-bedroom, two-bath place in a nice area of San Jose near San Tomas Expressway, for $165 per month. I made $64 gross per week, so the $55 tariff for rent was workable. This was the autumn of '69, and I just turned eighteen. The apartment was perhaps ten miles from Los Gatos, but a new world for me. San Jose was the big city, and I was on my own, like many other young people. As with most of them, I had the same struggles of getting to work on time, learning how to pay bills, budgeting meager assets, figuring out how to prepare food, etc.

Rick and Nate had a lot of friends, many of whom were a few years older than we were. Drugs were everywhere and cheap too. Our apartment was a few miles from the Westgate Mall, which was a popular hangout for druggies on that side of town. Besides marijuana, which was a staple for just about everyone, reds (seconal), were popular. A lid of weed was ten dollars, and a "nickel" bag or jar of reds, as the name suggests, was five bucks. The trading point was—how many reds to a bag? The standard was about thirty-five. Those were cheap highs (or lows, as the case may be).

I saw a lot of drug use from up close over the next several months. In addition to the staples of weed and reds, there was plenty of hash, LSD, psilocybin mushrooms, and even some peyote, which was kept in the freezer. Our place was kind of a hub for people to gather. It never got out of control or frenetic and I never felt as if it were a "drug house." I had my room, and my privacy was respected, along with my decisions not to partake in the drugs. Oh, I tried a few, sure. However, most drugs just didn't have much appeal to me. I found weed to be too much bother. You had to work too hard at just getting a decently rolled joint. Plus, the smell of pot is lost on me. Over the years, people who are fans of weed have always implored me to, "Smell this, man . . . smells great, huh?" Well . . . *actually* . . . *no, it doesn't*. It smells like all the other pot to which I'd been exposed—no better and no worse than any other does. Guess I'm just not an aficionado of marijuana aroma.

As for the harder drugs, I never saw the allure. This stance was not based upon any pious view of the world. If others wished to get high, and they did, then so be it . . . have fun. I rather figured that getting through daily life took all my faculties, and I liked at least to *feel* as if I were in control of working things out. Most of the time, however, I was probably as inept as the next person was. I don't remember ever trying LSD, shrooms, or peyote and the like. Taking reds made little sense to me. All the people who routinely took lots of reds had stories of how they wrecked their car, or been beaten up because they were unable to defend themselves, or some other ridiculous misadventure that was directly attributable to being so stoned on cheap pills that they couldn't function in a crisis situation. It wasn't that I didn't enjoy getting high some myself, but I suppose I cared more about maintaining some control over my environment. Or, maybe I just bought in to the ad campaigns run by straight society and stayed on the outside edge of the drug scene.

My roommates were certainly in the scene, however. Nate was a good guy who considered me pretty square. Fair enough. Nate genuinely liked getting high. Moreover, he liked talking about how terrific it was being high after he came down from being high. Nate adopted the hippie credo of sex, drugs, and rock and roll with gusto. He worked some part-time jobs, as a fry cook I think. However, mostly Nate worked at getting high, as many young folks did during the early 70's. Even so, Nate was a great roommate. He always pitched in to help with the place. He paid his portion of the expenses on time. He was also quite handy at household repair, which was perfect, since Rick and I were not. A few months after I moved in, Nate's girlfriend moved in to our place. Her name was Pam. She liked getting high as much as Nate did. They were perfect for each other. They seemed truly happy in life . . . *and why not?* They had everything they needed . . . sex, drugs, rock and roll, and each other.

See, in those days everyone closely followed the rock bands and all the kids would eagerly anticipate the new album release of their favorite groups. It was a monumental event, something to be celebrated. When the Rolling Stones, say, or Lee Michaels or Creedence would release an album, one person would buy it and bring it around for everyone to listen to and comment on . . . usually, while getting high, naturally. We didn't have a lot of food in our apartment, but we always had a stereo and plenty of albums. People would trade albums and loan them all the time.

It was a time of sharing. Food, drugs, music, sleeping space; hey, if you needed it, there was usually someone there to help you. It was us against them—the counterculture versus the culture—and of course, it couldn't last. It wasn't that we were a commune or anything, but the people in your circle cared about you. The kids down the hall in the apartment complex, or the other friends of my roommates . . . these were our "support group". It was a good feeling to have folks there. It couldn't last because people move on, relationships change, people argue, things happen. It was cool while it lasted, and I was accepted even though I wasn't the coolest guy around.

I was one of the kids who had a real, full-time job. Quite a few of the other kids were just living off their parents, part-time work, hustling around town for a few bucks, or some combination thereof. My friend Rick was one of those. Rick had no job, and saw no real reason to get one. He had grown his hair long by this time, so the chances of being hired by someone were slim. However, Rick had no use for employment anyway. He would get some pick-up job occasionally, but mostly he lived on the edge of the system—getting a little from his parents, a little from county programs, or panhandling. Rick was a master panhandler. He was always exceedingly polite and looked quite sincere. He was adept at selling himself. If Rick needed a meal, and there was no one from the group to help him out—no problem. He'd spare-change from strangers at the mall for cash. Besides, his needs were small, a bowl of rice, and some milk perhaps. Rick didn't work because it interfered with his philosophizing. Rick was into Hinduism, Buddhism, and Scientology (before any celebrities were) . . . almost any kind of out-of-mainstream philosophy he could find. Rick was always challenging my middle class and (relatively) straight-arrow lifestyle, too. I learned to challenge and question right back.

Rick attracted all kinds of interesting and varied people around him. Wes was one of his old friends who knew all kinds of things about music. Mark was a stoned-out hippie type who always told everyone "I'm hep, man, I'm hep." Fred was an Army veteran who had gotten out of Vietnam alive and who, along with his brother Alan, tried to consume all the reds available on the West Side of San Jose. Fred took the drugs so often that his tolerance skyrocketed. Soon he would have to take thirteen or more just to get high. Glad I stayed away from those reds.

Then heroin came on the scene, and things got worse. Drugs were so easy to come by back then—and so cheap—that it was hard to believe it sometimes. I don't remember who first brought the heroin around, but soon there were outfits stashed in the refrigerator. (Outfits or "fits", were the drug user's paraphernalia, to use a current term, needed to inject the heroin into the vein). To be clear, these were *not* antiseptic hospital type syringes, but homemade needle rigs, a giant rubber band, a spoon, and the little squeeze dropper from nose drops bundled up in a baggie. I had a goodly fear of needles anyway, and I wasn't about to try the stuff, so I couldn't tell you the exact procedure for shooting up, it's been so long, but I remember it wasn't a pretty sight—or safe. Rick developed an abscess on his forearm that grew to the size of a golf ball. Others had purple and blue marks and splotches on their arms. That wasn't even counting the fact that everybody who took heroin always threw up.

Later, some people thought it would be great to shoot up reds, so they broke open the capsules, heated up the powder, and shot that up. Eventually this phase passed with no full-blown overdoses, but not for want of trying.

Rick would try all these drugs. He was the quintessential experimenter. Rick took Timothy Leary's teachings to heart, continually trying to expand his mind. Getting high was not the process for Rick that it was with Nate, Mark, and most of the others. Rick was one of those guys who seemed to get high to find some ultimate truth on the other side. I don't know if he ever found that ultimate truth; but, if not, it certainly wouldn't be for lack of effort.

It wasn't all music and a few drugs for me during this time frame. I managed to acquire a little of the other piece of the trinity—sex; although, not to the degree which I would have liked. I had a couple of girlfriends during this time, although nothing of much duration. I vowed to continue with the effort, though.

Maintaining a running auto was tough. I got into wrecks with two different cars within a year, neither of which was my fault, thankfully. Nevertheless, it still made getting to work difficult; also, the attendant insurance hassles were a drag. I started feeling a little jinxed with all the wrecks. It was as if Bob Sr., and his penchant for wrecking vehicles, were cursing my driving or something.

A lot changed over the next few months. We moved to different apartments a time or two, and then Rick took off on one of his long distance hitchhikes. He had been hitching for some time—he and I ended up hitching to Los Angeles a few times during those years. I don't actually remember why we went, but I'm sure Rick had a legitimate reason at the time. We usually ended up in Westwood or Santa Monica. I can't recall anything unusual happening when we were in LA. Mostly, I just remember the process and time on the roads. Rick honestly liked hitching. However, to me, it was too much hassle and too time consuming. We would be stuck somewhere for hours, waiting for the next ride. Rick never wavered. He was constantly upbeat on these sojourns. He would spur me on to have a positive outlook, as well. Hitchhiking back then was safer than now, and more common. You could always rely on other "longhair types" to give you a ride, too. When you saw a Volkswagen bus approaching, your spirits lifted. We got plenty of rides from people in VW's.

One day, hitching our way back from Los Angeles, we were dropped off at a freeway on-ramp in Salinas, in Monterey County. Rick and I were burnt out and dragging ass. To make matters worse, there were five or six people already queued up at the on-ramp, each waiting their turn to hitch a ride north. The hitchhiker protocol dictated that we had to wait our turn, so we could see that it was going to be an even longer day for us.

We took our place along the roadside, sat down on the asphalt shoulder, and leaned against a metal light pole. We had nothing but time on our hands, so I began reading the messages scrawled on the pole from previous hitchhikers. One missive especially dampened our already low spirits. It read simply, "No wonder Steinbeck left this."

Once, in the winter of 1971, I believe, when we both had pretty long hair, we were dropped off near Santa Barbara, in the town of Isla Vista, near the University of California campus. It was the middle of the night and quite cold. We were hanging out at an all-night restaurant, wondering why the only customers were a large number of police and the two of us. We left, and sometime later managed to get a ride from one of the rare cars we saw on the streets. The driver was a local who told us that Isla Vista was under curfew because the local Bank of America had been firebombed just a day or two before by some radical types . . . for the *second time*. The driver let us crash at his place until daylight. We were amazed that the cops at the restaurant had paid us no mind. Maybe they knew we were just harmless fools in the wrong place.

Not long after Rick left on his cross-country trek, Nate, Pam, and I, briefly got a place together. It was near my work on the other side of San Jose, and was a basement apartment in a rundown area. It was the type of place where you could hear mice munching in the walls while you were trying to sleep. It didn't take long before Nate and Pam struck out on their own, which was okay with me. With both Rick *and* Nate gone, the network of people on the West Side was changing; and besides, I was spending more time with people from the McDonald's area.

During my time at Mickey D's, I had become friends with Roy Givens, the assistant manager who first trained me, and whom I had found to be my (brief) college classmate. Givens (pretty much everyone always called him Givens) was a couple of years older than I was, and lived a few blocks across the street from the "unit." Givens had electric guitars and amps, and as I was trying to learn the guitar, he gave me a few tips. He also had a pool table in the front room of his one-bedroom apartment, so quite a few of the guys from Mac's would hang there on their off hours. An added bonus was the number of young, single female type personnel who were living at the new apartment complex where Givens lived.

After Nate and I left the dumpy place with the mice, Givens was kind enough to offer his place to me. For about the next six months, my sleeping quarters were under his pool table. It was perhaps a little cramped, but the commute was nothing, the company pleasant, the billiards free, and I met some fun people. As I said, the day the *Angel* with the Conchos pulled into McDonald's, I had a vision of someday becoming a scooter tramp. At least I was well on the way to the tramp part. However, the acquisition of a real motorcycle was still a distant dream.

It was at Givens' pool table one day when I met Drew. I had no clue what an influence this one person would have on my life; but then, I suppose no one can see these kinds of things approaching.

Drew Hilliard lived in the apartment complex with Givens, and Roy met him a few times and invited him over to shoot some pool. We all started playing, and from the git-go, Drew had me laughing. He was unlike anyone I had ever met. Drew was upbeat, energized, and all *go-*

go-go. He provided a running commentary as each of us took our shots at the table. Drew had a novel way of speaking and used terms and phrases that I never heard before. He'd say things like "Oh, you just face-raped me there" or "I just got porked in the asshole with that shot." He had me laughing non-stop. Drew started calling me "The Kid" that day because I looked so much younger than the two of them. It turned out, however, that I was older than Drew was, and we had been born at the same hospital in San Jose just eight days apart. His mom was going in practically as mine was coming out, I guess.

Drew had a tough upbringing. His parents divorced early on, and his mom had taken up with many different guys. She was an alcoholic, so all things considered we had quite a bit in common. Drew hardly knew his dad when growing up, and I believe his father had died some time before we met. Drew had a stepsister, but they didn't get along too well. He got his high school girlfriend pregnant just before graduation, and he and Linda lived in an apartment across the complex. Sadly, the baby died a few months before I met Drew, from Sudden Infant Death Syndrome, commonly called, "crib death".

Over the ensuing months, Givens, Drew, and I spent a lot of time together. We would play pool, or fool around with guitars and such. Drew and his wife, Linda, worked their night shift jobs, and after a time, Givens and I ended up on the night shift too . . . at McDonald's. We would stay up late and watch the only all-night movie channel in San Jose, play some music, or go late-night bowling. Givens and Drew were in competition over everything they did; guitar playing, drinking, bowling, billiards, eating, boasting about sexual prowess, it didn't matter—they were always trying to one-up each other. Then each would try to win my approval over the other, as if my opinion would validate their view. This was a constant source of laughter to me, and to Givens and Drew as well, but not so funny to Linda.

She didn't like Drew leaving her behind, so sometimes he would bring her along. Unfortunately, all she would do was bitch the whole time. Linda was a very unhappy person, and I don't think that Givens and I were the source of her unhappiness. Having your only child die when you were still teenagers must have been devastating to Drew and Linda. They seemed doomed as a couple. Added to Linda's trouble was Drew's desire to be a biker. In fact, he was dressed like a biker when we met.

Drew, at that point, was one of those wannabe bikers I mentioned earlier. Drew had long hair, a beard, and wore biker clothes.

The problem was that he had no real motorcycle. A fact which Givens and I reminded him of many times. Drew wanted to be known as "Satan", and was determined to get a bike. Linda was just as determined *not* to be married to a biker. They did eventually divorce, which was much better in the long-term for each of them.

Meanwhile, I was going in all different directions. I was trying to figure out what to do with myself. I drifted around a lot for the next couple of years. I quit work to grow my hair and be a little rebellious. Then I went back to junior college full time for a while, this time at San Jose City College. I moved back in with Mom for a few months, then back with Givens for a time. Along the way, I had some part-time and temporary jobs.

Then, a car or two came and went. It all kind of runs together in my mind now and it probably did then.

Then, Givens and I enrolled in a trade school. He did great, but I only did, so-so. Eventually, Givens got a good electronics job, saved his money, and bought an old, small house in west San Jose right before the real estate market began to take off in the middle of the 1970's. In retrospect, I could have used the guidance of my stepfather, Clay, to help me through this difficult time. I bet all nine kids from our family could have said the same.

One direction I did figure out was the military option. Uncle Sam was moving from a full draft to an all-volunteer military, and the bridge between the two was the draft lottery. In the lottery system, all American males who would turn nineteen in a calendar year were subject to conscription based upon a random drawing of birth dates done late in the previous year. That meant all of us who were born in 1951 were in the drawing pool of 1970. The idea was to eliminate the deferral system of the full draft, with all its inequities, by a purely random scheme.

For example, if July 10th was the first date drawn, every guy born on that day would be number one for the draft call-up to meet the manpower needs of the Armed Forces. Every calendar date would be assigned a number, and the military would then estimate where the cut-off line would need to be to meet the upcoming year's demand quota. Needless to say, almost everyone hoped for a high number. A high number meant you could make plans for your future, knowing you almost certainly had no military obligation. A low number meant you probably needed to enlist, so you could at least choose your branch of service. Other options were moving to Canada or facing prison time, which a few guys did.

The Vietnam War was the big elephant in the room, and the 1969 lottery needed up to around number 195. With all the anti-war sentiment in the country, and with the policy of "Vietnamization" taking place, work force demands were thought to be on the decline for ensuing years. Still, my birthday was selected 131; so, in all likelihood, I was going to be called up.

Most of the guys my age wanted nothing to do with the Vietnam War, just to add some perspective. There was a big distrust of the "establishment" and any gung-ho, military fever, had become a victim of the nightly news and body bags laid out on an air base runway. There was a lot said about how the World War II generation didn't hesitate to fight for America when their turn came. However, to almost everyone I knew, WW II had nothing to do with Vietnam. If we had been attacked, as in 1941, the same rush of manpower would have occurred. However, as the 1970's came along, the Vietnam War was seen as a never-ending mess that had only been started to protect the interests of the oil, rubber, and tin companies in the first place. The military leaders inspired zero confidence in the younger generation. Almost to a man, returning vets who were slightly older than us told us to stay away from the current military, if we could. I remembered my stepfather Clay had been against the Vietnam War from the start. This was another example of a time when I could have used his guidance and advice.

However, the real kicker for my assessment of the military situation was George Graves. George was a kid from the neighborhood in my high school class. He was small; in fact, we were just about the same size. George was an excellent athlete and pretty much a jerk, like most of the jocks were at Los Gatos High. George had a brother named Steve who was also in my class and a real good guy who worked at Magoo's Pizza in Los Gatos. Anyway, George was too small to compete in varsity sports, except for wrestling. Our senior year, Los Gatos had two State wrestling champions. One of them was Graves, in one of the lowest weight classes. Yet a few months after graduation, Graves was called in for the draft physical and *failed*. Because of a sports injury, Graves couldn't fully extend one arm (perhaps a degree or two shy of full extension) and thus was exempt from service. Therefore, Mr. Super Jock who could out-muscle anyone his size in the state couldn't serve in the military, but, nobody schmuck guys like me, could. No thanks, Uncle. They probably would have used me as a tunnel rat, because of my size. Tunnel rats were small guys who were given a .38 revolver and a flashlight, then told to go down a tiny hole in the ground and take out any

Viet Cong hidden there. I wouldn't wish that duty on anyone . . . even George Graves.

My decision to enter the military or not, became moot when Senator Alan Cranston and others delayed the necessary legislation long enough so that the time it would take to induct and train the nineteen-year-olds of 1970, had grown exceedingly short. The call-up for that year ended at lottery number 125. I skated by six numbers.

Amidst all my bumming around, I did manage to connect with a real girlfriend during this time. Givens had an off and on girlfriend named Chris who had a friend staying with her for a few weeks. Sarah and I hit it off from the start. She was from the San Diego area and was really cute. Sarah was also bright, kind and talented. She wanted to be a gemologist and was always making jewelry for people. Sarah extended her stay for some months, and we got pretty close, at least closer than I had been with any other girl. We even started talking about long-term plans a little, although, I hadn't actually figured out what I was going to do with my future.

Then Sarah's parents got her into a gemology school in Santa Monica, near UCLA. I had no faith in long distance romances, but it was too good of an opportunity for Sarah to pass up.

Fortunately for me, I had experience in traveling to Southern California via the old thumb route with my buddy Rick Wilson, and so I would go down to visit Sarah when possible. Unfortunately, for me, Sarah met and fell for somebody else at the school, but didn't bother to tell me in any of her letters. Consequently, on my second or third trip hitchhiking to LA, I was greeted at Sarah's apartment door by the look of a girl who just OD'd on Novocain. It was essentially, "And your name is _____?"

That was one . . . Long . . . Hitchhike . . . Back . . . to old St. Joe.

"Then I headed back for home
And somewhere far away a lonely bell was ringing.
And it echoed through the canyons
Like the disappearing dreams of yesterday."

Kris Kristofferson, "Sunday Morning Coming Down"

ꞇ❧ *Chapter Five* ❧ꞇ

"On The Fringe"

San Jose City College had some outstanding teachers. One of my instructors was an older guy who lived through the Nazi occupation of The Netherlands as a teen. Jan Groenen emigrated to America post-War and learned English as he put himself through college in only three years. Then he worked on the staff of Tennessee Senator Estes Kefauver before becoming a teacher. Mr. Groenen picked me up hitchhiking to and from school a few times. He gave tough History exams, but always assured the students that everyone would get at least one question correct. You could hear the laughter at different times across the classroom as each student came across the particular question. Both the question and all possible multiple-choice answers were in Dutch . . . pretty clever. Groenen would mark any answer given by a student as correct.

Of course, there would always be some Gomer in class who would say, "Mr. Groenen, I just can't seem to read what number thirty-eight says."

I took two or three classes from Groenen . . . he was that intriguing. He even ran for the State Assembly one semester but didn't win. After a time, I quit that school, too. More rambling to do, I suppose.

Meanwhile, Drew and I were hanging out quite a bit. Drew bought a 1957 Chevy that was all black and had a jacked-up lift kit on it. We cruised around town a lot and that car got *lots* of attention. We'd buy a large bottle of Coke and a small bottle of Ten High whiskey. We knew it wasn't exactly Crown Royal, but it was cheap. Drew later sold the Chevy when gasoline started becoming too expensive. Besides, he was always being pulled over by the San Jose cops for operating an "unsafe vehicle."

Drew had a factory job as a machinist, and when he put his mind to it, could accumulate some cash. When he sold the '57 Chevy, he bought a VW bug, and then put all his money toward a bike. He bought a three-wheeler, an old "45" that had been a police bike some years before. It had a long, extended front end and was ugly and slow, but it was a motorcycle.

Around this time, my mom, brother, and sister moved from Los Gatos to a mobile home park in San Jose that wasn't too far from where Drew, Givens, and I lived. Drew would sometimes come over to the park, and we'd hang out at the clubhouse and shoot pool. One day, Drew was riding out of the mobile home park on the trike as I followed in his car. I don't know what the hell happened, but the bike suddenly went squirrelly, went airborne, and crashed back down on Drew, slamming and dragging him along the asphalt. When the trike stopped bouncing around, I loaded Drew up in the car and took him back to Mom's place where she cleaned him up as best she could. Drew wasn't too seriously hurt, and he sold that trike soon afterwards. With that long front end and the altered center of gravity, it was just too dangerous to ride.

After Drew and his wife split up, he became a full-fledged biker when he bought a Harley Panhead. This was a real chopper, though pretty basic and needing some work, but a definite step up from the trike. By then, Drew was spending most of his time with bikers, and I had gone back to school (again), this time to the west side of town at West Valley College. West Valley had a brand new campus in Saratoga that was fancy. I'd go to class and half expect some French waiter with a towel on his arm to say, "Table for one, monsieur?"

I got some steady employment for a spell, and managed to buy a 1957 Oldsmobile. She had a big back seat and a large trunk (sounds like a country song). The extra room in the Olds worked out well for me since I lived out of that car for a month or so. I had a sleeping bag, guitar, and a trunk of clothes, and that was about it. I lived off and on at Givens' place, Mom's (who moved back to Los Gatos after her short stint at the mobile home park) and various crash pads of friendly folks.

My focus was going to school and scratching out a living, but more and more I was beginning to live on the fringe of Drew's world of motorcycles. I'd never given up my dream of becoming a biker, which started a few years earlier when that *Hells Angel* rode into my McDonald's. I hadn't made any tangible progress toward that goal, however. I wasn't even thinking in terms of goals, really. What was changing was that I was beginning to learn some of the biker ways from Drew. He was getting to know and experience the world of scooter tramps, and in turn, would tutor me.

Drew soon joined up with a car club in San Jose called the *Vi Kings.* It wasn't the "Vikings", but the "Vi Kings", with a pair of dice between the two words. They wore a club patch that looked just like a bike club patch. Since only a few members like Drew had bikes, officially, they were a car club; but, with the back patch they looked like a bike club. The whole thing was really quite confusing.

The *Vi Kings* soon were taught a difficult lesson. They were paid visits by the local outlaw bike clubs, the *Hells Angels* and the *Unforgiven Sinners*, and told to disband. Back in the 60's and 70's, the outlaw clubs in many cities would try to control who would wear back patches and who would not. This control varied from city to city. Cities with one dominant club tended to be tightly controlled. Those cities with no dominant club, or which had competing clubs vying for dominance, tended to be more open. San Jose was tightly controlled. Los Angeles, for example, with its tremendously high population, was loosely controlled. I'm sure the situation was similar in other states. The dominant club could be a local one, or one of the large national clubs, such as the *Outlaws, Bandidos*, or *Hells Angels*, for example.

In San Jose, the *Hells Angels* were dominant. In fact, the San Francisco Bay Area was their largest region of influence. The *Angels* had over half a dozen chapters in the Bay Area. The San Jose chapter was one of the newest, formed in 1969. The history that I was told, later verified by some participants, was that there had been a momentous biker war in the 60's between the Bay Area *Angels* and the biggest outlaw club at that time in San Jose, the *Gypsy Jokers*. After a bitter struggle, the *Angels* won. Some of the *Jokers* retired, some of them joined the new San Jose *Hells Angels* chapter, and a number of them moved to Oregon and kept their club going there. The word was that a few even stayed in San Jose in defiance of the *Hells Angels* and kept a low profile, only wearing their patches (or "colors") on certain safe occasions. Occasionally *Jokers* could be seen riding on a freeway through San Jose . . . always in a group, and always moving fast. The enmity between the two clubs wasn't my concern. I just thought they had a cool name, *Gypsy Jokers*. That had a good ring to it.

The dominant outlaw clubs essentially gave two reasons why they attempted to exert control over any new clubs that wished to form. First, was the notion that too many clubs would cause confusion and lead to more biker club wars, so limiting and controlling the proliferation of bike clubs would impose a stabilizing equilibrium on the chopper scene. Second, was the idea that any criminal behavior or negative publicity generated by the actions of the new clubs would be blamed on the dominant club. The principle invoked here was that most citizens, upon seeing biker types, especially ones wearing club patches, immediately call them all *Hells Angels* or *Outlaws,* or whichever club was dominant in a particular locale.

Neither one of these arguments holds water, however. In fact, they are nearly laughable. I will grant that many people, and I can attest to this from experience, will insist that they saw *Hells Angels* when in reality the bikers weren't even wearing club colors at all. I'm sure the *Bandidos, Outlaws, Angels,* etc., are blamed for many things they never do. I'm also certain they don't really care. It adds to their image and, besides, they *are outlaw* clubs, right? It comes with the territory. No, the real reason for limiting the number of smaller bike clubs in a city is "We are in charge, and you're not." Since that was the order of things, then so be it.

Therefore, the big thing in San Jose was to take patches. If you wore a bike club patch without permission, you could lose it. It could end up being a trophy on somebody's wall. Now to clarify, this situation didn't apply to clubs that were strictly car clubs. They usually wore a kind of windbreaker anyway, so there was usually no confusion with the bikers' colors, which generally were sewn on to denim or leather vests.

Dresser clubs didn't count either. A dresser club was a group of guys who rode full dress motorcycles, that is, the ones with the big fairings, fancy fiberglass saddlebags, windshields, CB radios, and at least a dozen extra gadgets that made them dressers. Usually these clubs were in the AMA, the American Motorcycle Association, and were populated by straight citizens who had nothing to do with the scooter trash scene.

The *Vi Kings* trouble came because, although they called themselves a car club, they had biker looking patches, many of their members looked like bikers, and some, like Drew, had choppers. They also hung out at the San Jose cruise scene located in downtown San Jose, in the area of First Street and thus were highly visible. The kicker against them was that the bottom rocker of the club read "San Jose." The dominant clubs didn't like anyone sporting San Jose bottom rockers. I never quite understood this dictum. Neither one of the clubs, the *Unforgiven Sinners,* nor the San Jose *Hells Angels,* had "San Jose" on *their* bottom rocker. (The *Angels* used to have the chapter city as their bottom rocker, but had some time previously switched to the state, or in the case of international chapters, the country as their bottom rocker).

The *Vi Kings* quickly disbanded. Drew never gave up his colors, but I guess a few of the guys were not as fortunate. Soon, Drew took a big leap and became a hang around for the *Sinners.* A hang around was the first step toward becoming a full member, and just to achieve the hang around status meant some people in the club liked you.

After a short time of hanging with the *Unforgiven*, Drew had some bad luck when his Harley was stolen. It had been parked in the County Courthouse parking lot when it was taken. Drew was inside for only a few minutes paying a ticket when the bike was stolen. Since he had no bike, he couldn't be a hang around, so he left the company of the *Sinners*. Drew was devastated, and I felt badly for him. The count was now at two bikes that had come and gone within a year or so for Drew.

The good news, from my perspective, was that I started spending more time with Drew and meeting some of the guys from his old car club. Soon, I quit junior college (this is getting to be habit-forming) and got a job at an electronics manufacturing company. Givens, my old buddy who worked there, put in a good word for me.

Drew introduced me to a guy named Bret Hayes, and his nickname, given to him by Drew, was "Angel". Bret was a few years older than I was and a tough dude. He was not overly tall, but he was strong and sturdy, and well respected by the club bikers, even though his bike was a Honda. In fact, Bret's bike was a chopped Honda that was still in the shop, so he had multiple strikes against him, really. I mean, if you did have a bike, you were supposed to be riding it. Still, everyone seemed to treat Bret with great respect. The three of us began hanging around a lot. "Satan" and "Angel" were now flanking me. However, I rarely used those nicknames. I still called them Drew and Bret. They called me Kid, as did everyone whom I had met through Drew.

We'd hang out at parties together, along with a few other guys like Ralph and Dennis McGinley, who were not bikers but car people and decidedly upbeat and fun to be around. I had turned twenty-one, and it was my first serious partying time. We would go to the Bodega, a nightclub in Campbell that had terrific bands and many women, although we tended to get into fights there. We were just stupid guys looking for women or trouble, and we generally found one or the other. One night we got into a decent-sized brawl, and the bouncers threw all of us out. The owner told us not to return. Sometimes, we would go to Jake's, a topless bar in East San Jose where a lot of bikers gathered.

During this time, Drew would tell me stories and share his experiences with the different bikers he hung with over the last year or so. I was determined to get a bike and try the lifestyle. Drew still looked and acted like a biker, and tried to get me to do the same. He was always attempting to get me to buy a denim vest, add biker buttons and pins to the front of it and have Harley wings sewn on the lower back of the vest. This was the standard look for independent Harley chopper riders in those days. I demurred. I didn't want to dress like something I was not; and at that time, I certainly was *not* a biker.

I wasn't a hippie, either, at least not in my mind. Oh, I had long hair, took a few drugs, had trouble maintaining a steady income, and had no real address much of the time. These were all things that would identify me as a hippie in many people's minds, I suppose—but I never considered myself a hippie. I hung around with some folks whom I thought of as hippies—and that was cool—but we didn't have the same mindset or values.

Besides, I was never able to pass the tests to make it as a certified hippie. First, I tried tie-dyeing a tee shirt. That was a disastrous mess. My shirt looked like Ken Kesey's Merry Pranksters dyed it when they were *not* high on acid. Then I tried throwing Frisbees with the hippie types. You know . . . the guys with the bell-bottom pants who would throw the Frisbee a mile and their dogs (with headbands tied around their necks) would catch the disc in mid-air? My tosses were embarrassingly shoddy. Even the dogs seemed to roll their eyes at my feeble throws. Then some hippie chicks tried to teach me to roll a joint.

That was a total failure. After fumbling about for a few tries, they reclaimed their pot before I could drop any more of it on the carpet. It was one more reason that I never cared too much for weed. It was . . . too . . . much . . . work.

I guess that I just wasn't skilled at any of the practical applications of hippiedom, although I did get decent marks in the political rhetoric exam. See, and all this time you hadn't realized there were tests for this counterculture stuff back in the 70's.

I was on the fringe of the biker world and on the fringe of the hippie scene during this time. One place where everything came together was a small nightspot in the Santa Cruz Mountains called *The Chateau*. It was located deep in the hills and was hard to reach. *The Chateau* was at the bottom of a twisty, narrow, pot-holed road. My '57 Olds could barely make it back up the road when I would leave. A lot of the other older cars and VW buses had the same problem. The difficult access was a blessing, though. Being so isolated, *The Chateau* rarely had any cops come around. Whether the club was located in Santa Clara or Santa Cruz County (the boundary line was close by) I don't recall. In any event, it was a long out of the way drive for any deputy on patrol.

The Chateau had some big-name bands appear there. Mostly, though, it was just a cool little party haven situated in the middle of towering redwood trees. The crowd was a mix of hippies, heads, bikers, rockers, stoners, college types, and regular folk. I wasn't there a whole lot, but I did go as often as I could.

There were some cottages across the road and above *The Chateau*. These were rented out, mostly to young people, and I briefly dated a girl who lived there. We were at her place one night when I heard a massive roar outside. It turned out to be the arrival of most of the *Hells Angels* San Jose chapter. They would sometimes come up to *The Chateau* after their club meetings on Friday nights. That was the first time I ever heard the sound of a pack of Harleys together. The noise of the engines filled the mountain air and echoed throughout the canyons.

I never met any of the *Angels* at *The Chateau*. (I was a little occupied the night they showed up. I think we were practicing political rhetoric or something). However, I did meet a few bikers on my trips to the club. I even met a couple of the ex-*Gypsy Jokers*. I was still on the fringe of the scooter world—not a biker, not a hippie—just a longhaired guy bouncing around the San Jose scene.

Things changed a bit one night in February of 1973. It was a Friday night, Bret's birthday, and the three of us were at Bret's duplex on the East Side, getting ready to go out, along with Bret's girlfriend Barbara, Drew's girlfriend Lisa, Bret's roommate, a stocky guy named Charlie, and a few other guys from the old *Vi Kings*. Just as we were about to leave, a thunderous roar came from down the street. In a few moments, most of the *Unforgiven Sinners* parked their bikes out front, and they were on their way in to the small duplex. Turned out that Drew told them that it was "Angel's" birthday and invited them to come by and "just say hi" to him, since their weekly club meeting was being held only a few blocks away that night. When Bret's girlfriend found out what prompted the unannounced visit by the *Unforgiven*, she stared daggers at Drew.

In no mood to make a quick exit, *The Sinners* continued to hang out. The thought of the two girls in the middle of that crowd convinced Bret to have the girls go on ahead to the party. Most of the other people left too, or at least tried to do so. As it happened, one of the guys from Drew's old club who was there, named Danny, was on unfavorable terms with the president of the *Sinners*, a guy named Eddie. Eddie recognized

Danny's car when they arrived, and positioned his bike about three inches in front of Danny's Chevy, effectively blocking him in. Eddie had been Drew's sponsor when he was a "hang around" for the *Sinners*, and Eddie was big into mind games. When Danny tried to leave, Eddie refused to move his bike and allow Danny room to maneuver. Danny struggled for ten minutes trying to get the car out without hitting any bikes, with Eddie watching from the porch the entire time. Finally, he made it out. I figured then that as long as the *Sinners* were there, my chances of getting to know real outlaw bikers in an all-too-up-close and personal manner were, unfortunately, excellent.

Soon the impromptu Birthday Party consisted of Drew, Bret, Charlie, about eight *Sinners*, and me. I was wearing a V-neck sweater and cords, in my Joe College look. I thought back to the words of George Gobel, who once said, "Did you ever feel that the world was a tuxedo, and you were a pair of brown shoes?"

The *Sinners* got bored, but not bored enough to leave. Maybe it was a slow Friday night for them and they were waiting around awhile before heading off somewhere else. I wasn't going anywhere, either. Drew always told me that one of the big sayings in the biker world was, "Go for what you know." I determined just to be myself and see what happened.

Some of the *Sinners* started roughhousing amongst themselves, crashing into furniture and walls. Then the toughest looking *Sinner* of the lot, the Sergeant at Arms named Richard, punched out Bret's roommate, Charlie. It was quick, decisive, and bloody, although it was just one on one. Charlie must have said the wrong thing. At least he did in Richard's mind. I reckoned somebody else would soon take exception to something that I would do or say.

Then someone found Bret's birthday cake in the refrigerator, untouched. The *Sinners* quickly started a cake fight among themselves, making sure they paid close attention to Birthday Bret in the process. When things died down, there was beer spray and cake residue all over the kitchen floor and walls, and in the faces and beards of Drew, Bret, and all the *Sinners*.

The only person still untouched was me, Mr. Brown Shoes. A large *Sinner* named Slice walked up to me.

He said, "You're not wearing any cake."

"No," I replied, "it clashes with my maroon sweater."

Then I got nose and face full of birthday cake, courtesy of Mr. Slice. I quickly assessed the situation. Yep. Devil's Food, with a not-too-sweet icing . . . tasted good. I then scooped a handful of cake and returned the favor to Slice, compliments of The Kid. Slice just smiled, took another swig from his bottle of Jack Daniels, and walked away.

A while later, the *Sinners* all left. We cleaned up Charlie. Then we cleaned up the duplex. Then Drew and Bret called their girlfriends and went out together, with Barbara's stern lecture to Drew added, at no extra charge. I went home and relaxed. I didn't wear the maroon sweater much after that. The college look was fading away, although I still wasn't ready to wear a denim vest with Harley wings just yet. It had just been one night, but I felt good about things. Maybe someday I could exist in the world of *Sinners*, *Jokers*, and *Angels*.

Drew and Lisa were married not long after Bret's birthday party. Lisa Martinez was cute and a genuinely nice person. The wedding was pretty normal, not a biker wedding or anything. My mom and kid sister Nancy even attended. Mom always liked Drew. Some of the *Unforgiven Sinners* were there too. They half-threatened to kidnap Drew and keep him from making the matrimony mistake. Most of the family and friends at the reception were a little nervous about a bike club being in their midst, but the *Sinners* were on good behavior. There wasn't even a cake fight.

Drew and Lisa rented the Martinez home from her parents, as they just moved up to a better place. Drew was in heaven. They had a real house with three bedrooms, plus a garage . . . for cheap. Lisa hated it, though. She lived nearly all her life there and would have preferred something else. Financially, however, it was a terrific set-up, even though the place was on the East Side of San Jose. Lisa was devoted to Drew, and it showed.

A few months later, Drew offered me a spare bedroom at their house. I said sure, since the price was right—free. Lisa wasn't crazy about that idea, but she always was kind to me. I tried to pull my weight around the place—cleaning up the kitchen, doing some yard work and such. Lisa wasn't much of a housekeeper and Drew was zero help. Besides, they commuted to Palo Alto every day for their jobs, which was a fair distance away, so they weren't around much. I worked much closer to the place, so I had time to lend a hand.

The guy who put in some serious work was Drew's new father-in-law. David Martinez was a real hard-working guy. He reminded me of my step-dad, Clay. He would finish his shift at the cannery and then head over to his rental to do hours of yard work. Drew never left the couch and his television programs to help Mr. Martinez out with the yard work. Sometimes, I would help David out. I don't like seeing others work while I sit. Drew, however, seemed unmoved. Lisa was too, for that matter.

I guess they figured that the rent they paid covered the gardener too. I would often tease Drew.

"You've got your own Mexican gardener."

"Yeah Kid . . . My own personal *bracero*."

Drew and Lisa made good money . . . and spent a lot, too. Still, they managed to save up quickly for Drew to buy yet another bike. Lisa was into motorcycles, too. She met Drew when he was riding, so they had bikes in common, unlike some other couples I had seen in which the wife wanted no part of the motorcycle or the expense required to own one.

The new bike was a 1958 Panhead. It had a super long front-end, the kind that made people gasp when they saw it. The front forks were extended thirty-three inches over stock. That bike took up the same parking footprint as a small car. We added some locks and security to the garage, and Drew set out to customize his new ride even more. For the next few months, I received a little hands-on training about the care and mechanics of a Harley.

Drew kept encouraging me to get my own bike. I didn't have all the necessary cash yet, so Drew suggested that maybe I should begin with a Triumph or a Norton instead.

"Uh, that would be a big *No*, mister. My first bike will be a Harley Davidson, just like yours was."

Still, I knew I couldn't afford a gleaming customized ride like Drew found. My sights would have to be set a little lower.

About this time, I was given $1,200 from a trust fund that my grandfather had set up. He put away two dollars per month per grandchild, payable at age twenty-one. Thanks, Buck; I appreciated it. I took the money from the fund and, along with what I had saved, paid all my bills. Then I put some needed maintenance into my '57 Olds, bought some clothes, and took the rest on a road trip, looking for an old bike at a reasonable price. I went out on weekends from Santa Rosa to Stockton and down to Fresno, to check motorcycle shops and want ads for a workable deal. I found nothing.

I returned to San Jose, a little forlorn. I bought a local newspaper and for about the tenth time looked in the want ads. For Sale: 1947 Knucklehead . . . $800. I called the number. The cycle was in Santa Cruz. It ran, but wasn't rideable. That weekend Drew and I rented a trailer, then drove over the hill. I hoped the Knucklehead would be in halfway decent shape.

It was. It was black, brown and ugly. It had no chrome, a large front tire, a crummy seat, a cheap gas tank and stupid foot pegs . . . and, it was . . . wonderful. The owner started it up after only about five kicks. The Knuckle sounded strong. Drew looked at me with surprise. He nodded his approval. It had a suicide shift and a cracked wheel nut, and there was no way I could test ride it, but there was also no need.

The $800 changed hands. We trailered the bike over the hill to San Jose and its new home . . . next to its good-looking cousin in Drew and Lisa's garage. The Knucklehead needed lots of work and re-fitting to be ready for the road . . . ditto for its new owner.

I had a beer that night, June 17, 1973 . . . my first cold one as a Harley owner. Then I spent an extra five dollars, got one of those Harley wing patches, and asked Lisa to sew it on my new denim vest.

I could wear it now.

⚬ *Chapter Six* ⚬
"Shiloh"

Harley Davidson produced the Knucklehead engine from 1936 through 1947. The term Knucklehead came from the shape of the valve covers on the twin cylinders. This new "V Twin" design proved to be popular and durable, and that basic look remains the standard for most of the big bikes today. The prewar Knuckles were 61 cubic inch displacement, about 1000 cubic centimeters, or cc. During World War II, production of street bikes ceased and Harley built motorcycles for the military. After the War HD resumed the Knucklehead line; this time with a 74-inch engine option, about 1200cc, which had been introduced in 1941. I was lucky. The bike I bought was a "74", the same displacement as new bikes in 1973.

In 1948, Harley came out with the Panhead engine. The Panhead name derived, again, from the valve covers, which somewhat resembled upside down wash pans. The cylinder barrels and the lower end of the engine were similar to the Knuckleheads, but the Panheads had internal oil supply to the valves at the top of the engine, and fewer parts in the valve cover assemblies. Pans were superior and stronger than Knuckleheads, but the gulf between the two was not a chasm, and it's not as if the Knuckles were looked down upon.

The biggest problem, I would soon find out, was the availability of parts. By 1973, the Knuckleheads had been out of production for over twenty-five years. Back then, the aftermarket industry was not nearly as large as it is today. Since the production run only lasted about eight years, there weren't very many around either. The popularity of motorcycling took off about the time that the Panheads emerged. Panheads were out of production too. Harley switched to the Shovelhead line in 1966 (which, among other changes, featured a return to the outside oiler system like the Knuckleheads). Harley produced loads of Panheads for eighteen years, so obtaining parts for them wasn't a problem.

The other model Harley Davidson produced that was suitable for chopping was the Sportster. These bikes were a little smaller than the "74", displacing 1000 cc, and so were more affordable to own. Sportsters were acceptable in the biker scene, but weren't as highly regarded or as desirable as the larger "74's". Fortunately, a lot of non-engine accessories and parts would fit on all three of the Harley "74" product lines. That was one of the beauties of a Harley—you could swap an engine out, or a transmission, even a frame. A 1973 off the shelf transmission, for example, would fit nicely in a bike made in say, 1952. Alternatively, you could buy a brand new Shovelhead, tear it down, and put the engine and transmission in a 1950's frame and have the better of two worlds—a newer, stronger drive train coupled with the classic lines of a vintage bike. Harley switched from a fully rigid steel frame, commonly called a "Rigid," to a more forgiving and comfortable frame, called a "Swingarm," in 1958. Swingarms essentially had shock absorbers in the rear. The Rigids looked much better because the lines of a rigid frame just flow perfectly in a customized chopper. However, the Swingarms were more practical, especially on longer rides. Street chopper modifications were a continuous blend of what looked good versus what was practical; with a healthy dose of individual economic constraints mixed in.

The Harley Davidson Company had undergone a significant change a few years before when they sold the firm to AMF Corporation. AMF was a large sporting goods company making, among other items, bowling balls . . . groovy. AMF made a number of changes to the Harley line. They added new, sportier factory models to complement the full dress look Harley had always marketed. In addition, the Shovelhead engine received a makeover, mostly to the crankcase, or lower end. The shovel valve covers, again named for their appearance, remained intact. This new engine was called the FX.

Quality problems in the manufacturing cycle plagued the new Harley product lines, however. The word on the street was that the FX bikes didn't measure up to the older, more trusted Harley models.

While that may have been true, it certainly didn't stop guys, both dresser and chopper riders, from buying new bikes. Another favorite tack was to buy a new FX engine (still backward compatible) and install it in an existing bike. In 1973, an engine sold for about $735, which was a large sum. My *whole bike* cost $800.

This combination of desirable older models—already modified to choppers or still essentially stock—coupled with the economic reality meant most chopper riders customized their bikes a little at a time. Sometimes a guy would buy a new bike, but that was a rare occurrence. Many guys, though not everyone, did a lot of this work themselves.

There were also shops that specialized in customizing, along with guys who had expertise in specific areas and who would take in work on the side.

My new bike needed quite a bit of work, far more than my limited mechanical knowledge would allow. Drew provided some advice and instruction, but it was a long, slow process to get the rebuilding job off the ground, much less completed. Drew had me take the bike down to the frame. That was probably a reasonable idea if one were well versed in re-assembly, but I was not. Looking back, I realized I shouldn't have tried to perform such an extensive re-build with my limited funds and knowledge. Getting the bike up and running was a learning experience; I should have only replaced the necessary items. Through trial and error, though, I came to understand the size of the task I had in front of me.

The biggest obstacle was the transmission. My Knucklehead came with the factory, stock-issue jockey shift, called a "suicide" which was cumbersome to operate. The suicide shift had a foot clutch on the left side and the gearshift below and to the left of the rider. To ride, one had to remove the left hand from the handlebars and quickly reach behind and locate the shifter at each change of gears. For a novice rider on a big bike, this was difficult, and a safety concern. I needed to buy a "ratchet top" to convert the transmission to the standard foot shift. That was expensive. I had to save up and buy the part, and then repeat that same process with successive items that needed replacing or re-fitting on my 74.

Fortunately, one of Drew's friends from the *Vi Kings* was a biker named Lenny McLaws, who was a whiz at transmission rebuilding. McLaws, nicknamed Snatch, was thin and wiry, and had a pretty blue Panhead that he built himself. McLaws knew a lot about choppers for a young guy, and the transmissions he built were super. The problem with McLaws was one many guys had—dependability. Lenny meant well, but getting him to commit to a schedule was problematic. Many bikers, I would discover, had haphazard schedules at best, and were terrible at following through on commitments. Eventually, McLaws delivered my new tranny, and it was perfect—super tight performance with no problems, and a smooth kick-through start.

Over the summer, I slowly bought needed new parts; had the frame worked on to add back some mounting tabs that some previous owner removed, cleaned up and maintained existing parts which were good, and various other tasks everyone must go through to learn motorcycle rebuilding. Drew provided direction, although his bike was running so he was out riding and partying much of the time. His lifestyle was one of constant motion. He would go on bike runs with his riding buddies on weekends and help me with my bike and continue to party around San Jose during the week. Still, Drew made it to work every day. He was even helping Bret (Angel) with his rebuilding job. Bret sold his Honda and bought a Harley. It was a Knucklehead, like mine.

Drew would work on his bike in the garage and would sometimes bring bike parts into the house and do some piece work while watching television. Bret and I picked up this habit, and soon were doing likewise. Once, I stopped by my mom's house—I don't remember why—and had some of my disassembled parts in my car. Mom just had new carpeting installed in her living room. I casually brought my oil tank, which had been drained, inside her house to work on. I was sitting in her family room, which was behind the living room, quietly working away on the oil tank. Mom was seated nearby, watching TV.

My teen-aged sister Nancy, the last child still living at home, appeared in the doorway with her eyes the size of silver dollars. She motioned me over to her. Then she pointed to a trail of old, used, black motor oil spread across the width of the newly- carpeted living room. What I thought had been an empty oil tank dripped some old residual oil on Mom's brand new carpet. At that moment, I seriously considered silently packing up and leaving her place—never to return. It would just be better that way.

Nancy took charge of the situation right away. She found some kind of cleaner; I didn't know what it was, and she and I feverishly worked to clean up the oily trail as best as we could. Mom finally figured out what was going on and, surprisingly, took it all in stride—if you can call locking herself in her room and not talking to anyone for hours—as "in stride". The cleaner Nancy chose worked pretty darn well. The carpet wasn't perfect, but much better than I expected it would be. This was the first time, but certainly not the last, when I would see a female's quick thinking save a dumb biker from his own actions.

Although I was making progress toward getting my bike on the road, albeit slowly, one factor remained unresolved. I had never actually *ridden* a Harley Davidson. True, I did own one, but I had not driven it . . . or any other Hog, either. In fact, I had only ridden a motorcycle once, and that was for five minutes. My sister Embry bought a Honda 90 when she was at college, and once managed to bring it down to my mom's place during a summer break. I had ridden it there one time, and that was my total sum of hands-on biker experience. Drew offered his bike for me to try, but I was reluctant to get on my first Harley with the front end extended out 33 inches. I could just see his bike in pieces scattered along the street. Nobody else who had a bike (at least one that ran) knew me well enough to offer me the use of his bike, which was just as well. I resolved that when I rode my first Harley, it would be my own.

I thought my motorcycle had a good symmetry of numbers to it. It was a '47 "74". Harley stamped the engine cases with engine numbers that consisted of the model year, the model designation, and the serial number of the engine produced. Mine was 47FL3447. I liked that . . . a lot of fours and sevens.

Then, I named my bike Shiloh. I didn't name it for the Civil War battle, although I am a Civil War "buff" as the saying goes. I named it for the song by Neil Diamond, even though he spells Shiloh differently. I had a feeling that this bike was a turning point for me and that we would be together for a long time. Turned out, I was right.

Not long after I bought my Harley, I started going out with a woman I just met. Veronica and her close friend were passing through San Jose when I met them. We hit it off right away. Veronica was older than me . . . and divorced. She had a young daughter who lived with her dad in Washington State. We had a few things in common, even though our backgrounds were quite different. She and her friend ended up staying in San Jose, her friend also hooking up with a local guy.

Veronica's last boyfriend was a biker from her hometown, Yakima, Washington. He was in an outlaw club there called the *Ghost Riders*, so Veronica knew the whole biker routine all too well. In fact, she almost dumped me early on when she found out I had a bike, except I wasn't a real full-fledged biker yet, so she gave me the benefit of being only a chauvinist in training. As Hawkeye Pierce from *M*A*S*H* said, while channeling Ethel Merman, "There's no *vinism* like chauvinism."

By 1973, I was no longer a mere 110-pounder, as I had been back in my McDonald's' days. No, I was all the way up to 125 pounds, and just short of six feet. I was no longer the shortest guy in a crowd, but more often than not, I was still usually the skinniest. My jeans had a twenty-nine inch waist, with an inseam of thirty-three. That meant one tough shopping trip for pants—since there weren't too many jeans in that size. Veronica was built the same as I was. She was tall for a girl, about five feet-eight, and was thin, like me. People said that when we stood together we looked like a relief poster for a third-world country.

Veronica and I got a place together not too long after we met. It was a little studio apartment on the East Side, not far from Drew and Lisa's house. Veronica had gotten a job at a retail clothing store in downtown San Jose, in the area of "head shops" near the San Jose State University campus. I was still working at the electronics company. My bike remained at Drew's, in various stages of work. It was a tough balancing act—living with a woman for the first time, working, and rebuilding a bike.

Drew and Veronica didn't get along too well. She was older and wiser than most women Drew had been around. She was also pretty sassy, which I liked. Drew was well set in the biker ways by then, and was doing his share of getting high and partying quite a bit. The two of them were kind of an oil and water thing. Veronica didn't take crap from people and stuck up for herself well. Some guys don't like that. Each of them kind of put up with the other, however, because of me I suppose.

The friend Veronica traveled with to California didn't cotton to me much, though. The two gals didn't hang around much with one another, once Veronica and I moved in together. Veronica took a big chance in hooking up with me. She was a long way from home and family and still took a flyer on a guy who was potentially heading down the same path as her last boyfriend, which hadn't ended well for her . . . as I said . . . sassy.

Just after Labor Day weekend, Drew told me of an upcoming meeting of local bikers that was to be held in town. Drew heard about this meeting while on a motorcycle run to the Ukiah area with a bunch of guys over the long weekend.

I drove over to the site on the scheduled evening. I had never seen so many choppers before. It seemed like half the scoots in San Jose were parked outside the small meeting hall. Bike numbers are deceiving though. What seems to an observer to be ten is usually about six. If you think there are fifty, there are probably around thirty, and so on. Nevertheless, there were dozens of bikes there that night, with perhaps eighty people there altogether.

The subject was the rights of California motorcyclists. Riders in the state had been fighting the passage of a mandatory helmet law on an irregular basis over the prior five or so years. The bill had come up a few times in the state legislature, but had been narrowly defeated by various grass roots organizations, sometimes quickly thrown together for that sole purpose. Virtually no one in the chopper scene wore helmets when riding. Being completely in the wind was half the idea. More important was the feeling of freedom, of making your own choices when riding. Mandatory helmet laws went against that whole credo. A few guys did wear helmets; that was their choice. To most bikers, however, a mandatory helmet law was the worst thing that could happen . . . next to wrecking your bike, of course.

As we found out that night, a new motorcycle rights group recently started up. This group was called the Modified Motorcycle Association, and was headquartered in Sacramento, the state capital. Similar meetings to the one that night in San Jose were being held at different locations across the State. The "MMA" had hired a full-time lobbyist. They were now a tax-exempt non-profit corporation—the first of its kind in the nation. The guys in attendance, nearly all independent riders in small groups of friends, such as Drew and his buddies, were being asked to join this new MMA and support the bikers' rights movement. The cost was five dollars per year.

The men heading the meeting were the president, Flint Cramer, and vice-president Lyle Grisham, of the San Jose *Hells Angels*. I'd heard some of the guys mention those names before. The president and VP of the *Unforgiven Sinners*, Eddie and a guy named Miguel were also there. They helped to organize things and get the word out. I met them a few times previously, starting that night at Bret's birthday party. Even though I was new to the bike scene, this type of activity seemed unusual to me— you just didn't hear of the outlaw clubs brass reaching out to the general chopper riders. Drew and some other guys in attendance, including a man named Phil who just moved in to a house across the street from Drew and seemed to know many of the bikers there, confirmed this.

The idea of a bikers' rights organization had merit to me, although I couldn't see how five dollars per person would make any appreciable difference in California politics. I certainly wasn't keen on being forced to wear a helmet. California at that time was the only state never to have enacted a helmet law, and I didn't much care for the notion that, just as I was about to get my first bike on the road, new laws might be coming onto the books. I shelled out my five bucks and signed up. Plus, what the hell, I had never seen *Hells Angels* up *that* close, and I might never again.

Quite a few guys in the crowd signed up that night. I went home feeling good. I met some new people, and discovered there were some folks in the biker community looking beyond their own immediate concerns.

About a week later, Drew called me up one evening after work.

"There is going to be another biker meeting. You should come."

"Another one so soon? When is it?"

"Tonight . . . in about an hour."

"What? Hey, thanks for the notice, man." I was not happy.

"All right then, man. Don't come if you don't want to."

Testiness aside, I said I might show, and he gave me directions to some guy's house where the meeting was to take place. Veronica was even less happy than I. She wasn't keen on me spending too much time with bikers, especially the one named Drew.

I drove to the house, which was in a nice middle-income area of South San Jose. There were only a handful of bikes out front, perhaps ten. Strange, I thought. Unless maybe a lot of guys were thinking like me—too soon for another MMA membership recruiting drive. When I walked inside, I saw Bret, Drew, and Phil, the guy from Drew's neighborhood. A few others looked vaguely familiar.

Once the meeting started, things became clear. This wasn't a general MMA meeting. The guy talking had a different agenda entirely. His name was Howie, and he seemed to know almost everybody who was there.

The subject was a motorcycle club; a *brand new* motorcycle club. Right here in San Jose. Not an outlaw club, but an MMA affiliated club. A club that would work as a group for the benefit of the MMA, and also be a close knit brotherhood for its own members. I looked at Drew. *Wish he had given me a heads up*, I thought.

I learned more as the evening progressed. The idea for a new club started among some brainstorming by Howie, Drew, and Phil. Each invited a few of their friends whom they vouchsafed to the other two organizers as trusted and dependable fellows. Drew had brought in Bret and me. There were about twelve guys that attended.

Over the next few hours, ideas were brought forth, strategies emerged, different options discussed, and pros and cons were debated.

Forming a new club would be a big deal. Both Howie and Drew were former hang arounds of the *Sinners*, and although the theory is that hang arounds have no obligation to a club, and can leave at any time with no "hard feelings", no outlaw club looks with favor upon the former hang arounds joining another club, much less going out and forming their own.

We also discussed what priority the new club would take in each member's life, in relation to family and job commitments. A lot of the married guys weren't about to put a brand new club, which might not even be in existence in six months, ahead of their family.

The idea of back patches was discussed. Most guys said that was a tough sell to the local outlaw clubs. I never imagined myself being in a club. However, if I were to join this one, then why would I settle for anything less than a back patch?

Then too, would the MMA even agree to this? They didn't know us. Would the MMA take on the risk and liability?

I knew less about the biker life than anyone else present did, but I contributed my share to the discussions. Overall, the guys there who were new to me seemed pretty sharp and sensible. Everyone contributed to the discussion.

We agreed to meet in one week to continue the effort. After that, the meeting broke up for the night. We decided a lot that first night.

First, family and work took priority. I knew, and I'm sure others did also, that peer pressure to put club activities first would certainly arise. That is just the way of things when men form into groups. Nevertheless, we were not going to be an outlaw club, so the club was not to rule over family.

Second, we would draw up a proposal to represent the MMA at car shows and help organize other fundraising efforts in the region, holding to the MMA's position of inclusion to all bikers. This meant we would be dealing with all sorts of street motorcycle riders, from outlaw types to mainstream bikers.

Third, since the look of most of the guys was that of a typical "biker", a few key individuals would approach the outlaw clubs to get their okay to form. We wouldn't push for back patches, at least not at this time.

Last, we would use the MMA logo, which consisted of the letters MMA in gold in the shape of a motorcycle, for the center of our patch, and our club colors would be black and white.

We had our strategy set—we had chosen our look—now for some tactical decisions. Like who was in and who was out. Twelve guys were present. Ten committed that night. The other two weren't sure. Soon they both dropped, with no hard feelings. Their names were Jeff "Wax" Patrick and Dave Bellagomba, called "Bubbleagumma."

Then officer elections were conducted. Bret was elected President, Howie was VP, a mountain of a guy named Keith, a friend of Howie, was Sergeant at Arms; and Phil's friend named Mitch was elected Secretary. The rest of us were regular members.

We bounced ideas around for the name of the club. Then John, the guy whose house we were at, said, "What about *Wheel Lords?*" Everyone liked it. John could draw fairly well, and he sketched out the lettering with the MMA bike logo in the middle. Everybody liked the look. *Wheel Lords,* San Jose, it was.

I started out Thursday, September 13, 1973 simply going to what I thought would be a quick meeting. Three hours later, I was in a motorcycle club. I got home and told Veronica the news.

One of us liked the idea.

☙ *Chapter Seven* ❧
"Men and Machinery"

The *Wheel Lords* met on Thursday nights. Club meetings were called "church". The officers would caucus first. After that, the full Club would discuss business. Outside of church, each of us was getting to know one another. This process would take some time, but we had to start somewhere. I thought I had been learning quite a bit over the last six months or so, but I soon realized that I didn't know jack shit. I mean, I met Jack Shit, but I really didn't *know* him. That was okay—we had a mix of people with varied skills and backgrounds, and some were more seasoned than others in the scooter world. I had thrown my lot in with these guys.

Bret Hayes was our president. As I said earlier, he was a solid dude and a loyal friend. The kind of guy you wanted on your side in a tight spot. "Angel" was respected, but he, in reality, wasn't a leader. I had some doubts about his ability to take charge and inspire the guys. Angel was fun to party with and was a regular guy with no pretensions. Bret spoke up reluctantly, and he didn't show that "take charge" personality. Still, Bret enjoyed the enviable position of having good things two ways—everybody respected him . . . and nobody messed with him. Angel was about thirty and was building up his first Harley chopper, a 1946 Knucklehead. Bret lived with his girlfriend Barbara, who was older than he was. Bret liked getting high, and he and Barbara went through cigarettes like Sherman through Georgia. Angel had long hair and usually wore a tank top and vest to show off his muscles.

Howie Heath was the Vice President. Howie was a driver. He set a lot of things up in the Club using his forceful personality to good effect. Howie was probably in his late twenties, married with kids. He had a nice house and a respectable job. Howie usually got his way. He was a smooth operator politically and could "talk shit" well. Howie had been around the bike scene for a long time and knew most of the angles. He was adept at assigning tasks and much of what we accomplished early on was due to him. Unlike most of the guys, Howie didn't sport a nickname. But Keith, his best friend in the Club, called him by his first and middle name, so some of the guys copied that and referred to him as Howie Dee. Skilled at building coalitions, Howie knew how to get his way. My partner Drew was one of those whom I thought was too easily swayed by Howie's arguments. Howie was rather short, maybe five-eight. He had piercing eyes and a full beard. Howie was the kind of guy who got a lot done, but left you kind of questioning the methods. He was a good bike rider, and something of a neat freak. His bike was a new 1973 Shovelhead, already customized and nice looking. When Howie rode somewhere, the first thing he would do upon arrival was to comb his hair and beard and make sure he looked sharp. He didn't drink, but liked weed.

Keith Wilcox was Sergeant at Arms. That position was primarily the club enforcer, keeping the members in line when necessary. Keith was just the guy to do it. He was about six feet three inches and 325 pounds. Keith was about the same age as Bret and Howie. He was married and had kids. Keith had long hair and a beard and looked like the stereotypical big, bad, biker dude. Keith was no oaf, though. He was smart, and would speak up intelligently when he felt it was needed. Keith smoked weed, I think, but I don't recall if he took many of the other drugs that were passed around. I do know he could chug a beer in about a half-second, however. Keith had a regular job and was a real family guy. He was a straightforward dude. If he didn't like something you said or did—he would tell you. Keith rarely used his size, however, to an unfair advantage. I think Keith was a regular-sized guy stuck in a big man's body. I also think he would have loved to have been about five-ten and 180 pounds, and not have the expectations put on him that came with being an oversized guy in a bike club. Keith loved rock music and was fun to party with. He also liked to tease, a trait always held in high regard by the Normans. Keith would call me "juesos" which he said was Spanish for bones. I took his word for it. I hoped it didn't really mean dipshit. I'd have to kick his ass. Keith rode a 1962 Panhead that was nicely built out. He called it "Rosebud." Like *Citizen Kane*. Cool.

Phil "Wrinkles" Early was the oldest in the group. He was thirty-two—but looked older. Phil was acknowledged as the best bike mechanic around, and just about *everybody* came to Wrinkles for tips and assistance at some time or another. Phil rode a rigid frame chopper with a 1972 Shovelhead engine. He didn't do many drugs—but drank regularly. Phil had already been through a couple of marriages. His dad, a real crusty old guy, owned a Texaco station on North First Street and Phil was a mechanic there. Phil was one of those guys who looked like he never changed his jeans. They were the same greasy pair day in and day out. Phil was a great guy, very generous with his time and knowledge. In fact, Phil's biggest problem was that he was too nice. He would commit to anything that was asked of him and then, being spread too thin, would have trouble keeping those commitments. Phil helped out a lot when I was building up my bike. Savvy in making things work and fit together on a scooter, he was also an excellent bike rider. Phil was called Wrinkles because of all the lines on his forehead, but soon most of us called him "Old Man Phil." I hadn't seen the old movie *The Treasure of the Sierra Madre* at the time the Club was formed. Had I done so, Phil's new nickname would have changed to Dobbsy. Phil looked just like the Humphrey Bogart character Fred C. Dobbs in that movie. Same height, same build, same beard, same receding forehead, same disheveled and dirty look . . . man, he was Dobbsy all the way.

Miller Mahone was the other guy (besides me), of the original ten who didn't look like a typical biker. "Tank" was tall and athletic looking. He rode a 1972 Sportster that was hardly modified. Tank was undoubtedly the richest guy in the club. He owned a nice house and worked in Fremont, just up the freeway from San Jose, at BART, the Bay Area transit agency. Tank worked nights as a maintenance-type guy and made six dollars an hour straight time, and much more than that on the routine overtime that BART always seemed to require to keep the trains running.

Once, Tank told me he couldn't make it to a Club function because he was asked to work on the holiday weekend at triple time and a half pay—$21 an hour—and couldn't pass that up. I wouldn't either. That would be over $100 an hour in today's world. Tank was also into old cars. He had a clean, old coupe, something like a 1940 or so. Tank seemed smart and capable, about thirty years old, and was the business looking type with short hair and a beard, which helped when we needed someone to talk to business owners and the like. Guys in the club, who knew Tank well, spoke highly of him, but since he missed a lot of club functions, we never saw all that much of one another. I don't even remember his old lady. There were some times that I thought Tank was only a *Wheel Lord* in his spare time.

The other guy who was in the thirty-year-old age group was John Fowler. John was married and had a cool wife named Shawna. He rode a 1951 Panhead that was in nice shape—when it was running. There always seemed to be some problem with John's bike. John had no nickname. Most of the time guys called him John Howell. He looked a little like a young Wolfman Jack, with that kind of fifties hair and a small goatee. John worked at some kind of auto parts distribution job I think. Like a number of the guys, he was a car guy too. John Howell liked to have a drink in his hand, and wasn't much into drugs. See, a fifties guy

79

all the way. John Howell reminded me of my cousin Buddy Michael, who was older than I was and had a bad ass '66 Chevelle SS in the Fremont area. John had a low tolerance for bullshit, and would argue his point with conviction if he thought he was being conned. John was about average height, a little stocky, and quite an extrovert. He loved to laugh, and would always be grabbing my shoulder or poking my ribs to do the same. Just about everybody liked John Howell a lot, including me. John was a cool guy to be around. He could be a pain when he got impatient, but he could also be a voice of reason and amusement too.

Drew Hilliard and I had been friends for about four years when he backed my entry into the *Wheel Lords*. Drew had his 1958 Panhead and shortly after the club started he ditched the thirty-three-inch-over-springer front end, for a more reasonable, ten-inch over-wide glide. Drew was about five nine, and powerfully built. His weight would fluctuate up and down depending on how much he worked out and how much junk food he ate. Usually he was around 180 pounds. Drew wasn't into sports, but he was athletic. He was one of those people who could do a standing back flip, even while wearing heavy biker boots. Drew liked to drink, but never, ever touched tobacco. Drew's drug theory was quite simple; if one dose were good, then two would be better, and three must be *great.* "Satan" reveled in being a biker. He also was a sap for those cutesy animal shows on television. A man of many contrasts, Drew could instigate a brawl one minute, then sit down and want to play a Bee Gees tune on his guitar the next. Sometimes Drew would tend to overplay his hand while trying to impart his wealth of experience to the Club. "I've seen it before, man," he would say. This would cause much groaning and Keith would call him "Windy" because he was full of hot air.

Lucas Rodes was about six months older than Drew and me. His nickname was "Weasel." Lucas had moved to San Jose from Washington a few years earlier. He was one of Phil's friends. Lucas had a terrific running '58 Panhead. He had been a hang around for a club in the Pacific Northwest and was extremely street smart. Lucas was an outstanding chopper rider. Some guys take to it naturally, and Lucas was one. Lucas was about five nine and medium build. He had kind of wild hair that, while not overly long, looked kind of like a lion's mane, especially after riding in the wind. Lucas was one of those binary guys. There is right and wrong, good and bad, black and white, or as Lucas would say, "the best" and "all fucked up." In Lucas's mind, there was little room for shades of gray. Naturally, in Lucas's view, his way was "the best" and if you disagreed with that, you were "all fucked up." Lucas was, without a doubt, one of the most stubborn people I've met. Consequently, we communicated on different levels for a while; but, it all came together over time. Though Lucas had little formal education, he did have keen insights into people. Lucas was 100% committed to the club, and had little patience for anyone who didn't feel the same. Just the kind of dude you need to have, luckily for us. Lucas had a girlfriend I only saw a few times, but she seemed pleasant. Lucas liked to get high about as much as the next guy, but of course, whatever he drank or ingested had to be "the best, man."

Mitch Moss was our first Club Secretary. Mitch was a year or two younger than Drew and me . . . but didn't look it. He rode a 1963 Panhead that was rather basic. That was because Mitch was the poster boy for 1970's scooter trash. He was always unemployed and didn't have the coin to spruce up his bike much, but it ran well. His mentor Phil saw to that. Mitch came from Illinois and was a real hell raiser. His nickname was "Sleaze", and it fit. Mitch was an extrovert like Drew and was always at ground zero of any club partying and high times. If Mitch was near, you could be sure something was about to happen. Although he liked to cultivate the image of a fuck-off, Mitch could handle the duties of secretary quite well, wrote fine Club letters, and knew how to talk to people in a business setting. I didn't know, but I wouldn't have been surprised if Mitch had been one of the better students in his high school class, but that didn't fit the biker image. Mitch's girlfriend's name was Connie. She was older than he was, liked bikes; and, *unlike* Mitch, she worked for a living. She also thought Mitch walked on water. Most of the guys thought well of Connie and looked out for her—hey, and why not? She was a scooter tramp's dream.

Add Kid to this mix, and you have the ten original members. It would show to be a strong group. A mix of older and younger guys, these were biker novices and old hands; street-wise guys and guys who could run public meetings and deal with the MMA business requirements. I felt fortunate to be a part of this group. It would be a good environment in which to learn—about scooters, bikers, and as it turned out, myself.

One of my first lessons, as part of the club, had to do with motorcycle colors. Black was the most popular chopper color, and probably still is. Red and blue were common too. Sometimes, there would be a gray or a yellow, with other, rarer colors. Our Club followed the norm, mostly black and a few red, perhaps a blue or two.

One color that was *never* seen was green. Drew told me, and others agreed, that green was bad luck for a chopper. I was skeptical. Wasn't the Kawasaki racing team a light green? They said, "Yeah, but those aren't choppers, so they don't count." Then Drew told the story of how this guy he knew, painted his bike green; then shortly after had been killed in a wreck. I turned to Keith.

"Is this some kind of 'Windy' moment?" I asked.

He said, "I don't know about that guy, but green *is* bad luck, for real. That's all I'm saying."

I thought about painting Shiloh green anyway, just to be contrary and to fuck with everybody.

Then I reconsidered. Maybe I shouldn't. Maybe the guys wouldn't even ride with me then. I mean, even *Lords* shouldn't tempt the Gods . . . *right?*

Chapter Eight

"Sanction"

The next few months were busy ones. Veronica and I were getting along well. We were both working and were slowly adding some home touches to our little apartment. I put the rest of my spare cash into building up the bike. There were new parts to buy, and old ones to refurbish. Drew helped me quite a bit. I couldn't afford to make the bike pretty with a lot of shiny new chrome, but mechanically things were coming together. I was hoping to be on the road in a month or so. I was getting impatient to ride.

We continued the weekly club meetings. It was great to see most of the guys on bikes. I couldn't wait to join them. Bret, our President, was not yet up on his bike either. Neither was John Howell, for that matter, but everybody else would roll in to the weekly meeting site with pipes roaring. The sounds were terrific. Smells were too, for that matter. Nothing beats the aroma in an open garage full of Harleys. The mixture of motor oil, exhaust fumes, gasoline, burned rubber, and the distinctive smell of the hot cylinders permeated the environment. The scent of action and excitement lingered in the air.

I tried to arrive early. The time before meetings was a beehive of activity. It was great to see the guys pull in, sometimes singly, sometimes in pairs. There would be greetings, jokes, laughter, backslapping, and needling all around. If one member had just done some improvement to his bike, he would want to show it off to the rest of the guys. If someone had problems with their bike (and there were always problems), the other guys would give a look and perhaps offer some advice. The better mechanics in the bunch, like Phil and Lucas, would give hands-on help—tuning carburetors or adjusting lifters or playing with clutch or throttle cables. I would listen to everything, attempting to learn as much as I could about the tricks to bike building.

There was no restriction on drugs or alcohol before meetings. Nobody got wasted or anything, but it was clearly a time for fun and relaxation. It was an arena for coming together and getting to know each other, with a healthy dose of teasing thrown in for good measure. Everything was open for ridicule. If you had something that you didn't want talked about . . . your covers would be pulled. And, if a guy had problems with his old lady—look out. He was an easy mark.

It was the usual bullshit that happens when guys get together in a macho setting. It had just been ratcheted up a notch or two because of the presence of motorcycles. I don't want to attempt an explanation of the psychology of motorcycles as phallic symbols, (especially ones with extended front ends as choppers have) but I found the atmosphere heightened when the club would gather on bikes. The back and forth joking and needling was at a higher level, the senses were a little sharper, and the machismo was a little more apparent if bikes were in the mix. When we would travel by car, if it was raining hard on meeting night, this swagger was not as apparent. There was an edge, a kind of synergy in the air when the boys and the bikes were together.

I never missed a club meeting. Other than time with Veronica, it was the highlight of my week.

We did have disagreements in our meetings. That's only natural. One of the larger points of contention, at least among a few of us, was the officer meetings. Club officers would meet first to formulate strategy and build consensus. Then all the membership would meet. This system was an effective political tool. What tended to happen was that two or three officers would push their agenda at the officer meeting. They would weather the blowback and any disagreement there and emerge with the final proposal, by then fully hashed out, at the full member meeting. Then the officers would present a united front so that any opposition would have a tough task to override the proposal. Somewhat like how congress works, I guess, with committees; you build a coalition, and make the work of anyone on the other side of the issue, more difficult. John Howell and I were the most vocal opponents of this practice. We thought everyone should participate in one big debate and then we would all vote. We didn't win that argument. It wasn't a real big deal. Most decisions would likely have ended up the same. The method to get there just didn't sit too well with some of us.

Over the next weeks, most of our meeting time was spent drawing up by-laws and rules and developing our proposal to the MMA. This effort was an inclusive process, and everyone had input. It was amusing for me to see the members express their opinions. Some of the guys lacked the basic comprehension skills of group organization, and the fundamental rules structure, that I took for granted. But then, I lacked any real knowledge of engine sprockets and primary chain tension settings, so we were all learning something.

My opinions and my lack of biker experience generally left me in the minority on most things. It wasn't as if I were shunned, or excluded by the guys. Everybody was really pretty helpful to me. It's just that sometimes I felt like the last man on a major league baseball-pitching roster. You had the starting pitchers, those guys who were dependable and got the ball like clockwork every fifth day. In the *Wheel Lords'* early days, those were Howie, Drew, Lucas, Keith, and Mitch. Next, you had the relief specialists, the guys who were quite valuable in a different way. For us, that was Phil and Bret. Then there were the long relievers, maybe not used all the time but still essential to the team's success . . . Hello Tank and John Howell. Last was the guy you were bringing along to be a key contributor in the future. Now warming up . . . The Kid.

We added some new members over the next two months. Some of the guys, Howie and a few others, were anxious to grow the club quickly. Friends were recruited to hang around, and then be voted to prospect status. Only, we couldn't call them prospects, at least officially. "Prospect" was a term the outlaw clubs used, so we came up with "potential member." The thought was the MMA wouldn't agree to support a sanctioned MMA club that had "prospects"; so, the term "potential member" went into the MMA proposal. I thought the phrase too cumbersome, but so be it. Amongst ourselves, we still called new guys, prospects.

The first new member was a guy named Rollin Pickett. He was a riding buddy of Drew's. I think they met because their wives worked together. Rollin was a nice guy and super straight. He had a new '73 Shovelhead and rode all the time. Unlike most guys, Rollin rode through rainstorms. He was quite capable of presenting the MMA to a conservative business crowd.

Rollin brought one of his friends around to the Club. Jason Hood became our next member. He was just as clean cut and straight as Rollin. Jason had a '73 Shovel also. Because of their similarities, the two of them came to be known as RollinandJason, since they acted and voted pretty much the same all the time. I wasn't sure if either guy would really fit in with the club long term, but I had no problems with them.

Lenny "Snatch" McLaws got into the club around this time too. McLaws was Drew's old friend from his car club days. He was the transmission specialist who re-built mine only a few months before. Snatch rode his blue 1950 Panhead a lot. He was a good guy to have around because of his bike knowledge. Lenny's problem was he just wasn't truly dependable. I was beginning to learn how much personal discipline was required to be in a club. I wasn't convinced Snatch had enough.

Our rules said a potential member needed a unanimous vote to make them a full member. Most clubs have this same rule. Outlaw clubs usually have a six-month minimum term for a prospect. Some even have a one-year requirement. Non-outlaw clubs have less stringent policies than their counterparts did. A newly formed club like ours doesn't start at the same level as an existing club. There are trials and errors to endure. It's easier to get into a club during the formative time. For instance, the *Hells Angels* who first formed in 1948 in San Bernardino almost certainly bore little resemblance to the *Hells Angels* of the 1960's, when the *Angels* first gained notoriety. All clubs evolve over time, and our club was still in its infancy.

The upshot was that RollinandJason and Lenny were voted in after only a month or two as prospects—and good for them. I had made it into the club at the beginning with less scrutiny than the other members did. I'm sure some of the original guys had doubts about me.

We started talks with the business manager of the MMA. His name was Ron Roloff. Ron was also the registered lobbyist for the organization. He was a chopper rider and very clean cut, about thirty-five, and a tireless worker for bikers' rights. Other than an office secretary, Ron was the entire paid MMA staff. Ron reported to a Board of Directors that ran the MMA. We heard a rumor that the Board was all *Hells Angels*, but no one we met would confirm that as fact. It was a private, non-profit corporation and didn't have to tell us anything, we supposed. We really didn't care if the *Angels* were behind the organization. A good idea is a good idea. In fact, if some *Angels* were on the Board, it might be to our benefit. We figured that bikers like the *HA* could readily see the benefits of a sanctioned MMA club. We could deliver twelve or so committed people to a project on quick notice. Trying to organize a group of independent bikers to do the same, would take much longer.

Ron met with us and listened to our proposal. He reviewed our by-laws, and we got to know each other a little. Ron was big on appearance and public relations. He was wary of guys representing his organization who would reflect badly on the MMA or him personally. Many of us had long hair. Most had beards. That didn't bother Ron. After all, it was the *Modified* Motorcycle Association—chopper riders were expected. Ron wanted assurances that we knew how to act toward business owners. Bike shops and other retail outlets catering to bikers were being courted by the MMA as sponsors. We would have to approach these owners on a business level to gain their support. Ron also told us we would have to abandon any notions of acting like an outlaw club while in public places. A bar brawl or a few arrests didn't bother an outlaw club. In fact, they were almost expected. However, that couldn't happen to an MMA sanctioned club. The MMA couldn't afford bad publicity one day and go to state legislators the next to ask for considerations.

Roloff had other concerns. One was that any MMA club would need to wear only black leather vests—no denim. Also, no Nazi paraphernalia, or patches or pins with swear words either, or any of that kind of stuff.

Forget it! I'm out! My heart was set on denim. I loved my Levi cutoff. I even had some SS badges on the collar. Besides, who could afford leather?

Roloff's pet peeve was nicknames. He hated nicknames that were over the edge. He would always tell us how he saw one guy somewhere with a patch on that said his name was "Pigpen." Ron said, "Please guys, no Pigpen."

We had other visitors at our meetings. A couple of times we were blessed by the appearance of some *Unforgiven Sinners*. Their president Eddie seemed to take an especially close interest in our progress. Eddie and another member or two would stop in and give us the benefit of their wisdom—free of charge, even. Some of us truly felt fortunate. It became obvious that Eddie and perhaps a few other *Sinners,* weren't too keen on the idea of another club in town—even if it weren't an outlaw club. Some of our guys said we needed to walk a fine line there. It wouldn't do to start off on a bad footing with an established outlaw club in town, especially one that knew several of our guys pretty well.

Typical of that attitude was our VP Howie, their former hang around, who said, "I like the *Sinners* but I don't like their ways." I could never figure that one out. Don't somebody's ways make them what they are? So, you like them, but you don't? Or is it that, you don't like them, but you do? Oh well . . . *whatever*. Hey, I'm just the new guy.

At any rate, I liked the *Sinners*, even with their continued poking around. I might have done the same in their position. I just felt that we didn't need their cachet. My opinion was that we needed the approval of

Roloff, the MMA Board, and the San Jose *Hells Angels* . . . and it didn't matter what the *Sinners* might say. If the MMA Board did have *Angels* on it, then it *really* didn't matter.

Eddie and the *Sinners* tried one ploy that I thought would be bad for us, but ended up working in our favor. The MMA had four levels of membership: the standard $5 card, a $25 "Blue Card" for those who could afford more, a "Silver Card" for $50, and a "Gold Card" $100 membership. Very few people bought Blue or Silver. It wasn't like American Express where you would get special deals or status recognition or anything. Gold Cards were another matter. The MMA targeted those sales to businesses. For their one hundred dollar, yearly contribution, the shop would be recognized in the MMA monthly newsletter—standard stuff for non-profit fundraising. The MMA had a few Gold Card shops in the Sacramento area and we were trying to sign on some businesses in San Jose.

Eddie came to one of our meetings and suggested that every member in our club should become a Gold Card member. This would show our commitment to the cause—both to the general biking community that we would be approaching to enroll, and to the MMA organization as a whole. I think Eddie thought that an extra $100 to each of us would cause a lot of internal dissension and maybe even cause some guys to drop out and weaken our group.

We discussed the idea later. One hundred dollars in 1973 was a lot of coin to guys who had low-paying jobs—or no job at all. It meant my bike rebuild would be delayed by a few weeks. Nevertheless, we agreed the Gold Cards were the way to go. Besides, the MMA Board would have an extra $1300 on the table when they considered our proposal. That was not an insignificant sum for a struggling nonprofit organization in those days. That is probably close to $7000 today.

Rollin, one of our new members, sold a Gold Card membership to a leather apparel shop in town. Their name was *Just Leather,* and they catered to motorcyclists in the area. The guys who owned the store were older dresser rider types. They were just what the MMA needed—helmet wearing guys by choice who valued the right to choose whether to don the helmet or not. *Just Leather* ended up doing a lot to support the MMA and all bike riders in California over the ensuing years. A lot of our guys started going to *Just Leather* and buying a few items there. They even had a black leather vest that I rather liked. I still couldn't afford it, though. Besides, I wasn't ready to give up my Levi cutoff just yet.

Roloff and our officers worked out the final details of our proposal; our by-laws as written . . . check, a Gold Card for each member . . . check, we would act as business reps for the association . . . check. There was more . . . we ran our own club with no interference from the MMA or the local clubs . . . check, no "dumb shit" activity to bring discredit on the MMA . . . okay, we would try . . . and no "Pigpen" patches . . . check. Denim vests (as long as they were relatively clean) were okay, although Roloff still liked the black leather look for our future . . . and no back patches . . . *what? Whoa there*—hold up mister . . . I wasn't ready to hymn *that* tune. However, that was the deal. The *Angels* weren't going for the back patches at that time. Resignedly, I joined the choir and opened the hymnal, but it was tough to carry the tune with gritted teeth.

The next MMA Board meeting was November 1st, 1973 . . . a Thursday. That date would also be our usual Club meeting night. The MMA Board would consider our proposal, and then decide whether to sanction the *Wheel Lords* MC. Roloff would call us with the news sometime that night. Everybody was energized. We wanted to have all bikes up and running that night. Every Thursday after church, we would go out and do some barhopping and partying, just to get tighter as a club. We looked forward to November 1st, as a time to celebrate.

Old Man Phil rented a house across the street from where Drew and I lived. Mitch and his girlfriend, Connie lived with Phil too. This was on Virginia Place in East San Jose, near Story and King Roads. Phil's place backed up to a rundown public golf course called Thunderbird. Thunderbird was the kind of course where local kids and derelicts would have beer parties at night on the grounds. You would see leftover bottles strewn about the trees. Behind Phil's house was a good-sized garage and behind that another small building. Then there was an alley behind which fronted the golf course property. The garage and Phil's tools and his expertise were available for anyone to use. You could access the place from the front or from the alley. Soon, I had my bike over at Phil's garage, as did Angel. We were furiously trying to get the two Knuckleheads up for the November 1st deadline.

It was going to be close. I was at Phil's garage right after work the day of the board meeting. Bret was there too, as were Drew, Phil, and Mitch. Lots of guys were lending a hand. I was determined to ride to the night's meeting, which was being held at Howie's house, perhaps six miles away. Since Bret was the president, his bike got the most attention.

Just after dark, Angel's bike was finished. He rode down the street and back . . . it needed a little more work on the carburetor. Okay, no big deal. Now for The Kid's ride.

Drew and Phil were helping me with the final assembly. Now to be clear, there were not a lot of frills on the old Knucklehead. It was spray-can black paint, with a spray-can black paint springer front end. I managed to chrome only a few parts, like some of the shift linkage, so most of the bike wasn't awfully pretty. I still had the original sixteen-inch, large front tire, but with no fender. I got a Panhead oil pump to replace the archaic, original one. I'd installed a twelve-volt battery and generator in place of the old six-volt system. Clutch plates were replaced. New throttle, wiring, and drive chains. I'd added a small Sportster gas tank because the price was right . . . zero.

Some things I didn't have. I had no front brake. It was a significant expense and, besides, you weren't required to have a front brake on a bike built before 1966. There was no electric start. Most of the older choppers didn't have them, and mine was no exception. No speedometer either. Again, there was no legal requirement for one. I did have a headlight, taillight, and brake light. They worked . . . more or less. It had a horn. It was the little hand squeeze type for bicycles, but it was legal.

There was no seat. Seats were expensive, and I had not been able to save up for one yet. I took an old towel, folded it a few times, and put that over the battery—there . . . one instant seat. I hoped the battery wouldn't leak any acid. The Kid might not ever have any kids of his own.

We got down to the final items. It was fully dark now. We poured some gas in the tank, rolled the bike to the driveway, primed the carburetor, and I kicked on the pedal.

And kicked.

And kicked.

Phil made some adjustments.

A few more kicks.

Drew kicked for a spell.

Then we got an engine fart—*progress!*

Then we shot some more starter spray down the throat of the carburetor.

A few more kicks by me, and then flames leapt out and died down.

All right . . . *even better!*

A kick or two more and then *BAM* . . . we had a running engine.

Then it died.

No matter, though. I had started my own Harley—*my own fucking Harley!* I did it once. I'll do it again.

I started it up again. There were lots of adjustments needed. There was a small air leak in the intake manifold.

"No sweat," Phil said. Soon, that was fixed.

The old Lenkurt carburetor needed tweaking. That took awhile, revving and adjusting . . . revving and adjusting.

Then the lifters needed some adjusting. Drew did that.

Then the clutch was slipping. More time spent adjusting that. I felt like I was a racecar driver and I had my own pit crew.

At length, we got to where you could put the tranny into first gear, and the bike wouldn't lunge forward underneath you. It was time to ride.

I let the clutch out and gave her gas. I went down the street smoothly . . . made the U-turn a little shaky perhaps, but no big deal. However, I couldn't get her into second gear. I just couldn't get the left foot to find the proper correct click for second.

Drew tried it out. He roared down the street, first, second, third . . . no problem. Then back to the house the same. What the hell, I thought. Okay . . . one more obstacle to overcome.

The meeting time was getting close. It wouldn't do to have so many guys show up late. Besides, some of the *Unforgiven Sinners* were supposed to be there, and we needed to make a respectable showing. (The *Sinners* just couldn't stay away from our meetings, it seemed). Bret, Drew, and Phil took off. Mitch would stay and ride with me in a few minutes. I got in a few more practice rides down the street and back. I still was unable to shift with my foot, so I improvised.

When I needed to shift, I would let off the throttle completely with my right hand and move it over, across, and down to the shifter near the left foot. Then pull in the clutch with the left hand, bend down and pull the lever into the next gear, and then quickly replace my right hand to the throttle. It was cumbersome, and I would lose speed with the hand off the throttle for a few seconds, but it did work. I must have looked like some kind of epileptic seizure in motion.

Mitch and I cleaned up the area and grabbed our jackets. We started up our bikes (mine did take a while) and headed out for the meeting. My first real ride . . . side by side with one of my club brothers . . . I was a little apprehensive about starting from a stop at the signal lights, but things weren't too bad. I didn't know how Mitch felt about riding alongside a novice, but he seemed okay with things. It was a straight route to the meeting. We went up King Road for about four miles, passing the gas station that everyone called Mexico Texaco, and then right on Berryessa Road for a mile or two.

The night air was crisp. The two bikes motored smoothly, punching their way through the darkness. We never got above forty-five miles per hour because of traffic. It didn't matter though.

Your senses were alive.

You *saw* everything.

Heard everything.

Smelled everything.

Felt everything.

Riding was even better than I had imagined. All the work and hassles over the last four months had been worth it.

We turned on to Berryessa Road. Mitch punched it and I followed suit as best as I could with the crazy shifting. We were side by side with just a few minutes to go when it happened . . .

I ran out of gas. I *ran out . . . of, fucking. . . gas.* The constant revving of the engine and the repeated adjustments made at idle sucked up all the gas we poured into the small tank. The gas petcock did have a reserve setting. The problem was the reserve had already been turned on, unbeknownst to me. I must have missed it with all that was going on.

Mitch had to get to the meeting. He was club Secretary. I told him to go ahead. I would push my bike to the meeting. Howie's townhouse was just a few blocks away. By the time somebody could get some gas and be back to me, I could already be there. Mitch took off, and I pushed Shiloh across four lanes of traffic and headed towards the townhouse complex. It wasn't exactly going to be the kind of entrance I had planned. The first time I rode my bike was also the first time I pushed it . . . *not* an auspicious beginning.

Along the way, I thought about things. What else do you do when pushing 400 pounds of iron with a 125-pound body?

On the plus side, I did have a running motorcycle. Or rather, I *would* have one in thirty minutes or so. A lot of my club brothers really helped to get me on the road. Some of them wanted me to be up almost as much as I did.

However, the minus side of the ledger had a few entries too. It was time to get some different clothes. I still didn't look like most of the guys. My cutoff was passable, and so was my coat. It wasn't a cool leather jacket, but was one of those green Army coats that some guys wore. It would do for a time.

No, as I had my head down, pushing the bike I realized I had to change out . . . my pants. I wasn't wearing jeans. I had cords on. Maroon cords. I don't even like maroon. This pair of cords had gotten too short, so I had Veronica sew on an old guitar strap to the bottom hem of each leg. So, here I was, sporting this kind of, semi-flowery design on the bottom three inches of my red cords. I mean, I did *own* some jeans—I just wasn't wearing them. Levis would wear much better against the elements. I made a mental note to ditch the cords . . . *fast*.

My boots had to go, too. My pair was soft brown leather with fringe down the side. They looked like hippie boots. Most bikers wore a sturdier black cycle boot, usually with a steel toe. That's probably why I had so much trouble shifting, I thought, it was the stupid, soft boots. I would dump them straight away along with the cords. With those boots and pants, I must have looked like a dropout from the casting call of *Mod Squad*.

As I neared Howie's garage, I remembered that some of the *Sinners* were going to be there. I wasn't going to make a tremendous impression—pushing my plain-looking, old bike in and being late to boot. Oh well. At least I actually had my bike with me. In all likelihood, the baddest of the *Sinners* wouldn't be there. Eddie, the president, would surely be there, and sometimes Gordy or Darren might accompany him when he dropped by. I knew all of those guys a little, and they were okay. I would get a few comments, but that was expected. Hell, I would get some needling from my own guys, too. However, the most imposing of the *Sinners*, Richard, wouldn't be there. He generally didn't socialize with our guys much.

Richard was the *Sinners* Sergeant at Arms, who punched out Bret's roommate at the birthday party months before. That, however, was trivial compared to Richard's reputation around town. Drew told me the story some time before.

Richard had been at a bar in Santa Clara one night with a girl, who was not his wife. A couple of guys began to hassle them, and things escalated into a fight . . . a *knife fight*. When it was over, one of the guys was dead, and the other was badly hurt. Richard didn't have a scratch. It was kind of like a Jim Croce song, I guess. Richard did about a year in county jail for the killing. Being the one who was attacked and defending himself helped his case, I suppose. As did the fact that Richard, despite being in an outlaw club, had a family, a nice house, and a respectable job. His occupation?

Richard was a meat cutter—a butcher by trade—at your local *Safeway*.

I was huffing and puffing when I finally pushed my bike into the open garage. The crisp November evening wasn't evident on my face. I was sweating . . . *a lot*. Our officer meeting started, and the rest of our members in the garage came over to say "hi" and see my bike.

Then I looked over at a large figure seated on a big bike. He was wearing sunglasses, a wide brimmed hat, a brown leather jacket, and a Levi cutoff with the *Unforgiven Sinners* patch on it.

Richard.

Fucking perfect.

Richard slowly looked me up and down—all 125 pounds of me (soaking wet), the bike with no chrome front end and a towel for a seat, the maroon cords with the guitar strap bottoms . . . the fringed hippie boots. Then he just grunted and shook his head. He must have thought I was from Mars . . . or Berkeley.

I put gas in my tank as the meeting proceeded. After some time, we got the phone call from Ron Roloff in Sacramento. The MMA Board approved us. We were officially a club. Everyone was happy. (Well maybe not everyone, but every *Wheel Lord* was). It was time to party hearty. We went out to celebrate at a tavern. I don't remember which one. I don't even remember if the *Sinners* came along. It didn't matter to me.

As we were leaving, I fell in at the back of the pack. This would be my first ride as part of a group. We roared off, with a dozen or more

Harleys screaming down Berryessa Road, and I was doing my best to keep up with my crazy shift routine. I think Phil rode alongside and mentored me down the road.

The air was brisk, and the wind was free. We were the *Wheel Lords* Motorcycle Club.

And, I was one of them.

"Got a one-way ticket to the open road, come on.
Got a red line engine and I'm raring to go . . .
If you want to ride
Let's go."

John Fogerty, "Hot Rod Heart"

❧ *Chapter Nine* ❧

"Early Daze"

Our first task as a club was the San Jose Car Show. This was an auto and motorcycle show held at the County Fairgrounds every year. It started the day after we became official and ran through the weekend. Drew set us up with the show's promoters, a couple named Paul and Vicki Bender, with the assumption that we would be sanctioned. I'm not sure how Drew managed it, but he had everything all set with the Benders by Friday afternoon. The Benders, especially Vicki, were extremely helpful to us. They were business people, not bikers at all. Vicki and Paul donated a booth space and provided tables and chairs too. It wasn't a space off in a dark corner either, but right on the main floor next to some hot cars.

Even though the MMA was a non-profit group, we weren't sure we would be welcomed to the show. There had been a bike show in Cleveland, Ohio, a few years before. The *Hells Angels* and a rival club called *The Breed,* had gotten into a giant brawl with dozens of the bikers involved. Some of the guys were killed, and many were injured. The massive fight made promoters nervous all over the nation. Ever since that event, bikers weren't exactly welcomed at the car or bike shows. The Benders took a big chance with us.

Everything worked out pretty well. All of us got to practice some of our PR skills. We sold some MMA memberships and spread the word about the organization. Most important, other promoters who were there were able to see how we conducted ourselves. We gained entry into many of the upcoming car shows throughout the area. Within a month, we had worked the San Francisco Show. Lucas and Mitch had even gone to Southern California and worked the entire weekend at the Long Beach Car Show. Promoters donated all the space. We paid all our own expenses to these shows. By the end of the show season in April, we had worked eleven shows from Santa Rosa to Anaheim and brought in well over $3000 to the MMA—$5 at a time.

A few of the San Jose *Angels* dropped by the car show that weekend. There was Lyle Grisham, the new president, Jack Elroy, and a few others. They were checking us out. We figured they would.

Just after the car show, Bret stepped down as president. It seemed to me that he never felt comfortable in a leadership role. Howie moved up and became president, while Lucas was elected VP. That move worked out well. Lucas was a hard charger and took care of business.

There was a lot of club activity over the winter months. In addition to the car show circuit, there were MMA Blood Runs in San Francisco and Sacramento. The MMA opened an account with the Red Cross, and staged a "Blood Run" to solicit donations to the account. Members of the Association who needed blood would be eligible for free or discounted services. It was also a good PR vehicle for the MMA. The Association would get their name out in the public eye and attract the attention of the local motorcyclists. Local papers would run stories with headlines proclaiming "Bikers Invade Town for Blood Letting" and other such nonsense. We got a kick out of that stuff.

The club staged quite a few runs of our own, too. These were usually quick one-day or two-day runs, about one per month, to the Pinnacles, near Salinas, or to Boulder Creek, in the Santa Cruz Mountains. There were work conflicts, and some guys would be working car shows, so there might be half a dozen guys who could make it to these short runs. It was just another way to get the guys together and get tight. I made a few of these runs and missed a few. Winter was also the time for guys to rebuild and upgrade their bikes, so the number of bikes on the road was reduced anyway.

Over the winter, Old Man Phil donated the use of the back building at his place. He gave it to the club for use as a clubhouse. At that same time, many of the guys happened to be out of work—even some of the guys who always had jobs, like Drew and Howie. Those two factors—a place to party, and bikers with plenty of time to party— combined to make for some lively times in the new clubhouse. Every Thursday night at church, we would hear the stories and jokes from the guys who had been hanging around with each other all week. Half the club was living a wild time with all kinds of drugs, booze, women, and partying day and night; or, so the stories said. The other half of us were pretty much on the outside of this scene. That didn't bother me and, from what I could tell, didn't seem to bother the other guys who weren't included, either. Veronica and I were still together, and I wasn't looking for any outside action. Drugs weren't a big attraction to me, although I would indulge from time to time with the guys.

I did find I was a little envious over the way those guys who partied a lot had grown tight with each other. They were kind of their own inner circle. I was still in the process of establishing myself in the group, and wasn't to that level yet. However, I knew there was plenty of time. I wasn't going anywhere.

Some more guys joined the club over those first six months or so. Like I said before, it wasn't super hard to join the club, or any club, early in the life cycle. We had about five new guys come in to the club that winter and spring. Another ten or twelve guys came around to check us out, too. Some of them made prospect, oops . . . I mean potential member. Most guys left when they found out that we didn't just party all the time. The biker lifestyle attracted guys, but the work of pushing the MMA drove some away. It became apparent early on that just being a righteous biker wouldn't get you far in our club. You had to be able to conduct business for the MMA on your own, at least to some extent. We knew not all of our members necessarily needed to have the skills to conduct a public meeting or talk to business owners, but each would have to be able to communicate well with other bikers in some fashion. We loved having members who were the typical big and bad biker dudes, but brawn alone wasn't enough in our club. You had to have brains and balance—and heart, of course . . . if you had those, and you happened to have brawn as well . . . even better.

One of the men who joined early on and who had it all was Dennis Kempton. Dennis was new to bikes and rode a slightly chopped '73 Shovelhead. Our president, Howie, had met him while on a ride and invited him to come around. Howie was always trying to get our numbers up. He would ask almost anyone to come around. In this instance, though, Howie's instincts were dead on. Dennis was a solid contributor to the club from day one. He made it to full member quickly and soon became one of our mainstays. Dennis was medium-sized, but a martial arts guy who knew how to take care of things. He was married to a woman named Joann, a good-looking lady who was fun to party with.

We added some members, but we also lost some. In February, one of the guys, Rollin, got a three-week suspension. I don't recall what the reason was. I do know that Rollin and Howie didn't like each other, and whatever Rollin thought, Jason pretty much thought, as well. Then Bret, our ex-president, got involved on RollinandJason's side. Then the officers backed up Howie, and there was a big Peyton Place drama going on for a few days. I didn't know the details even then, but the upshot of it all was that *all three* guys quit in one night. Drew and I walked across the street to the clubhouse (nice having a clubhouse so close) and there was Bret, (Angel). He was cutting off his patch. We were stunned. I couldn't believe Bret would throw everything away so easily. He and

Drew were tight from the old days; or, so I thought. However, there was Bret giving up his patch for two guys he had known for less than six months. I mean, I wasn't too keen on a lot of Howie's bullshit politics either, but I wasn't about to quit the club—*my club*—over it. Give up on my brothers . . . over some in-house beef? Give up my patch . . . *are you kidding?*

I learned a valuable lesson that day. Fortitude takes many forms. Angel was a tough and respected guy. Once he and Keith, our 325-pound Sergeant at Arms, had a friendly wrestling match and Angel more than held his own. No one could have ever pushed Angel out of the club. However, he let himself be pulled out over trivial matters. He let Howie get his way.

Drew was bitterly disappointed. So was I. To our mind, Bret had chosen RollinandJason over us. Enjoy the ride, guys.

Bret and I later worked at the same electronics company. People there knew him as "Biker Bret." I didn't tell them that I knew him even better. I still liked Bret on a personal level. But, on a respect level, forget it. I never called him "Angel" again. He was a guy I knew at work who sometimes rode a bike.

We lost one of our original ten members, but the rest of us were still going strong. One Friday night, after MMA booth duty at the big Oakland Car Show, John Howell took me on a wild trip through the East Bay. We were in Jim's '58 Chevy wagon, along with his wife Shawna. We had all been drinking some beers at the show. Our booth was very near a booth run by some of the wives and girlfriends of the *Hells Angels,* Oakland charter. They were raising funds for the legal defense of Oakland *Hells Angels* President Sonny Barger by selling "Free Sonny Barger" T-shirts and other items. I guess John Howell knew some of the women there from back when.

By the time we closed the booth, all of us had gotten a pretty good buzz on . . . especially John Howell. He continued drinking as we sped away, carrying us to some party site in Contra Costa County. John was the type of drinker who would get louder and funnier the more he drank. He was also the type of driver who talked all the time and liked to look at the other person instead of watching the road. That is a bad combination. Soon we were careening through the Caldecott Tunnel and weaving around traffic. I didn't have a clue where I was. I never heard of Caldecott *or* his tunnel.

I was in no shape to drive, even if I had known where I was. I looked at Shawna . . . worse than me. John wasn't concerned though. He turned to me.

"No problem, Kid. I know this area. This is my old neck of the woods."

"Will you watch the god-damned road, John?" I blurted out.

He just smiled and slapped me on the shoulder . . . and I was sitting in the *back seat*. It wasn't so much the thought of being creamed in a car wreck that had me worried. (Well, not totally anyway). No, it was the thought of being creamed in some unknown *place* that bothered me . . . Contra what . . . And Calde who? Get me back to St. Joe! We finally made it back in one piece. John Howell had one hell of a good time that night . . . me . . . a little less so.

Two months later, John left the club. He got a job out of state. It was in a small town, in Missouri, very near to where a number of my cousins lived. I hated to see John go. Everybody did. John Howell thought up the name *Wheel Lords* and the patch design too. John was a good *Wheel Lord* and fun to be around. The Missouri thing didn't work out, and he and Shawna were back in California a year or so later. However, he never came back with the club. I think that was John Howell's way. He seemed to be a rambler. I'll bet he has had thirty jobs in thirty different towns over the years. I'm glad our paths crossed, if only for a short time.

In later years, whenever I would hear radio traffic reports about Caldecott and his fucking tunnel, I would think of John Howell.

Once I had my bike up and running, I began keeping it at the apartment Veronica and I rented. The place was on the first floor just inside the courtyard gate. I would shut down the bike on the sidewalk and push it into the courtyard and then over the stoop into the apartment. We kept the Harley in the front room. Actually, it was the *only* room since it was a studio apartment. It was a tight fit with two people and a bike in a studio. Veronica was a good sport about it. She loved riding. We would go on club and MMA runs together as often as we could. Veronica still wasn't exactly crazy about some of the other guys in the club, what with their womanizing ways; and, sometimes we would argue over the behavior of other people. We argued more than either of us liked to, but those fights were almost always about others—her family or mine, her friends or mine. When we could keep the subject to just the two of us, things were great. Things are never so simple though.

Soon, Veronica's sister, Yvette, came down from Washington to live with us. Now we *had* to move. The studio was just too small. We found a place in downtown San Jose near the San Jose State University campus. It was plenty spacious and affordable. It was an upper floor place, so I kept the bike at Drew's house, which wasn't too far away. The new place did have a couple of drawbacks. First, it was in a high-crime area. That in itself wasn't any sizeable concern. Most of our members lived on the East Side of San Jose, which was the rougher side of town. We were used to being in the tougher neighborhoods. It wasn't that big of a deal. You did worry about your old lady, though. As guys, we could take care of ourselves; but, the women were a different matter. You worried about the old lady when you were gone.

Bikers, however, had a sort of "de facto" self-insurance policy. Once people in your neighborhood figured out you were bikers, you generally didn't have a crime problem; at least, not at your house. Petty criminals just don't want to risk messing with bikers; there are easier, more vulnerable targets to be had than bikers . . . especially if there are lots of bikes coming and going at all hours of the day and night. For example, the street where our clubhouse was located *never* had any problems. Phil and Mitch lived in the front house, Drew lived across the street, and somebody was usually sleeping over, inside the clubhouse. There were bikes in and out constantly. That block had to be one of the safest in East San Jose.

Our new place in downtown had no such advantage. We were just another group of young people living in an apartment. Veronica, Yvette, and I had to be constantly vigilant.

The other problem with downtown was the loonies. Governor Reagan closed a lot of the California mental hospitals and those patients were now living at halfway houses in urban areas . . . like downtown San Jose.

We were always chasing away some nut case from our property who honestly shouldn't have been wandering the streets. These people were more or less harmless; but still, you never knew what might happen.

The only time we had a real problem was once when Veronica and I were doing laundry at the laundromat a few blocks away. We just pulled all the clothes out of the washers when I heard a scuffle outside. Some black guys were beating up some hippie looking guy. They were cursing and attacking any white person on the street. I figured they would come after Veronica and me soon enough, so I found a pay phone

101

and called the clubhouse for help. Drew answered the phone. I knew he would be over in a flash. The black guys weren't hurting people too badly, just roughing them up some. Nevertheless, it was the principle to me. People should be able to walk the streets without being hassled.

Drew, Lucas, and a new prospect got there in just a few minutes. Drew was the first one out of the car, as I knew he would be. I told him to follow me and back my play. That was one of the good things about Drew. He didn't need any explanation in a jam. If one of his club brothers decided that something needed doing . . . then let's *do it*. We found the black guys around the corner and pitched into them. It wasn't much of a fight. I squared with one guy, and Drew took another down fast. While Drew was pounding him pretty good, a third guy jumped on his back. Drew just grabbed his shirt and put him face first into the asphalt. Then Lucas came up, pulled a shotgun on the black guys, and told them to get lost—which they did.

Lucas took all the fun out of things. Drew and I wanted to fight, not pull guns. After the black guys had taken off, Lucas and the guys left. Veronica and I had to lug our wet laundry back to our place and hang dry everything. What a drag that was. However, we were never hassled at the laundromat again.

I never did that many drugs. Certainly not like some of the other guys. However, on occasion, yes I did. One such time was when Drew and one of the other members, "Snatch" McLaws, had real LSD. You must realize that by the mid-70's, the days of purple haze and orange sunshine being handed out freely were long gone. The acid that was prevalent by 1974 was usually heavily laced with speed or other cuts. It was rare to find the real LSD. Snatch insisted he had some, and he and Drew were going take some one night and invited me to join them . . . so I did.

We piled into a car along with a bottle of whiskey. Drew was very big on "taking the edge off" drugs. He always countered one drug with another. If he took uppers, he would "take the edge off" with hash or booze. If he took Quaaludes (a big favorite for some of the guys) then some speed or coke to "take the edge off" that.

I don't know if it truly was the old time LSD or not, but it was different from anything I had taken before. We were all pretty buzzed. Then Lenny said he needed a new battery for his car.

"At this time of night?" I said.

"Yeah. Midnight Auto Supply," Snatch replied.

We drove around for the next three hours with Lenny. Constantly looking for just the right battery to swipe, Lenny or Drew ruled out every car that was a potential candidate for some reason. Too old, too well lit, too hard to get at, etc., etc. We must have driven half the neighborhoods in south and east San Jose.

Finally, I asked McLaws, "Lenny, even if you do manage to swipe a battery, *and* you don't get caught, *and* it is the right fit for your car . . . what makes you think that the battery you get will be in any better shape than yours?" I thought that was a tremendously profound question, given my mental state at the time.

Lenny wasn't convinced. However, he and Drew were hungry. We abandoned the great farcical battery caper and went to an all-night café for chow. Munchies *always* supersede greed. We never did get a battery that night.

This was just the type of frolic that guys would discuss on meeting nights before church. Half of these capers were just this stupid. The other half were cool. All were hilarious to hear.

Drew dropped me off at my place near daybreak. I was still buzzed. I tried to sleep . . . no way. Veronica had one of those hippie posters on the wall. The kind that had naked bodies and flowers and all kinds of hippie looking crap intertwined. In the half-light coming through the windows, I found myself staring at the poster. The poster turned into a ram's head and seemed to loom over me, getting larger and larger by the minute.

I shook my head hard from side to side. I turned away and tried to force myself to sleep. Light slowly filled the room. Veronica woke up and said, "Where the hell have you been all night?"

"Someplace I don't think I'm going back to."

"Huh?"

"I'll tell you later."

I finally came down and nodded off. I think my last waking thought was "Sergeant Friday of *Dragnet* was right. That real acid is some nasty shit."

I was fitting in more and more with the hardcore guys in the club. Still, a lot of them didn't understand or appreciate my thought patterns. Once, around this time, about five of us were walking down a street somewhere. I don't recall exactly where it was, or who was there. I'm pretty sure Drew and Lucas were there.

We were just walking along when I noticed something. Everyone was walking in symmetry. The two guys in front were followed closely by the three behind . . . all perfectly spaced. Then I looked down. All of us were walking in exactly the same step . . . left, right, left, right. How often does that happen?

I was suddenly struck by the thought of . . . *West Side Story.*

The Jets and The Sharks . . . my mom used to drag all of us to the movie musicals when we were kids.

I couldn't resist. I started snapping my fingers to the downbeat of our left feet hitting the pavement. The guys looked at me as if I were, well . . . on acid, I suppose. Nobody got it yet.

I couldn't stop there. I had to try for the full effect, so I broke into song.

"The Jets are gonna have their way—tonight!"

"The Jets are gonna have their day—tonight!"

I didn't know the next lines. I just faked it after that. Those guys didn't know the difference.

Oddly enough, none of the guys joined in . . . imagine that. Oh, Drew recognized it, I'm sure. He knew all kinds of music. He even played violin in his high school orchestra; but no, I was a solo act that day. I just kind of fizzled out, right there on the street.

I guess some people just don't see the humor in things as other people do.

Spring brought several new members to the club. Kenny Hampton and Timmy Stuart moved to San Jose from Texas. They both rode Panheads. Kenny had a '62 Pan, and Timmy had a 1954 model. They were both wiry guys and Kenny was short. Kenny was one of those guys who could rebuild a bike any time, any place. He once decided to change his frame out from Swingarm to Rigid. That is a complicated process. Many of the parts won't fit from one frame to another, and there are always a few surprises along the way too. We had a run coming up in two days, but Kenny was undeterred. He went straight ahead with the rebuild, working day and night. He had it ready in time for the run. Kenny and Timmy were buddies like RollinandJason had been. So everybody called them KennyandTimmy. They didn't have nicknames either. They were just KennyandTimmy.

Matt Bartlett rode a brand new 1974 Shovelhead. Matt was really young—no more than twenty—although he looked a lot older. Matt had a bum leg. He had been recently injured in a car crash. He had received a lump-sum settlement. He used the money to buy a new Chevy El Camino and a new Harley . . . our hero. Matt was a burly guy, although not real tall.

Leo Hernandez rode a '73 Shovelhead. It was pretty stock. Like most of the other new guys, Leo had no nickname that I remember. Sometimes Keith or Drew would refer to him as our token Mexican, but that was about it.

Lenny "Snatch" McLaws dropped out of the club about this time. He was a good guy, but he just didn't have the makeup to be in a club with rules and mandatory meetings and commitments. Who knows, maybe he needed more time to find a battery. Lenny continued to do transmission work for some of the guys from time to time. When they could nail him down with a commitment, that is.

By the start of the serious run season, late April, we had about thirteen members, plus a few prospects and hang arounds. The first significant run was going to be the First Annual MMA Statewide Run. It was a big step forward for the Association. Roloff, the business manager, found a County Park east of Fresno that he reserved. It was centrally located between Northern and Southern Cal. The MMA hoped they would have a large turnout of bikers for the weekend. They also hoped that things wouldn't get out of hand, what with a few hundred bikers partying day and night. To that end, Roloff asked the *Wheel Lords* to provide the camp security. We weren't real keen on trying to control a bunch of bikers who didn't know who we were. Bikers don't much cotton to being told what they cannot do when they are partying. Nevertheless, we agreed to give it a try.

We worked hard to get all the gear gathered for camp security. Walkie-talkies, rope, flashlights, sign-in tables, barricades, etc., in addition to the usual camping gear, tents, and assorted items for living three days outside. Everybody who could get away was going to Fresno early Friday to set up the site.

I had gotten a new job, so I couldn't go down to Fresno until Saturday. We had been holding local MMA monthly meetings at a 24-hour restaurant in downtown San Jose called Sambo's. It was a chain like Denny's. The manager, named Dave, rode a Sportster. He let us use the group area for the meetings. We publicized the Statewide Run at the meeting and scheduled a time early in the morning on the Saturday of the run for folks to gather at Sambo's and form a pack to ride to Fresno.

At our weekly church the Thursday before the run, the club decided that we needed one of our guys to lead the San Jose pack to the campsite. A quick check around the room showed that only one member would be in town Saturday morning . . . me. Everyone else would be at the run site by Friday night. I pointed out the fact that I had: A) never led a pack of any size, *anywhere,* and B) never ridden my bike anywhere even close to as far away as Fresno. It didn't matter. The club thought it was essential for one of us to lead the first organized pack of riders from San Jose to the MMA Statewide Run. I got the job. Phil and Drew gave me some pointers on corralling the independent riders together who (we hoped) would show up Saturday. I checked the map for the best route to, and through, Fresno for the 175-mile trip.

Saturday morning, before dawn, Veronica and I headed over to Sambo's. We were bundled up against the cold. I like hot weather and I looked forward to going over the Coastal Range, and getting to the warm San Joaquin Valley. Riders began coming in. Everyone was waking up and grabbing a quick breakfast or some coffee. Three of the Sonoma County *Hells Angels* even showed up. They were on their way to the run, although, they weren't about to ride down with our little group. Just checking things out, I guess.

When sunup came, thirty bikes had gathered. It was a decent turnout, especially for so early a departure. Soon, it was time to leave. When we got on the freeway on-ramp, I looked back over the pack. It looked in pretty good shape with no stragglers. We rode down Highway 101 and headed south towards Gilroy and the garlic fields.

A lot of thoughts were in my mind . . . *don't set too fast of a pace. Don't go too slow, either. When we stop for food or gas, make damn sure everybody leaves together.* Mostly, however, I was hoping for no breakdowns.

Cresting Pacheco Pass on Highway 152 was terrific. The fully risen sun warmed us as we headed east, passing the shimmering San Luis

Reservoir off to our right. I'd been over the route many times in a car, but never on a motorcycle. The change in setting was palpable, distinct. We left the city behind. You could see the broad expanse of the San Joaquin spread out before you. The air smelled of the dusty aroma of agriculture. As we neared the small town of Los Banos, a crop duster sprayed tomato fields in the distance. The thirty engines hummed their way through the slowly warming Valley.

Road trip . . . life is good.

We stopped a couple of times for gas and food. I wanted to make sure everyone had a chance to scarf some burgers for lunch since the campsite wasn't too near any services. Fortunately for me, we had no problems or breakdowns. Twenty miles or so east of Fresno, just where the hills begin their climb to the Sierras, we saw the site. It was a good spot alongside a small river. The road approached the site from the opposite bank, and you could see the people in the camp, as they could see us. There weren't many bikes visible, but there did seem to be a few people starting to stir.

We made the last turn to the camp and pulled up to the sign-in area at the front gate. All the club members gathered there, along with Roloff and the other MMA volunteers from the Sacramento area. They seemed kind of excited. There were shouts and slaps on the back all around. Then I realized why everyone was hyper. Virtually the only people in the campsite were the volunteers. Roloff and the MMA knew that riders would show up, but until that first pack actually rolled in, they were a little apprehensive.

Howie, Lucas, and Roloff came up to the bike as Veronica was stepping off from the back seat.

"You just brought in the first pack to a Statewide Run," one of them said.

"I'm not surprised," I said. "You had us leave San Jose at zero dark thirty. I figured we should be one of the first ones here."

As the afternoon wore on, packs came in from Sacramento, Concord, Marysville, Los Angeles, Orange County, and other cities, as well. There was a steady stream of twos and threes showing up also. By late evening, we had over 500 bikers at the site. The MMA made money and soon started planning for more runs. The club got its feet wet on how to provide security for hundreds of bikers, and I made my first long ride.

The putt back to San Jose on Sunday afternoon was great. Most of us in the club rode in one pack. It was just us, no independents. That was a fun ride.

The next weekend we had our first big club run. This was our first long distance, good weather, no MMA business, just-for-us run. We went to Black Butte Reservoir in the upper Sacramento Valley, about a 200-mile ride, each way. The small town of Orland was about ten miles from the Reservoir. We partied in town, at the campsite, and had a great time.

Then we had another run three weeks later to the Frog Jumps at Angels Camp in the Gold Country. That weekend was always a big biker gathering. I didn't make that run. Some other guys didn't either. There was a lot going on for some of us. Phil was having old lady problems, and he needed to clear all the guys out from hanging around his place— so we lost the use of his back building as our Clubhouse. I was scrambling for work and found a new job. I couldn't take off all the time to make *every* run. Other guys had similar matters to address. It was the usual stuff of life, it just got a little more complex because it was spring and the run season was in full swing.

Then the club decided to add one more run to our already busy schedule. I knew I couldn't make it to this one. My bike had just gone down with a mechanical problem, and I was working the new job and couldn't afford to miss any time. When I found out what the run was to be, I was doubly disappointed.

The San Jose *Hells Angels* invited us to their club's annual California Run to Bass Lake. I never contemplated going on a run with the *Angels*. As it turned out, by not going I missed out on a lot . . . a *whole* lot.

ᥰ✍ Chapter Ten ᥰᐛ

"Bass Lake"

All of us heard about the Memorial Day Weekend Bass Lake Run. It had been featured in Hunter Thompson's famous book about the *Angels*, and every year it got lots of coverage from the media. The press threw numbers around that stated hundreds of the *HA* made the run every year. We didn't know if that were true or not, but it was certain that there were going to be a great many *Angels* there . . . and darn few *Wheel Lords*. Our guys were definitely going to be small fish in a big pond, as were any other guests, for that matter.

Mitch and I missed the Bass Lake Run. Everyone else made it. Even Tank showed up. He hardly made it to any runs at all. I don't remember why Mitch didn't go, but it had to be something major for him to miss it. Mitch made it to nearly every club function, especially runs.

The gathering place was the Truckadero Café. That was a truck stop on North First Street in San Jose. Many bikers used it as a jumping off point for runs. Truckadero was conveniently located near the junction of Highway 101 and Highway 17 with quick access to the north or southbound freeways.

I stopped by Truckadero the morning of the run to see the guys off. If I couldn't ride, at least I could watch the others take off. Our guys were there, along with the *Angels* and the *Unforgiven Sinners*. A short time later, the Daly City *Hells Angels* pulled in, having come down 101 from San Mateo County.

When the pack formed up and headed out, it was an impressive sight. I'd never seen so many club bikers at one spot before. We had about thirteen scooters just from our club and there was easily well over forty bikes heading onto the freeway from the truck stop. I watched the pack disappear down US 101. In about an hour, they would be over the Pacheco Pass and be riding past San Luis Reservoir. They would stop at a bar in Los Banos. They would ride past the fields of tomatoes, peppers, and cotton on their way to Fresno and beyond. The same route I took with the MMA pack a month before. They probably made a few stops at bars and cafes along the way. Then they would roll up through the Southern Sierras to the Run site. Only I wouldn't be there. *Damn*. I drove back home. For this weekend, I was back on the fringe of things . . . and very disappointed.

I was at home Monday afternoon with Veronica when I got a phone call from Drew. There was going to be a special club meeting— *right now*—at Lucas's place. Get here.

Obviously, something was wrong. When I got to the meeting, the guys laid it on me. There were some unhappy, seriously pissed off folks there. They were unhappy with each other, they were more unhappy with those of us (Mitch and I) who didn't make the run, but they were most unhappy with some members who weren't there at all. Then I noticed we were a few people shy of a full house. There were about three guys missing.

Eventually, with a lot of tempers being vented along the way, Mitch and I got the story.

One of the *Angels* from the Nomads chapter, named Eric Salisbury, had known Howie, our president, some years back. As I remember, they lived in Vallejo, a blue-collar type city in Solano County, in the North Bay Area. Evidently, there was some bad blood between the two families.

Salisbury, known as Eric the Red, happened to come across Howie at the Bass Lake campsite some time Saturday. I guess Eric had a score to settle, and he and Howie got into a fight. Eric won. There was no one else involved. There was no pile on against Howie; none of the other dozens of nearby *Angels* jumped in; nobody picked a fight with any of our other members. It was a personal issue between two guys. Of course, in these situations, the advantage always goes to the aggressor. That meant this guy Eric certainly had the upper hand, even without factoring in the element of intimidation that goes along with being an *Angel* in a large group of other *Angels*. Still, it was one on one. That should have been the end of the situation. According to our guys, as far as Eric was concerned, it was. Some of the guys in our club weren't too happy with our president being beaten up; but, such is life sometimes. It was a personal beef—and, it was settled. Maybe not to our satisfaction, but settled nonetheless.

Things got complicated when Howie decided to leave the run site and go home. I don't know the motivation for him leaving; perhaps loss of face to our membership played a part. It shouldn't have. There is no shame in losing a stand-up fight. The *Hells Angels* hadn't told Howie to split. That was his choice. Lucas, our VP, told Howie that he should stay around. Howie left anyway, and he encouraged others to leave with him. Lucas and Drew were going to have none of that. They made it clear to all our members that the club was staying at the run site . . . no

110

matter what. Despite their entreaties, some of the guys left with Howie, two of them new members. Matt and Leo had just become full members a month before. Maybe they figured that if the president of the club was leaving, then it would be okay for them to do likewise. Keith left soon after, too.

When the *Angels* found out later that night that Howie left for home, the situation for the remaining *Wheel Lords* worsened. A number of the *Angels*, now further fueled by a day spent partying, proceeded to lecture our members on bike club behavior. Our guys were put on the defensive in a couple of ways.

First was the matter of our president packing up and leaving. The *Angels* considered that an affront. It didn't matter the reason, you just didn't up and take off. They had respect for someone who took their lumps and hung around, but *leaving?* That was bad form.

The second part of the night's lectures centered on our Club's response to a crisis. The *Angels* point was, some guys stayed, some guys left—what's the deal? Do you have people running things, or do members do whatever they want? (Contrary to what some people think, there are rules and a lot of "have-to's" in a motorcycle club. Nobody is allowed to do whatever he feels like doing).

The *Angels* weren't wrong in pointing these things out to our guys. In fact, our guys were told flat out that things were settled and for us to stick around. Our Club, led by Lucas and Drew, held together through that night. At least, as well as could be expected, considering there were seven *Wheel Lords* among a few hundred *Hells Angels*. To be clear, not all the *Angels* were coming down on us; nevertheless, enough of them put in their two-cents-worth that, after a time, there was a sizeable pot on the table. Our guys weren't upset with the *HA*. They were angry with our own people for having put them in an uncomfortable position.

After the Saturday night lecture series had been concluded, the balance of the long Memorial Day weekend passed without any further incidents for our club. In fact, our guys said they were treated well by the other club members. The overall feeling seemed to be that things were square and let's party and move on. Our club stayed until Monday and then rode back to San Jose together. Lucas and Drew knew they had to get some big issues settled quickly. Therefore, they called the afternoon club meeting that Mitch and I had been called to attend.

Once Mitch and I got the full story of the Bass Lake Run, we understood why the guys were so pissed off. It was a pretty contentious meeting with a lot of charges and counter-charges made. Nobody came to blows, however. A couple of guys were pretty ticked at those who missed the run, which meant Mitch and me. However, mostly people were angry towards the guys who took off and left the rest of them hanging.

I think the biggest problem for some of the guys was just the fact of being put in the position of close association with the *Angels*. Most of our guys, with a few exceptions, had never been around the *HA*, and then their first time in the mix and—bam—everything blows up on them. It was a tough first day at camp. Some guys were questioning whether this was what they signed up for or not. We were supporting the rights of bikers and working our tails off within an organization that was largely run by the same people who just put us through the wringer.

Lucas and Drew, who had more experience being around outlaw clubs, held a different view. They said we needed to clean up our house, deal with the issues, and move forward. True, the run rules may have changed, but we all committed to the club, and there was no backing off. If being a *Wheel Lord* now included measuring up to the standards of clubs like the *Angels*, then so be it. Lucas, binary as ever, was the most vocal on this point. There was "the best" and "all fucked up." In this situation, "the best" meant standing together and dealing with the guys who left us, and "all fucked up" was any other option. Besides, he said, what did everyone expect when you joined? If you didn't know that something like this could happen (and really, no one did) then consider yourself better educated than you were a week ago.

In the end, we decided some things. Mostly we decided to let everyone cool down and relax. Every member needed to make up his own mind as to what he felt was right. We would have our regular Thursday meeting in a few days and continue from there. Matt and Leo, the two new members who left with Howie, were suspended. Keith was not suspended, and I don't remember why. Maybe it was because of his high standing in the club. The biggest change was that Howie was no longer president. That is because Howie quit the club. As it turned out, as soon as Howie made it back to San Jose a few days earlier, he quit his job and was in the process of selling his house. He sold some of his stuff to different friends, both inside and outside of the club. Within a week, he packed his belongings and his family up and moved out of state. That was the second president who quit on us in less than four months.

As for me, I wasn't going anywhere. One or two guys were still pissed at me for missing not only the Bass Lake Run, but a few other things, as well. That didn't bother me, though. I could handle that easy. What did bother me was that I had not been there when all the shit came down. I was determined to be there the next time . . . and every time thereafter. So, things have changed, and I need to prove myself to some guys in the club? No problem . . . The *Wheel Lords* need to stand together and show other clubs that we belong? Fine . . . tell me when and where and I will be there. I wasn't about to let my old friend Drew be disappointed in me; or Lucas, our new president, either, for that matter.

By the next club meeting, Matt and Leo quit, just as Howie had. Then our two prospects quit. We were down to ten members, just as we had started with the year before. Lucas and Drew preached to all of us about hanging in and staying committed. Some of the other guys weren't so enthusiastic, most of them from Howie's old clique.

Within a week or so, two more guys quit the club. Newer members KennyandTimmy made their choice and pulled a RollinandJason act, eventually winding up back in Texas. That left eight of us—seven originals and Dennis. Then, Tank stopped showing up to weekly church. In a few weeks, he also dropped out. Now we were only seven.

Meanwhile, I had been having a difficult time. Veronica and I had been together for a year, and she was seeking a long-term commitment from me. She also badly wanted to move back to her hometown in Washington to reunite with her daughter. I couldn't fault her on either count. Those were natural feelings. I wasn't going to leave the club and move out of state, and I didn't want to lose the best girlfriend I ever had . . . so, I had a dilemma.

About this same time, I found myself on the short end of a club decision. I don't remember the exact reasons, but I know that Drew, among others, wasn't too happy with me. Maybe it was because my bike was still down, although I was trying to get it back on the road. On the other hand, maybe it was residual fallout lingering from Bass Lake. Perhaps it was my general tendency to speak my mind, which some people consider cockiness . . . especially when coming from a skinny guy. At any rate, at one of the meetings a few weeks after Bass Lake the Club voted that I needed an attitude adjustment. I don't recall the actual vote count, except to say that I kind of felt like the Robert Redford character in the movie *The Sting* when he said, "I didn't have too many friends in the room at the time."

At the next church, Keith, our Sergeant at Arms, had me stand in front of him, so he could pop me one. Like I said before, Keith was a mid-sized guy trapped in a big guy's body. He weighed well over 300, and could have really done some damage to my 125 pounds if he had wanted to do so. Keith didn't enjoy that sort of duty; not like some guys I've seen. He didn't even hit me in the face. He hit me in the chest . . . only once, too. I was surprised and started to say something like . . . "Is that it?" Then I realized maybe I should let things alone, and said nothing. The meeting resumed, and I sat and thought for a moment. I concluded that my attitude hadn't really been adjusted, but maybe . . . *just maybe*, I was becoming a little wiser as to when to speak and when to shut up.

My newly found wisdom didn't last too long, though. Around that same time, it could have been a week or so after that meeting—I'm not sure, Drew ran a tear down session on me. A "tear down" is when one member rips into another for some perceived slight or misstep. I don't remember the whys or wherefores, but Drew tore into me pretty good. Of course, he made a big production out of the whole thing, in one of his "Windy" moments, as Keith would say. Drew liked "reading the words of the Lord" to folks, as he called it.

After he finished, Lucas started to move on to the next order of business, but I immediately spoke up. "Whoa there guys. Satan had his say—now I get mine." Then I tore down on him with equal enthusiasm. Drew was surprised, and he was none too happy with me. However, I didn't care. Drew had been my mentor, but I had just as much right as he did to speak my mind. I think Billy Shakespeare had it right when he said, "What goeth around cometh around" or maybe some words to that effect.

The attitude adjustment and the tear down weren't a concern to me. What was disappointing was that some of the guys seemed to think that I wasn't pulling my weight, or contributing my fair share. That bothered me. I determined right then to show them they were wrong.

Then the next week, Keith quit the club . . . that hurt. Keith had been one of the main guys since day one. He was smart, funny, and even-tempered—not to mention that he was about as big as a house. Keith carried a lot of credibility around with him, although he had lost some at Bass Lake. However, all that left when he went out the door.

Two weeks later Old Man Phil quit. Another original member was walking out the door. Another well-liked guy, who was a valuable asset, was leaving us.

Six weeks earlier, we had thirteen members and two prospects. Now we were down to five members. There were five guys to do all the work at MMA Statewide Runs . . . five guys to run the MMA booth at car shows . . . five guys to keep the club functioning and alive.

One fact we soon realized was that all the men who stayed in the club were young. Lucas was the oldest, and he was just twenty-three. The rest of us—Drew, Dennis, Mitch, and me—were around twenty-two. All our "old hands", who provided us direction—Bret, Howie, Phil, Tank, Keith, and John Howell—were gone. The young members were now running things. Drew and I joked with each other that one of three things was possibly true: 1) the older guys had the wisdom to know when to get out; 2) the younger guys were too dumb to know when to hit the fence; or 3) the hippies were right . . . "Don't trust anyone over thirty".

After we laughed awhile, we re-affirmed our original stance. Fuck those quitters.

That is not to say that all the guys who left were enemies to the club. Phil stayed around and was still a great friend to all of us, especially so to his buddies Lucas and Mitch. When the gas crisis from OPEC hit some time later, Phil would open his Dad's Texaco gas station to all of us after hours for fill-ups. Everyone still liked Phil a lot. Keith would show up at MMA runs and still supported bikers' rights. We'd see him from time to time. Tank, whom I hardly knew, didn't mix much after he quit. I ran into him a few years later, and we got along well. It was good to see him. KennyandTimmy later returned to California from Texas, before moving on yet again. They finally had some sort of trial separation I guess; because a few years later Kenny came back to the *Wheel Lords* as a prospect on his own. It didn't work out, though. Later Kenny took off for Texas for good where I'm sure he and his buddy became KennyandTimmy again. No one to my knowledge ever heard anything from, or about, Leo. Howie moved to Oregon. None of us in the club ever had any contact with him either, although I'm sure he and his buddies, like Keith for instance, stayed in touch. Matt remained in San Jose and talked with Dennis now and then.

Each of us who remained in the club had his own feelings about the guys who quit on us. I can only speak with real authority on my views. I still liked some of the guys who left. I also still disliked some of them. Regardless, all of them lost respect in my eyes. And respect always trumps like. Those guys missed the best times, which still lay ahead of us. And they missed out on the true brotherhood, which is worse. If I had to simplify some complex feelings, I guess I would defer back to Drew's original maxim.

Fuck those quitters.

My personal life was getting tougher. Through my own stupidity, I lost a good job. In addition, my bike was still down. Then Veronica decided she needed to move back home to be with her daughter. We resolved to stay together, and so began my second long distance romance, this time northward to Washington instead of southward to Los Angeles. I hoped it would work out better than the last time, but it was going to be difficult.

I had so many personal difficulties that I asked the other guys in the club for a short leave of absence. I felt I needed to get my personal shit together (at least a little bit) and not have the financial and attendance obligations that were required by the club. The guys said okay, although Lucas was skeptical that I would return. I didn't blame him since so many guys made recent exits.

Over the next few weeks, I made some progress. I managed to get Shiloh back on the road, and I found some part-time work. Veronica moved back to Washington. We called or wrote to each other every few days. She hadn't given up on convincing me to move up with her, but I think she knew it was a long shot.

Drew let me move into their house with him and Lisa, and I began to feel that I was a little more in control of events. This was in the summer of 1974. It was my first experience as an independent biker. I had no Club duties to perform, no meetings to attend, no dues to pay, and no places to be. It was unfamiliar territory for me. I hated not being involved in things.

After about four weeks, I came back to the club. Drew gave my patch back to me, and Lucas was pleasantly surprised to see me return. I was quickly back in the swing of things, doing my share of club business and helping to organize MMA events. The five of us were all over the place, showing people that the *Wheel Lords* were still around and functioning.

Some months earlier, before Bass Lake, Drew had designed a club tattoo. This was one more step in the growth process of a newly formed club. It was simple—*Wheel Lords MC San Jose* in a half circle design. Three of our members got inked right away—Drew, Mitch, and

Dennis. Everybody else held off. In those days, tattoos were not nearly as common as they are today, even among bikers. A lot of bikers did have tattoos, but a great many did not. Some of our guys just weren't into being tattooed; and others, like me I guess, were waiting to see how things in the club progressed. Lucas had also been one of the wait and see types. When I came back from my leave of absence, I saw that he had his done. Soon after, Drew and I went down to Chuck Marshall's studio in downtown San Jose and got mine. That made it unanimous.

My big problem remained—how do I stay in the club and keep my girlfriend? Veronica and I were still trying to work things out. Finally, after a few months of struggling with things, I scheduled a trip to Washington. I needed to see Veronica in order to bring this situation to a close, one way or another. In addition, if I were going to end up in Washington, I had to check out the area, at least. Yvette, Veronica's sister, was moving back, and she would accompany me on the trip.

One night in early October, we piled our stuff in my car and hit the road. My ride was a lowered '58 Chevy wagon. I'd bought it from John Howell, our former member who moved to Missouri. John had been driving the same car six months earlier when we were late night careening through the Caldecott Tunnel in Oakland. Two hours into the trip, the battery light on the dashboard came on. It was around midnight on Highway 505 in the middle of nowhere. I pulled off the road, and Yvette and I slept in the car until daylight. I didn't have the money for a battery, an alternator or whatever it was the car needed. Too bad "Snatch" McLaws wasn't around to find me some free replacement parts. As a result, we headed back to San Jose. We made it back on battery power, and I called Veronica with the bad news. Yvette made it on her own to Washington shortly thereafter. I planned for a second attempt once I got the Chevy squared away.

I never made it. One delay led to another and soon it became obvious to me that I wasn't going to move anywhere. My future was in San Jose as a *Wheel Lord*, and Veronica's was in Washington, at least for the time being. Perhaps it was a cliché, but we were moving in different directions.

The final nail in our relationship occurred a few weeks later when the club rode to a party in Concord. It was being put on by the brand new MMA club, which just started up in that area. I met a girl there and immediately hit the canvas. "Down goes Frazier! Down goes Frazier!" I mean . . . I fell *hard* . . . and so did she.

Veronica and I broke up for good. We never saw each other after she left California. Veronica was a big part of my life at a time when many things were changing quickly. Her love and concern helped a 21-year-old kid grow up a little. I hope both she and her family have fared well; and, if she does think back to those old times, doesn't judge me too harshly.

⚔ *Chapter Eleven* ⚔

"Club Friends"

The *Wheel Lords* were fortunate. We met and became friends with a lot of good folks through our involvement with the MMA. In addition, I got to know quite a few great guys from the San Jose area who were friends with some of the other members in our Club.

Jeff Patrick was one of those friends. "Wax" was buddies with a number of our original members, and was one of the men at our kickoff meeting when the club was formed. Jeff decided not to join the club, but he came to quite a few MMA runs and was always welcomed by everyone. Wax had real long hair. We had quite a few guys with long hair in the club—Drew, Dennis, and I had the longest—but Wax had us beat. When he rode, he had to tie his hair back in three places—top, middle, and bottom—just to keep the tangles out. Jeff was a little short, but solidly built. He had a pretty bike, and a good-looking girlfriend, too.

Patrick was a mellow guy and never spoke badly about anyone. He liked to drink and usually rode with at least one bottle of the hard stuff in his saddlebags. He would party hard with his bottle in tow, but never changed his demeanor no matter how polluted he became.

Jeff was riding with me the first time I ever dropped my bike. It was the weekend of a small MMA run to the tiny town of Hornitos in the Gold Country of the Sierras. This run wasn't too long after my leave of absence. I just spent all night on security duty, and the next morning I got some R&R time. Wax and I took our bikes out to explore some of the local back roads. The roads were small, windy, and had lots of potholes. On a tight curve, I hit some asphalt debris and missed making the turn. I ended up on the asphalt with Shiloh nearby. Jeff stopped, came back, and after seeing that I was okay, said something like "Kid, we're supposed to be on the road . . . not, *on,* the road."

"Yeah. Very funny, Jeff."

Patrick, like a lot of bikers, was very adept at riding his cycle while wasted. Jeff's problem was that he had difficulty navigating when he was high. Returning solo from a Fresno Run one year, I ran into Jeff in Los Banos, which is a small town about halfway between San Jose and Fresno. Jeff was glad to see me since he was wasted and wasn't too sure about the route home. We joined up and rode together. I could see that

Wax was toasted, but he had no problem riding. He just kept asking me every ten miles or so, "Do we turn here?"

I would yell, "No Jeff. Just follow me and turn when I do."

He would yell back, "Okay, cool."

Then a few minutes later, we would repeat the whole exchange.

"Do we turn now?"

I'd have to shout back, "No! *Just wait*, damn it!"

This exchange went on for the entire ride home. Eventually we made it back to San Jose, although, we had both become a little hoarse from yelling back and forth.

Another local biker whom I got to know fairly well was John Robinson. I think he originally was friends with Phil and Lucas. John had no interest in belonging to a motorcycle club. Nevertheless all the guys in the club liked him. He was a dependable, quiet, straightforward dude. John would accompany us at Christmas time when we would all ride to local hospitals and one of our members would dress up as Santa Claus for the kids who couldn't get home for the holidays.

John and his wife lived in a nice middle class neighborhood. They had me over for dinner a few times. I think they took pity on this struggling skinny kid. Most of us in the club ate more or less haphazardly. We would munch a lot of fast food, or if we did have bigger meals, they weren't too well balanced. However, John's wife would always cook up a real meal with the plates full of meats, vegetables and bread. It reminded me of my dad's relatives back in Missouri when I was a kid. They would always have heaping plates of vittles for everybody.

Everyone in San Jose knew Robert Planchetta as, "Planch". Planch owned a small motorcycle shop in an industrial area of the city. His shop catered to Triumphs and other non-Harleys. Planch bought an MMA Gold Card business membership, which is how the guys in our club got to know him. Drew and Dennis partied a lot with Planch over the years, as did most us, really. Planch gave a lot of support to the MMA, and got the organization known to a lot of folks who weren't into Harleys.

Planch didn't ride a Harley himself. He owned other types of bikes. Planch was constantly bad-mouthing Harley Davidson quality to us and would always needle any of our members whose bikes were down for repairs. Planch was one of the first guys around to shave his head. With his shiny skull and earring, we used to call him Mr. Clean.

Planch was full of contradictions. He was fun to party with, but he also enjoyed being a pain in the ass. Planch would point out to me how little I knew (compared to him) about motorcycle mechanics, then proceed to find bike parts I needed at a discount, and then spend extra time showing me how to install them properly. He would bitch about the MMA and Ron Roloff, and then spend hours lending a hand to our club with security duty at an MMA Run.

Planch was one of those guys who developed his stubbornness to the point of obstinacy. He would hold his position no matter how well he was proved wrong about it. Planch always seemed to consider himself the smartest guy in the crowd, but—surprise—a lot of guys thought the same about themselves. That led to some interesting and hilarious discussions whenever Planch was around.

It seemed that, every time I went to Planch's shop, there was a different set of flunkies around him. He had assistants, girlfriends, hangers-on, and other associated folks just lounging about the place. I'm not sure how much work was actually performed at his shop, but there was never a lack of people there. Planch seemed to enjoy being a big fish in a small pond.

After a few years of Harley bashing, Planch suddenly bought one for himself. It wasn't long before it was the *only* bike he'd ride. Then, of course, he told everyone how great Harleys were. This gave Drew and the rest of us lots of free ammo. Yep, being around Planch was a lively time.

Scott Catton was a San Jose biker who rode and partied with our club off and on for a few years. Scott was originally a friend of our member Greg, but quickly became a favorite of a lot of us. Scott was a big gangly guy, and young. He was one of those guys who wore key chains and wrenches and all kinds of stuff that hung off his belt loops. Scott wore rings on nearly every finger. When he walked, he seemed to be going in different directions at the same time. His bike was the same way. It was tall, with a high center of gravity, and had long extended forks and a tall sissy bar. The bike seemed to be like Scott, extending outward at all angles.

Scott was a great guy to party with. He was up front, and no bullshit, all the time. Scott would be around for a time, then would take off and ramble for some months, only to come back to San Jose and start the whole cycle again.

The MMA functioned as well as it did because of all the volunteers who would pitch in and support the goals of the association. One of the prime areas of support was the Marysville-Yuba City region. Sometimes referred to as "Twin Cities," the two towns lie in the Sacramento Valley about an hour or so north of the capitol. It's farm country mostly, with large crops of rice, walnuts, almonds, and the like. The whole Marysville area provides easy access to the Northern Sierras. Camping, boating, fishing, and gold panning are popular activities along the many nearby rivers and streams. It's also a great place to ride motorcycles.

Early on, a number of local bikers joined the MMA from the Yuba City area. Some had been involved with the MMA since the inception of the Association. Les Clayton owned a small bike shop in Yuba City. Les was always donating raffle prizes, organizing runs, soliciting memberships, and giving his time to the MMA. He was older than all of us in the *Wheel Lords* were, but we got along great. Les didn't party quite the same as most of us did. He was a little more conservative than we were. However, Les was very friendly and hospitable to us. Any time a group of us was in the Yuba City area, we would stop by. Les routinely treated everyone in our club as if they were special—which is really how he treated everyone, now that I think of it.

John "Turtle" Cox was a tight buddy with Clayton. I think John was a cabinetmaker by trade. He would make ornate cases and trophies that he would donate to the MMA to give away as prizes. John was a real friendly guy and another great favorite of all the *Wheel Lords*. Les and John could always be counted upon to help. They generated a lot of interest and enthusiasm for the MMA. Consequently, the Marysville-Yuba City region, though small in population compared to the bigger cities of California, probably had more per capita participation to support bikers' rights than any area of the state.

Another group of guys who helped us out at MMA events was a motorcycle club from Sacramento called the *Kinsmen*. They were a non-outlaw club like us, and roughly the same age group, too. The *Kinsmen* were a friendly sort, and they did a lot to support the MMA. Most of them were a little less rowdy than some of our guys were, and didn't party quite as hard as we did, but they were a big help at statewide runs.

If we needed some temporary, extra manpower, they were always willing to lend a hand. Some of the guys I remember were: John Fleming (a tight buddy of Ron Roloff) Bob Stine, Woodland John, Dave "Chief" Robbins, and Tommy Tufts.

Colin Oliver was a clean-cut biker from Sacramento. "Ollie" was at every MMA event. Essentially, he was Roloff's right hand man. Ollie hardly ever got to ride his bike to events. His lot was to drive the vehicle full of supplies and registration forms and such. Olympia beer was one of the popular brands in California back in those days, and Ollie usually had a can of "Oly" close by him. Ollie with an Oly, can in hand, just had a nice ring of symmetry to it . . . you know? Colin was a real upbeat person with a quick smile.

Roloff instituted an MMA Rep program to organize the independent volunteers across the state. The Area Reps would report through a chain of Regional Reps to one of two Statewide Reps, one from Nor Cal and one from So Cal. Ollie became the Nor Cal Head Rep. I think his counterpart was a guy from down south named Dave Phillips.

One year at a large Statewide Fresno Run, there was a massive tug of war between Northern and Southern California. The Head Reps took positions at the center of the long line. There was a large mud puddle between them. The MMA provided one of those super thick heavy-duty ropes. Then all kinds of people took places behind their respective Reps, ready to tug against the other half of their state. There must have been 200 bikers, and old ladies, ready to pull away. Our club wasn't involved. We were just the security detail. Besides, it didn't feel right to us. Drew and I looked at each other. He said something to the effect that something bad was brewing . . . he just didn't know what.

The signal was given. Both sides began to pull. There were easily over a hundred people on each end, mightily tugging away. Ollie and his So Cal counterpart were facing one another right up front. After about ten seconds, with no movement, there was suddenly a loud explosion—*BOOM*—the rope broke. Two hundred people hit the ground. That was pretty damn funny.

Then we heard Ollie yell out from the pileup. He was in bad shape. He held the rope tight against his torso. When it broke, it ripped across his chest. The exploding rope had torn off his nipple. *Ouch* . . . Ollie's wife and Roloff took him to a local hospital. He was better by the next day, and back at the campsite where he was making jokes about an instant mastectomy, if memory serves. I'm sure Ollie had his can of Oly with him too.

In the fall of 1974, a second club asked the MMA for sanctioning, following the model the *Wheel Lords* had developed. The *Centaurs* were from the Concord area of Contra Costa County. They were a small group, like us, and we got along well. The *Centaurs* received local approval from the *Hells Angels* Richmond chapter, and we got to know some of the Richmond *Angels* a little. However, the *Centaurs* didn't last too long. They folded up less than six months later. We were a little disappointed. If the MMA State Runs kept gaining popularity, we were going to need all the on-site security assistance we could get.

Sometime later, a third MMA club formed. They were from Sonoma County in the North Bay and were called the *Highwaymen*. They got local approval from the Sonoma County *Angels*, whom they seemed to know pretty well. We ended up spending a lot of time with the *Highwaymen* over the ensuing years. They worked just as hard as we did for the MMA, and together, we partied quite a bit. They were small in number too, generally around five members. The main guys in that club were Phil and Don (no, not the Everly Brothers), Steve, known as "Bones", and "Party" Marty.

The *Wheel Lords* and *Highwaymen* got along well, and everyone pretty much liked each other on an individual basis. However, on a club-to-club level there were some differences. The *Highwaymen* never took any advice we offered. Maybe they thought we were conceited to be giving them advice in the first place. We just tried to make them aware of the obstacles we had encountered in our tough first year. Nevertheless, the *Highwaymen* didn't care. They had the backing of Sonoma County *HA*. They nodded politely to us and then went on with their own agenda. Fair enough. They owed us nothing.

One other difference between the two sanctioned clubs was that we considered ourselves smarter than the *Highwaymen* were—not a *little* smarter either—*a lot* smarter. However, that wasn't an indictment of the *Highwaymen*. We considered ourselves smarter than any other club. Okay, maybe some of the *Hells Angel* chapters we had come across might be just about as smart as we were . . . but that was it. That might have been an arrogant attitude, but that was who we were. We had members who were adept at not only the usual motorcycle club skills, but who could run site security, organize meetings, speak in public places, talk intelligently with business owners and government officials, and party all night to boot.

These small matters aside, the *Highwaymen* were cool to be around. We'd go up to Sonoma and barhop with them all over the countryside. Unfortunately, one of our runs up their way wasn't such a pleasant occasion. One of the Highwaymen, Phil, was killed in a bike wreck. We all rode up to Sonoma for the funeral. Phil was a big favorite of some of our members, especially Drew and Lucas. That was a big loss for a small club. Nevertheless, the *Highwaymen* continued on, and were there at our side for the next MMA run season, working just as hard as we did. It was good to have them.

The President of the Modified Motorcycle Association's Board of Directors was Martin Carpenter. We first met Martin at an MMA Sacramento Blood Run in February '74. Marty owned a motorcycle engine re-building business called "Little Marty's Custom Repair". He shared a building with a chopper business owned by *Hells Angels* Sacramento chapter President, "Solo Steve" Gillette. Marty and Solo were good friends, and he was tight with a lot of the other Sacramento *Angels*. Marty was the same age as Old Man Phil from our club. Like a lot of the older guys, Marty was a car guy before he got into bikes. Marty owned a super nice, '71 Chevy El Camino that won a ton of car show trophies.

Martin didn't socialize with us too much at first, but over time he and Dennis, and later Drew, got to be good friends. It probably bothered Ron Roloff a bit that one of the MMA sanctioned clubs had a friendship with one of the board members of the association. Roloff liked to be in complete control of things, but he definitely wasn't in control of Martin. Marty always kept the confidential side of the business affairs of the MMA to himself. He was one of those savvy guys who seemed to have been around the scene forever. Between the car show crowd, the cycle shop crowd, the MMA people, and the *Angels*, Marty seemed to know everyone in Sacramento.

Martin would let whoever was in town for MMA business, stay at his place in Sac. After some time, he and I got to be very good friends. Marty was the type of guy who could listen well—not many people really possess that ability. He helped me out a lot, with tips on bike, and car repair.

Marty was like my dad in one way. He smoked constantly. Camel studs. That wasn't so bad except he insisted on smoking as he lay in bed. He told us that he would sometimes fall asleep with a lit cigarette in hand. Two or three times he ended up setting his mattress on fire. Sometimes, when we were in Sacramento, we'd end up crashing out in his front room. Marty would turn in and we could smell cigarette smoke drifting down the hallway from his bedroom as he lit up. One of us would end up yelling at him to put the cigarette out before he fell asleep—and roasted us all.

After a few years, Marty sold his business and left the MMA Board and pretty much got out of motorcycles altogether. He still kept his own counsel on all the details of his time on the MMA Board and didn't share much with us . . . and, we never asked. Martin remained a great friend to me and all the *Wheel Lords* for years.

All the bikers in the Sacramento area, including Martin, were always telling us how anti-biker the Sacramento County Sheriff's Department was. They said harassment was standard procedure for all chopper riders. We took their word for it, but then Marty told us they would fly a helicopter over his house just to mess with him. Drew and I were skeptical on that claim. We thought Martin was just exaggerating for effect. Back in those days there weren't as many helicopters in the air as today. Very few media stations had a copter. Police agencies didn't have that many either. We figured why would the Sheriff's Department waste a valuable resource checking up on Martin in his quiet South Area neighborhood?

Then one night when I was over at Marty's we heard a noise in the sky. It was a copter, hovering above the cul-de-sac. I went outside and looked around. There were no police cars . . . no fugitive being chased anywhere . . . no car wreck was evident. There was no clear reason for a helicopter to be there. Yet, there was an official-looking copter hovering over Marty's house, with a spotlight shining directly on it. After some minutes, it flew away. I went back inside. Marty never moved from his recliner. "Just my buddies checking up on me," he said. Like I said, everybody in Sacramento seemed to know Martin.

The *Wheel Lords* first met Don Lundberg at the small MMA run to Hornitos. That was the weekend I first dropped my bike when riding with Jeff Patrick. Don was an older guy who rode a full-dresser. I think it was a BMW or something like that. Don was quite a bit older than us and definitely not a scooter tramp as we were. He was a typical middle age guy who happened to love riding motorcycles. Don was an auto mechanic who lived with his wife, Betty, in Millbrae, which is right next to San Francisco International Airport. Don fell in with the MMA at Hornitos and became good friends with Roloff. Don was a real big guy and was nicknamed "Gorilla," which meant that his wife, Betty, was known as "Chimp."

Both Lundbergs were soon doing volunteer work all over the State of California on behalf of the MMA. They seemed to be everywhere. Don helped coordinate the onsite activities at MMA Runs. He could always be counted to lend a hand at the large events. Don was one of those rare people whom *everyone* liked. I don't think any of us ever heard anyone say *anything* negative about Don. He was also very generous in sharing his automotive knowledge with anyone who needed it. Sometime later Don bought a Harley, so then we liked him even more.

Don and Betty would drink beer, but they never were into any drugs like most of the other people in our circle were. We would all party together and have a good time. Still, there was a lifestyle separation in certain areas.

One of the great things about being in the world of motorcycles was the age range of the people we would meet. When I was in college a great majority of the other students were very close to my age. Night classes would have a few older, returning-to-school students; but, nearly all of the daytime students were in their early twenties. Likewise, for most of us in the club, the people at our job sites were usually near our age, too. There were some exceptions, of course; but, in general, most young people our age associated socially with others of the same age. Any interaction with older adults usually took the form of an authority figure—family members, bosses, teachers, and so on.

The biker lifestyle was cross-generational. We were able to become friends with many guys who were the age of our parents. They would treat us as equals—once we gained their respect, that is. Once a friendship was established, there was no parent/child dynamic. A good friend was a good friend—no matter the disparity in age.

Each of us in the club learned a lot from our older friends: Don Lundberg, Les Clayton, Marty Carpenter, Ron Roloff, and some of the older *Angels* and *Sinners*. All these guys served as unofficial role models for a group of 22-year-olds who were trying to get their shit together. All we had to do was be observant and pay attention. We felt lucky to have them around us.

ᐸᔍ Chapter Twelve ᐳ᎒

"Men and Machinery II"

"Tolling for the rebel, tolling for the rake
Tolling for the luckless, the abandoned and forsaked
Tolling for the outcast, burning constantly at stake
And we gazed upon the chimes of freedom flashing."

Bob Dylan, "Chimes of Freedom"

The *Wheel Lords* were made up of men from either a poor or lower-middle class background. We had auto mechanics and machinists, assemblers and maintenance men, sheet metal fabricators and machine operators, laborers and the unemployed. Unlike a typical Woody Allen movie, we had no architects or novelists in our group.

Most, but not all, of the guys graduated from high school. A couple spent a few semesters at a junior college. Even though as a group we were undereducated, knowledge and learning were appreciated talents. We were constantly searching to increase our education—whether it was improving our bike building skills or learning how the political process worked. We looked up to people like Ron Roloff, who knew the ins and outs of political maneuvering within the legislative process.

Most of us were one-generation-removed from Depression era children and Dust Bowl emigrants. A few of the guys had close relationships with their fathers; but, most of us knew our dads only a little, if at all. A surprisingly high percentage of our guys were the oldest or the only son in the family. Only a few of the guys had an older brother. Maybe we were subconsciously looking for a father figure or an older brother. We didn't think along those lines . . . but who knows? Regardless, each of us was on his own in the world. There was no Daddy or Mommy paying our way through a college fraternity or finding us jobs or anything. That's not a complaint. It's just the way it was. Everybody understood that we were on our own. That is except for one another . . . and your old lady.

We got our full back patches in early 1975. That was a big deal for us. Some of us had a problem with all the political BS that accompanied the formation of the Club. To get everyone on board—the

128

MMA Board, the San Jose *HA*, etc—had taken over a year, with the approvals. However, once we got the full patches, the entire hassle was merely a speed bump in our past. We all got new black leather vests (goodbye old Levi cut-off) from our friends at *Just Leather,* which looked bitchin'. These vests were brand new on the market, and we were some of the first to get them. They were top quality and weren't too bulky or stiff, unlike some others.

The same people who produced the *Angels* and *Sinners* colors made our patches. The script of the lettering was great. We didn't know of any other club that used it. For that matter, we couldn't think of another club that had colors of black and white with gold, either.

We threw a patch party to celebrate. It was a small affair, just the members and their old ladies. We all got pretty ripped. We even raised a glass for the ex-members who quit on us. They should have stayed the course, but everyone has to make their own decisions in such matters . . . then live with them. It was a good thing that the party was just the members and old ladies. We got emotional and probably a bit cocky, too. But then, we felt as if the *Wheel Lords* MC had a lot to celebrate that night.

Lucas Rodes was President of the *Wheel Lords* for much of our existence. "Weasel" and I were different personality types, and the two of us had our ups and downs the first year or so. Once we came to understand one another better, things were great. We still may not have agreed fully on certain matters, but we respected each other's position.

Lucas's girlfriend, a lady named Amanda whom I only met a few times, suddenly became ill and died. This was when I was on my leave of absence. Lucas didn't invite me to the funeral, so I didn't go. All the other guys did attend. In retrospect, I should have gone. I was a fool to stand on ceremony. The right thing to do was to be there for my club brother, and I let him down. I like to think I learned from my mistakes of this kind. That point is probably open to debate, though.

On a happier note, Lucas had a cool family. His older brother Jimmy was a good guy. He was an independent biker from the Pacific Northwest. Lucas's mom was a hard-nosed broad in the best sense of the word. Lucas once described his mom as the type of parent who, if questioned by the police about her son, would promptly tell the cops to go screw themselves. In her mind, her kids could do no wrong. Anyone who even suggested the possibility that they had done wrong was an asshole. End of story. Hey, I love my mom, but I could never envision Anne talking to the police like that. However, Lucas's mom . . . yeah . . . I could see that. Lucas's mom perfectly fit (years later) the Jeff Foxworthy joke, "If the Marlboro never leaves your mother's lips as she tells the state trooper to, 'Kiss my ass' . . . you may be a redneck."

Weasel had a great running Panhead. Then, he modified the engine by adding Shovelhead uppers to the Panhead lower end. That improved the performance of his bike even more. Lucas, naturally, referred to this new engine set-up as "The best, man, the best."

Lucas had little formal education, but he was wise. Once, when somebody (I forget who) complained to him about me, Lucas listened for a time and then said, "What did you *expect*? That's Kid . . . you *know* him. And, you know that's how he is. Did you expect something *different*? Get real, man." That seemed to be a straightforward, universal truth that could be applied to anyone, really.

Dennis Kempton was a steady and sturdy guy. It was rare to see Dennis over-amped, or worked up about anything. Most of the rest of us were quick on the draw when we spoke out. Dennis, however, was a slow talker who measured his words carefully. Dennis was our sergeant at arms for some time and served as vice-president and president.

Dennis worked as a maintenance man at a large apartment complex and his wife Joann had a respectable job at an electronics company, so while they weren't rich, they did okay financially. Dennis and Joann made a strong partnership. She was smart, good with money and budgets and liked to party, as well. Dennis was nicknamed "Doctor" because he occasionally had a stash of high-quality drugs that he would share with the rest of the members. He reminded me of my stepbrother, Greg in that regard. Some of the guys would overuse Doctor Dennis's free pharmacy at times; at least I thought so. I wasn't quite so much into the pharmaceuticals as some others were, but I must say that I received my share of gratis prescriptions from the Doctor.

One night, near the end of our first year as a club, Dennis, Mitch, Drew, and I were out running around town. We were in a car, and none of us was wearing his club patch, so we looked like any other group of long hairs, I suppose. I don't remember what we were doing or where we went, except for the final stop of the evening. We ended up at the East Side apartment of some girl. She must have been a sweetie of Drew, I guess. I'd never been to the place or heard of the chick before.

Just before we left, two groups of guys from the apartment complex got into some beef with each other. There was a bunch of noise and shouting, but it didn't involve us, or the girls who lived in the apartment, as far as we knew. A short time later, we left, and as we were getting into our car, we heard some popping sounds coming from behind. It was some crazy whacked-out white guy on a second floor walkway shooting at us. I guess he thought we were part of the other group that he and his buddies argued with earlier. He had what looked like a small-caliber pistol. He was firing it from maybe 50 yards away.

As soon as we realized what was happening, Mitch started to go up the stairs after the guy, even though he was unarmed. Before he could get more than a few steps, though, Dennis went down with a yell. He'd been hit in the leg. At that point, we decided to vacate the premises. We put Dennis in the car and pulled out of harm's way. There was hardly any blood, but Dennis was in considerable pain. He kept saying, *"That motherfucker shot me! He fuckin' shot me!"*

We looked at the wound. None of us knew anything about trauma medicine, but it appeared like—dare I say it—just a flesh wound. We drove to Dennis's place, which wasn't too far away. When we got inside and looked closer, it seemed that we were right. There was some bleeding, a good-sized bruise, and a lot of pain; but, as far as we could tell, no bullet was lodged inside Dennis's leg, and no serious damage. Dennis was up and around in a couple of days. I don't remember what happened with the crazy people at the apartment, but I do know I resolved not to tag along anymore with guys on their sweetie trips. We ended up on the bad end of some dispute that had nothing to do with us, and we were lucky that we (almost) dodged a bullet.

We weren't quite so lucky with Dennis's wife, Joann. When we first carried Dennis into their house, she asked what was wrong. Satan, displaying zero tact, blurted out "Dennis just got shot."

Joann looked at the three of us for a moment and then very calmly and slowly said, "You . . . Mother . . . Fuckers."

Drew, Mitch, and I had no argument for that one.

Mitch Moss, "Sleaze," enjoyed acting outrageously. He liked to surprise and shock people. Mitch got a kick out of shaking people's sensibilities. He wasn't mean, but he did like to stick a burr under your saddle, and then see if he could get away with it.

His girlfriend, Connie, bolstered Mitch. No matter what Mitch did, or how much he screwed up, Connie always supported him. She worshipped the water Mitch walked on. In fact, most women liked Mitch a lot. He was that kind of roguish character their mothers warned them about.

The MMA would frequently hold local public meetings at restaurants. The group use area at a pizza joint or the back room at a Denny's—similar to a Rotary meeting, or a Little League party, that sort of thing—was often used. A couple of times after some of those meetings Mitch would suddenly stop on his way out of the main dining area of the restaurant and plop himself down at a vacant spot in a booth that was occupied by regular citizens. He would engage the couple or group in conversation and proceed to eat food from their plates. The people would be so stunned they wouldn't know what to say or do. Neither would we. The first time Mitch pulled that prank, we were as amazed as the unfortunate diners were. Mitch would be quite congenial and engage the folks in conversation as he was munching away on their french fries and the like. Sleaze wasn't trying to be mean or intimidating (much), just *outrageous*. He usually succeeded.

I got Mitch good, however, one time. He liked to call himself "Zelmo." He even had the word Zelmo tattooed on his arm. Nobody called him that, but Mitch would refer to himself as Zelmo on occasion. One day I started thinking about "Zelmo." The only Zelmo I ever heard of was Zelmo Beaty. He was a hot-shooting center on the St. Louis Hawks NBA team. This had been before the Hawks moved to their current Atlanta location. I followed the Hawks as a kid—they were the closest NBA team to where I had grown up in Springfield. Beaty, Lou Hudson, Joe Caldwell, Bill Bridges, Paul Silas, Len Wilkens . . . I still remember the core of that team. They were talented . . . but couldn't hang with the powerhouses of the day—the Celtics, Lakers, and 76ers.

Anyway, I knew Mitch came from southern Illinois, which couldn't have been that far from St. Louis. Since Mitch . . . oops, I mean Zelmo . . . was about my age, I thought it might be possible that he lifted the sobriquet Zelmo from the sports pages back in the day. It was just the type of quirky and outlandish move that fit Mitch to a tee. One day I tried out my hunch.

The next time we were in a conversation I said something like, "You got that right, Zelmo . . . Beaty."

"What? What did you say?"

"I said you got that right, Zelmo . . . Beaty."

"How do you know about Zelmo Beaty?" (I knew I had him now).

"Huh?" I said, matter-of-factly.

"How do you know Zelmo Beaty?"

"Zelmo Beaty? Well, gosh Sleaze, everyone knows about Zelmo Beaty." (Just call me Pope Innocent).

"*Nobody* knows Zelmo Beaty! How do *you* know that?"

"Mitchell, I know everything. Naturally, it follows that I know all about Zelmo Beaty. That's no big deal."

"No really, Kid," he pleaded. "How do you know about Zelmo Beaty?"

"Who?" (This was too easy now).

"Zelmo—fuckin'—Beaty, man . . . what do you think we're talking about?"

Poor Mitch. He was crushed that his secret connection was out. We continued the "Who's-On-First?" routine for a bit, but I never admitted to anything. I guess Sleaze never figured out that I grew up a few hundred miles away from his hometown and thus was able to put two and two together.

I never told anybody about Zelmo . . . well . . . you know who. I didn't want to pull his covers in front of the rest of the guys. As far as they knew, sporting a tattoo of "Zelmo" was just another example of Mitchell the Sleaze making something up and being outrageous, as per usual. However, I would have a quiet little chuckle to myself whenever I would spot a certain "Z" tattoo on Mitch's arm.

Satan would never pay his bills. He and Lisa charged everything and then did their best to avoid settling up. The Hilliard household must have had 20 credit card accounts—all of them maxed out. Even so, merchants and credit card companies continued to extend them credit. Drew and Lisa would delay payments until the last possible moment; then, trudge down to the store and pay the minimum required to free up their account so they could resume charging. It was crazy.

I didn't owe anyone anything. Of course, I also owned nothing (except my bike). Drew owed everyone everything. Yet, he owned nothing. (Okay, Lisa did have a little jewelry).

Drew and Lisa filed for bankruptcy. I think it was Chapter 7 or Chapter 13. Then, a few years later they were deep in debt again and ended up claiming bankruptcy once more. I thought two bankruptcies and that was your ass—they'd lock you up or something—but nope, a short time later the Hilliards were merrily charging away on a fresh set of credit cards. The consumer credit game was like a revolving door with them.

Satan would never pay his traffic tickets, either. His theory was a simple one, really. He would pay up only if caught and compelled to do so. All of Drew's unpaid tickets would become arrest warrants. Since we were always being pulled over by our friends in the San Jose Police Department (riding *or* driving, it didn't matter . . . it seemed as if somebody were always being stopped). Drew would end up being arrested on an outstanding warrant for a trivial traffic violation.

Then the club treasurer, who was usually me, had to go downtown and bail out our big criminal. What should have been a $40 fine became a $200 debt. This scenario played out about once per year. Drew would work to pay off his club debt; but invariably, just about the time he'd gotten square the police would pop him again because of another bench warrant. It didn't bother Drew, though. To him the whole scenario was just a minor speed bump in the judicial process. The chore of frequently bailing Satan out of jail gave the rest of us good ammo to needle Drew. We told him he must have had a secret thing for the desk sergeant or something.

Those of us in the club began to understand what it must have felt like to be one of Drew's credit card companies. Satan held club offices as secretary, sergeant at arms, and was a great club officer. However, needless to say, we never let Drew become club treasurer.

A few months after all the guys quit over the Bass Lake incident, we had one ex-member come back around the club. Matt Bartlett had been our youngest member and was one of the first to leave, along with a few others. When Matt came back to prospect, he knew it would be a tough row to hoe. It wasn't unheard of for former members of clubs to try to re-join; but, it was rare.

During our first winter car show season, a group of us went to the large car show in Los Angeles to run the MMA booth. We stayed at the house of a prospect for the *Hells Angels* LACO (Los Angeles County) chapter. His name was Jango, and he had been an *Angel* some years before, but left the club. Jango told us that his second go-round was brutal—as he knew it would be. A couple of his chapter's members were

134

going to need a great deal of convincing before they would ever give Jango their votes for full membership. Eventually, however, he did make it back. We saw Jango in San Francisco some time later. He transferred to the Frisco chapter and opened a motorcycle shop there. He supported the MMA and bought an MMA Gold Card membership for his shop.

Matt had the same struggle when prospecting for the second time with the *Wheel Lords*. He had a lot to prove to all the guys—and he did. After a long spell as a prospect, Matt was finally made a full member. He was the only guy to leave and come back.

Matt liked to party and could drink a lot of beer. Matt rode a 1974 Shovelhead that was chopped, but not radically so. Matt was smart, levelheaded, and he had a good business sense. He didn't have a regular nickname, but like a lot of guys with that name, we sometimes called him "Mattus." After he made member, Matt rather took over—from our ex-member Keith—the unofficial job of calling Drew, "Windy", when Satan would become full of his own hot air.

Matt had a quick laugh and was an approachable guy, so a lot of the people in the MMA or members from other clubs became his friend. Matt bought a house in East San Jose near the new Eastridge Mall. Since he didn't have a steady girlfriend Matt offered his house to the Club to use as a clubhouse, in exchange for some club help with expenses. How could we say no?

We gained another member when Frank Dinkins was voted in. "Fast Frank" was from the Concord area of the East Bay. Frank had been a prospect for the *Hells Angels* Richmond chapter at about the time we had first joined the MMA. Something happened; I didn't know what, but Frank never made it into the *Angels*. Frank was friends with the second MMA club, the *Centaurs,* who were from the same area around Concord, and so we got to know Frank through them. After the *Centaurs* folded, Frank decided to move to San Jose and prospect for the *Wheel Lords.*

Franky was somewhat older than the rest of us and had been around the bike club scene for some time. Fast brought a lot of knowledge and energy to our club. He knew a lot of people in the scooter world, loved to ride and party, and was a real instigator for hell raising— just like Satan. By the way, Franky wasn't called "Fast" because of his bike, (which was a nice 1950 Panhead). No, Frank was known as "Fast" because of his way with women—and how quickly he could get naked when the situation called for it.

Frank was tall and lean. He wore his hair long like most of us and generally had a full beard. Frank had quite a few divergent skills. He had served in the military as some sort of clerk in the Navy, I think, so he was very good with organizing papers and writing business letters and keeping track of things. Fast was good in a crisis, too. When he was a prospect for the *Angels,* he and another prospect were riding at high speed through town one night when the other guy, named Richmond Tony—or "RT," clipped a van and crashed his bike. The wreck nearly took off RT's leg. Frank stopped, applied a tourniquet, and saved RT's life. RT lost his leg, but he did later become a Richmond *Hells Angel.* He rode a three-wheeler trike after that. Franky saved RT, but did not become an *Angel.* Such is life.

Ben Pender became our first new member who had no connection with the early days of the Club. Matt and Franky had at least known the *Wheel Lords* from our first year, but Ben came into contact with us a little later. Drew had gotten to know Ben when they worked together at the General Electric plant in San Jose. After some time checking things out and hanging around, Ben made prospect, and then full member.

Ben was known as "Oso," or "Bear." The nickname certainly fit. Bear was about five feet ten and weighed about 325. It was kind of funny. There was a Mexican *Unforgiven Sinner* named Bear, and there was a white *Wheel Lord* named Oso (Spanish for Bear). Go figure. We referred to Ben as Bear most of the time, though.

Ben rode a Honda 750 when he first made prospect, and of course, we gave him lots of grief over that. Oso saved up his oro and later bought a '75 Shovelhead, which was a good thing since we weren't going to let a Honda rider in our club. I mean, there was no hard and fast rule stating that you had to ride a Harley. But hey, there was no way a Honda rider would ever become a *Wheel Lord.*

After Bear had become a member, it was hard to imagine the club had ever been without him. Ben was a super funny guy and looked a little like Orson Welles. Like Welles, Bear was a great storyteller. Everything about Bear was large. He drank large . . . partied large . . . laughed large . . . and, he ate large . . . *obviously.* In addition, Bear subscribed to the Satan theory of drug control. That is, if one dosage is good, two would be better, and three would border on perfection. Bear was most at home in a bar. In fact, he literally grew up in a bar. Ben's parents lived in town and had about six or seven kids. To keep them from causing trouble and off the streets, they built an addition on their house.

They turned that addition into a full bar, and it was no small place. The bar itself could seat about 15 people. They had a jukebox, a pool table, commercial refrigerators full of beer, and rows of hard liquor bottles lined up on the bar back.

Ben's parents were cool, and they would invite us over sometimes. Between us, our girlfriends, Ben's parent's friends, his siblings and their families, it wasn't uncommon to see 30 or more people gather at the Pender house on a weekend night. Ben's dad was a professional gambler, as well as having a regular job. He didn't play cards, though. Ben's dad played the ponies. However, he only played the quarter horses, not the thoroughbreds. Benjamin (Bear was named after his dad, but he wasn't a junior—they had different middle names) was a fixture at Bay Meadows and Golden Gate Fields Racetracks. Ben followed in his footsteps and was a gambler as well. He was very good at it, too. Poker, blackjack, ponies, sports book—Bear played them all. He didn't always win, but he always had fun.

Bear's extroverted personality made him a favorite with everyone in our circle of friends and acquaintances. Ben had a way of making those who were around him feel good about themselves. Bear's presence was writ large wherever he went. Whenever we went riding and barhopping, I made it a point to hang near Ben. He had a way of attracting people to him who would buy him (and those near him) drinks. If there was an old citizen guy in a bar, invariably he would end up telling Bear his life story while buying the drinks. Bear would make sure I got some of the overflow. Ben was a very good pool player, too. (Duh . . . he grew up in a bar). I played him many times and felt good about myself on the very rare occasions when I actually won a game.

Bear was like a cycle riding Jackie Gleason. He was Joe the Bartender, with the whole world as his Crazy Guggenheim.

Greg Gordon was the last man to join the *Wheel Lords*. Greg had been riding in San Jose for some time. We briefly worked at the same electronics company in Silicon Valley not long after the club first formed, although we didn't know each other then. I just remember having seen him on his bike sometimes at the plant.

Greg rode a 1948 Panhead. When he first came around the Club, he usually wore a soft leather pilot's cap, like the Snoopy character in Peanuts when he was fighting the Red Baron. Satan thought he looked like Rocket J. Squirrel from the cartoon show Rocky and Bullwinkle, so he nicknamed Greg "Rocky." That stuck, and Greg has been "Rocky" or "Rocket J", ever since.

Rocky was tall with a medium build. He had the longest hair in the club, down to the middle of his back. Rocky drank very little and never smoked. He was into weed, though. Rocky was one of those people I mentioned earlier who, when he had some extra-good pot, would want me to sniff the weed and then look for me to give some glowing recommendation of it. I hated to burst his bubble, but I wasn't a weed person, and I couldn't tell top grade Sinsemilla from ragweed . . . or possibly even lawn clippings, for that matter. I would just smile and say "Yeah, Rock. Sure smells like some fine marijuana to me, man. Enjoy."

Greg was one of the few guys who came from a family of motorcyclists. Most of us were first generation riders—Drew, Dennis, myself, I think Mitch, Frank, and Matt also—but Greg's dad had ridden Harleys for years. Rocky's brother, Skip, was also a biker around town and was friends with some of our guys. Bikes seemed to be in Greg's blood. He was the most machinery driven guy in the club—even more so than Lucas. Rocky was always reading the bike magazines, tinkering with his Pan, adding new gizmos, and talking about bikes.

Rocky, although about the same age as the rest of us, wasn't a car guy as most of us were. Classic cars of the 50's and muscle cars of the 60's seemed to have little allure for Rocky. To his mind . . . why should they? To Greg, a car wasn't a bike . . . so who cares? Cars and trucks were transportation. Motorcycles were the real and only deal.

There was a Winchell's Donut Shop just around the corner from Greg's house. I think Greg was their best customer. He seemed to eat there every day. We would tease Rocky about his fine dining habits. To Rock, a four-course meal consisted of: a glazed, a chocolate with sprinkles, two crumb donuts, and a maple bar.

Rocky worked graveyard shift at electronics plants, so his schedule was a little different than most of the rest of us. Still, Greg made every club function and more than held his own as a member. He was one of those guys that, if you looked up the word biker in the dictionary, you would find his picture.

These men were the real *Wheel Lords*. All the other guys who came and went in the first year were just part-timers. I mean, I still liked some of the guys from our original core group, and I appreciated their contributions. The reality, however, was that the guys I have listed here wore the back patch, carried the tattoo, and lived the brotherhood of our club. Not all of them would be part of the club to its end, unfortunately. Things happen, and people sometimes change. Still, I was proud to call each of them a brother member, and I think they all felt the same about me. Compared to these men, the guys who came and went early on were just temporary help.

As for me, I finally got my bike painted something other than spray can black. Lisa's brother-in-law, Frank Vasquez, made me a good deal and did the work. I chose a purple hue called Plum Crazy. Some of the guys weren't "plum crazy" about the color; but hey, I liked it. At least it wasn't unlucky green. One problem remained. I still couldn't afford to have my Springer front end chromed, so I had it painted purple, too . . . ditto for the oil tank. When I rode around, there was a lot of purple going down the road. Oh well, it would have to suffice until I got the bucks to upgrade. Everyone was always trying to make their bike look unique in some way. At the minimum, I achieved that. No other bike in town looked like mine did.

Another change for me was my old lady status. As I mentioned earlier, after a few months of being apart, my girlfriend Veronica and I had, for all intents and purposes, broken up. Then, I met a girl at a party, fell hard for her, and soon the break-up was official.

Marie was a good friend of one of Drew's sweeties. Yep, even though he was married and his wife Lisa worshipped him, Drew still had girls on the side. This particular sweetie, named Lacy, was no run of the mill biker bimbo, though. She was smart and biker savvy. She had been the girlfriend of a Daly City *Hells Angel* who was now in prison, and her brother was an independent rider well known and respected by the Daly City *Angels.* She knew her way around. Lacy was also very nice, and all of our guys liked her a lot. Over time, she became a kind of "kid sister" to a lot of us in the club. Lacy would send us greeting cards for our club anniversaries and stuff like that. Lacy was a kind person, but she had fallen for the wrong guy. Drew treated her well, and they would get together sometimes, but he was never going to leave his Lisa for anyone.

It was at one of those get-togethers that Lacy brought along her friend Marie. The two of us hit it off right away. Fast Franky would say frequently over the next few weeks "Kid, you've been dazzled." I guess he was right.

Marie was tall, dark haired and beautiful. She just turned 21, two years younger than me. She was trying to become a fashion model, and had gotten some work toward that goal. Her parents were French, with an Italian surname, and she had a classic look about her. Marie wasn't the

California surfer-girl pretty. She was the European continental pretty. She looked like a cross between Audrey Hepburn and Sophia Loren.

However, it wasn't just her looks. Marie was a kind and classy woman. She walked and moved like a model, and she treated everyone with great care. Okay, since she had also fallen for me, one could question her wisdom. However, her generosity and character were tops.

As we started getting more seriously involved, a few potential problems became apparent. First was the logistics. Marie, along with Drew's sometime sweetie Lacy, lived in Redwood City, about 30 miles from San Jose. Most of her modeling work was in San Francisco, which was even further from San Jose. However, since we both were used to being on the road a lot, we thought we could work that one out.

The second problem was financial. I had no job. Now, I had a new girlfriend who was quite likely a little more into the nicer things in life than the average biker chick was. I would have to get a regular paycheck coming in—and sooner would probably be better than later.

The third potential problem was the obvious one. How did I manage to get a girlfriend who was both beautiful *and* nice? And, oh yeah, how are you going to keep her as a girlfriend, bub? To those two questions, essentially, my response was . . . I have no clue.

The last problem might just be nothing. Then again . . . well . . . one big question loomed in my mind. Why was a head-turner like Marie even available in the first place? Lacy from Redwood City told Drew, and Marie confirmed to me, that she had recently broken up with her boyfriend.

Okay, fine . . . we're good to go then.

Then Marie said that she and the ex-boyfriend had been living together for nearly two years before they had broken up.

Hmmm . . . that's all right . . . we're still good.

And that said ex-boyfriend was a Daly City *Hells Angel*.

Well . . . now things could become interesting.

Shiloh 1973

The Kid 1974

WLMCSJ New Year's Eve 1974
(Top) Weasel, Fast Frank, Matt
(Bottom) The Kid, Satan, Sleaze, Dennis

WLMCSJ 1975
(Top) Fast Frank, Weasel, Kidd, Satan
(Bottom) Sleaze, Dennis

Shiloh 1976

Don Lundberg and Weasel 1976

Rocky, Dennis, Weasel, Matt 1977

Satan, Kidd, Bear 1977

WLMCSJ 1978
(Top) Bear, Weasel, Kidd
(Bottom) Matt, Rocky, Satan, Dennis

ᑖ *Chapter Thirteen* ᑖ

"Red and White"

T he *Hells Angels* are just like you and me . . . only different. All right, perhaps there is a little more complexity to the issue. I'm not saying I knew everything about the *Angels* (who are often referred to as the red and white . . . because of their club colors). I was never involved in any of their business and was never present at any of their club meetings. I have no clue to their inner workings. All I have are my own opinions, based upon my observations and interactions with some of the California *Hells Angels* of the 1970's.

I am unable to speak to the differences between the *Angels* of the 70's and the present day *Hells Angels*. I'm sure a lot of things are different now, just as I am certain that some things remain constant. I can only speak to what I saw and understood back in the old days. I do know there seems to be more biker club wars today than there were in times past. Why these various clubs can't at least tolerate one another is beyond my knowledge. It seems to me that these warring clubs are more similar than they are different; but, that is their own concern, not mine.

I'm also not competent to address any other major outlaw clubs from this period. Since the *Wheel Lords* happened to be in Northern California, we interacted with the *Hells Angels*. That is my frame of reference, and that is what I can speak to. Had I lived in say, Texas, then I guess I would know a little about the *Bandidos* of the 1970's; or if I were from Illinois, perhaps the *Outlaws* would have been known to me. I suspect the members from these other clubs were probably similar in words and actions to the *Angels* of the same time frame, but I don't know for sure.

All I can really talk about, with whatever credibility I may have, is how things were as I saw them back then.

First, I never knew Sonny Barger. The most famous *Hells Angel*, acknowledged club leader— and now I suppose, best-selling author, was in prison for much of the time that the *Wheel Lords* existed. I do remember seeing Barger in the late 1970's at a couple of *Hells Angels* funerals, but we never met.

Aside from the usual info everyone else knows about him, I only know two things about Barger. The first thing is that many of the *Angels* whom I knew and respected back in the day spoke very highly of him. Since these people's opinions were valuable to me, I figured Barger was probably a good guy. As indicators go, that was all well and good; but, a person needs to make up their own mind about such things. Since I never knew the guy, it's all academic, anyway.

The second thing about Barger was that I used a set of his gas tanks for a few months. At least I was told they were his tanks. An Oakland *Angel* named Choctaw, who was a friend to us, loaned them to me. I was at Choctaw's house one day and mentioned that my fatbob tanks had a few gas leaks and I was having trouble finding a quality replacement set. Choctaw walked to his garage, pulled out a pair of matched tanks, and told me to try them. He said they belonged to Barger, who loaned them to Choctaw. Maybe Choctaw was just bullshitting me; I don't know. Hell, maybe Barger had 50 gas tanks, for all I knew. At any rate, I took him up on the offer. The tanks worked great and looked cool too, with orange flames on the sides. I ran them for some months until I found my own permanent set.

When I first started hanging around with bikers, before the club days, people who professed some knowledge of the *Hells Angels* told me that the older *Angels* were a little more approachable, a little less intense, and not as rowdy as the younger *Angels* were. I suppose that was probably true, but I don't think that condition was limited to just the *HA*. That situation exists everywhere in society where men gather in groups. Young guys tend to be more "full of juice" and older guys a bit more wizened in a general sense. But yeah, I would say that the older guys, as a rule, had less of a tendency toward aggressive behavior than the younger ones. The *Angels* had a quite a few older members. At least they seemed older to us in our early twenties. The cross-generational mix I mentioned earlier was very prevalent in the *Angels* we met. They had lots of guys in their forties and fifties—some even older. Wide Clyde from Sonoma County was about 64, and Ancient Pete from LACO was at least that old. However, to be clear, none of those older guys was the kindly, old grandpa type. Every one of the older ones was just as dangerous as any of the younger members.

The *Angels*, like a lot of folks in the biker world, had a low tolerance for bullshit. That's not too surprising. What set them apart from most other people who were of similar demeanor was that the *Angels* were always the center of attention. They were used to being in the center. They liked it, cultivated it. In public, they knew they were always "on." All eyes would be on the *Angels*, especially if they were in a group . . . and they were often in a group. It wouldn't just be citizens who would focus on the *Hells Angels*. Other bikers watched them too . . . not overtly, but carefully so, just the same. Hey, it was partly out of necessity. You needed to keep track of things and not be surprised. It was safer that way.

We got a taste of that type of attention in the *Wheel Lords*, if only in a small way. If you rode a chopper, had long hair, and wore a patch, you got used to being stared at. That was fine with us. In fact, that probably was more than fine. It was fun.

The *Angels* usually downplayed this center of attention thing, but not always. They were quite aware of this situation and were aware that everyone else knew the way things were, too. They didn't really need to, if you will, "flex their muscles" in this area of being the dominant group. Nevertheless, sometimes they would do so anyway, just to remind everyone else of the order of things—or—maybe because it amused them.

Every *Hells Angel* had a network of people who made up his circle. We didn't use the term "network" then. I don't know what we called it in the 1970's, but it wasn't network. At any rate, most of those guys had one. This group would be made up of friends, girlfriends, ex-girlfriends, business associates, hangers-on, wannabes, and various other acquaintances. It was kind of like a pro athlete of today with his "posse"; but, really, it was more extensive than that.

This circle of friends would feed info to the *Angel* about all kinds of people and events. Hey, everybody wanted to be known as a friend to a *Hells Angel*. I mean, they were flipping famous, right? It was only natural for people to act this way. Our club would reap the dubious benefits of an *Angel's* info grapevine on occasion. Just when we thought the *Angels* didn't care a hoot about us, one of them would approach one of our officers about something they heard about us through their pipeline of friends. It was usually some minor matter, but it would serve to show how extensive these networks were. Sometimes, though, it could get a little aggravating.

Once, when I was club president, I had to call the president of the San Jose *Angels*— a man named Brian, about some matter. It was fairly early in the morning when I called him. I thought I might be calling too early, but no, Brian was already up and also up to speed on recent events. The first thing he asked me was what about the fight the previous night that Matt and one of our prospects had gotten into with some dudes at one of the local biker bars.

"Well," I said, "I haven't heard anything about that."

"Well, I have," said Brian.

That sound was my teeth gnashing.

The *Angels* weren't too keen with other people getting overly familiar with them. They wanted to be in control of the situation, and didn't like presumptiveness on the part of others. A typical example is the use of the word "brother." The use of brother or "bro" was widespread in the bike world. You'd hear it all the time. However, for many club bikers of that era, and to some independents as well, "brother" was usually reserved for members of your own club or very special friends. For these guys the word brother was used sparingly. Brother was a sacred word to us in the WLMC. That's just how we were taught. It seemed that way to the *Angels*, too. More than once I heard someone— often a stranger, but sometimes a friend or acquaintance—come up to an *Angel* and say something like "What's happening, bro?" Only to receive the icy reply "I ain't your fucking bro, pal."

Brothers were special . . . someone to die for or to kill for, if necessary. Dude, buddy, pal, partner, sir, hombre, man—any of these were acceptable forms of familiar address—but brother? No. It was somewhat funny to see how important semantics could sometimes become to men like the *Angels*, who mostly were steeped in action; but, that was the way of things.

Another mistake some people made when they were around the *Angels* was, for lack of a better term, to misjudge the third guy. Say you had a friend who was an *Angel*, and you could kid around with him. Then, say that you knew some other *Angel*. Maybe you didn't know him as well as your friend, but you were comfortable around him. He knew you and that you were friends with the first *Angel*. Things were groovy, right? Yes . . . except *all that* meant nothing to another *Angel*. I call him the third guy. The third guy could be one person or a group. The third guy didn't know—or if he did know, he didn't care—that you were buddies with another *Angel*. If the third guy decided he had a problem with you, your *Angel* friend wouldn't be of much help. Your *Angel* buddy's loyalty was to his club member, not you. Oh, your friend might try to defuse a problem situation for you; but, if push came to shove, he would back the third guy over you, even if he thought that guy was wrong. That is the protocol of bike clubs.

I saw a few people run into problems in this way. It was a mistake to believe that being friends with one *Hells Angel* would automatically give you a free pass with another. We were always aware of that fact, and took care not to assume too much around those guys.

Macho posturing or acting overly tough around the *Hells Angels* usually backfired on the guys who tried that approach. Not that the *Angels* didn't appreciate someone who was really big or very tough . . . they did. However, they saw and lived tough all the time. They could see through false bravado easily. It didn't matter how tough someone might act, or how brave he may talk. The *Angels* would figure guys out pretty quickly. It's what they did.

There was usually some testing going on with the *Angels*. That was just the lifestyle and the way of things to those of us who weren't in their club. You could be talking with one of them, as pleasant as could be, and another *Angel* would walk over and say something to you out of left field and you would have to re-calibrate your thinking and re-focus yourself. A lot of the clubs we were around acted this way, but the *Angels* were the most active and proficient at this technique.

Basically, when around the *Hells Angels*, you had to have your wits about you and not overstep the situation. At the same time, you couldn't be stopping every few moments to analyze things. Events happened too quickly for that. You had to develop a mindset, a way of thinking, and make it second nature to you. That mindset had to fit in with your basic personality. You couldn't try to be someone you were not. If you tried to act differently than your true character, your covers would soon be pulled.

I resolved to be myself, with an added dose of the new mindset awareness thrown in. Since I was generally a quiet person (with a slice of smart-ass thrown in), I usually got along with most folks. Besides, I'd enjoyed listening, learning, and observing people since I was a child, so it was fun for me to be around the Red and White. The old adage that said a person had two ears and one mouth, and they should be used in that proportion, is a good one. Add a couple of eyes to the mix and that ratio becomes four to one. So I tended to talk only about 20% of the time. I didn't brag much . . . mainly because I had nothing much to brag about.

One problem I would have around the *Angels*— in fact, around all other bikers really, was that a small percentage of guys thought I was a cocky little wise-ass. I disagreed with that assessment, of course. I thought I was a modest little wise-ass.

I noticed another thing about the *Hells Angels*. They continually seemed to have people copying them. Guys off the street would pretend to be *Angels*. These people would tell other folks that they were *Hells Angels* or, worse, dress up as *Angels* and go out in public. It seemed that most of these pretenders didn't even own motorcycles, much less belong to a bike club. The *Angels* we knew would frequently tell us stories of meeting up with some of these ersatz "*Angels.*"

When the real *Hells Angels* would come across the phony ones, they would beat up the masqueraders, and take and destroy their fake patches. Once, Stan Jennings and Artie, the President and VP of the LACO chapter, told us how they by chance met up with two guys in Los Angeles who were wearing high quality fake colors. Stan and Artie were in street clothes. The patches these guys wore were almost an exact match to the genuine, intricately constructed real colors. There was but one small color flaw in one area. Stan and Artie beat up the guys and took the patches, but they kept the phony colors as an example to show their other members.

Another time, a San Jose *Angel* named Brad said he was at the Santa Clara County Fair with a Daly City *Angel* named Dexter. They were wearing colors and, as usual, a few Sheriff's Deputies were following them around. Some guy saw Brad's vest with the chapter patch "San Jose" on the front. (The Daly City chapter didn't wear a city patch). This guy walked up to Brad and announced that he was a *Hells Angel*, but at the moment wasn't wearing his patch.

Brad said, "Oh really? From where?"

"I'm a Daly City member," the guy answered.

Brad pointed to Dexter and said, "Then you'll want to say hello to this man. He's a Daly City member, too."

The guy turned white and immediately took off. Brad and Dexter couldn't do anything with their Deputy escort a few feet away.

The *Angels* seemed to get this stuff all the time. Our Club would encounter people like this sometimes. We'd be at a bar and some drunk would start telling us how he used to be a *Hells Angel*. We'd just roll our eyes and get ready for the story. Matt got a particular kick out of this type of guy. He'd just listen earnestly to the drunk and say "Wow, that's a heck of a story, partner. How about another round of drinks? You buying?"

There must be a couple of thousand people running around this world telling others how they used to be *Hells Angels*. They could form their own club. You may have encountered some of them yourself. Heck, we've even had some people claim to be ex-*Wheel Lords*. That's how silly these things can get.

I had been around the *Angels* a little during our club's first year. My first time partying with a lot of the *Angels* happened toward the end of the run season of 1974. Just after I came back from my leave of absence, we made a club run through Northern California. We spent almost a week out on the road, no girlfriends or sweeties, and no friends along, just us. Veronica and I had just broken up, so I was glad to hit the road with the guys. Our MMA obligation was over for the summer, and we all needed to get away and have some fun just for ourselves. Our first stop was Sacramento, which was practically our second home.

We stopped to see Marty Carpenter, and later crashed at the house of the MMA Secretary, a cool lady named Susie. All the *Wheel Lords* liked Susie, who was kind of like an older sister to us. Susie tended to date *Hells Angels*, some of whom we knew a little.

While in Sac, we were invited to an all clubs party at the Sacramento *Angels* clubhouse. Every month or so, bike clubs from around the Sacramento and Marysville area would meet to discuss events and such, and then party a little afterwards. Since we happened to be in town, we were asked to come along.

I forget who brought us out to the site, but it sure seemed to be the long way around to get to the *Angels* clubhouse. The place was somewhere near the Sacramento River out in a rural area west of town. We arrived well after dark, and the meeting was over and everybody there was in party mode. There was probably five or six different clubs present. I don't recall all of them, but I remember our friends the *Kinsmen* MC were there. In addition, there were loads of *Hells Angels*. It wasn't just the Sacramento chapter. A lot of the Daly City chapter was there, along with some San Jose and Richmond members. There were a lot of guys from the Nomads chapter, and probably others as well.

To us, this seemed to be more than a local clubs meeting. This was a major party, we thought. We were the only club that didn't have back patches, so in an odd way we stuck out from everyone else. Aside from some of the *Kinsmen* and a few assorted *Angels*, we didn't know too many folks. Hey, we were there to party, and so we did. There were but four of us at this party. Sleaze didn't make the week-long run.

Lucas, Dennis, and Drew had been at Bass Lake a few months before, but this was my first time being around a lot of *Angels*. We had just fallen into this party by circumstance, and since I missed Bass Lake, it was more than all right with me. As the party wore into the later hours, we noticed that there seemed to be fewer and fewer members present from the local clubs. We hadn't noticed guys leaving, but I guess they did. There were only a handful of local club guys left—besides the four of us and all the *Angels*.

Drew and I were fond of gallows humor. That fondness served us well that night. There had been recent news stories about dead bikers being found in a few Bay Area locations. Supposedly, these bikers had been killed while partying with the *Hells Angels* some time before. Some bodies had been dumped down a well in the Ukiah area, and others from a separate incident were stuffed into 55-gallon oil drums and dumped in San Francisco Bay near the Richmond Bridge. Cops found the bodies and some *Angels* had been convicted and sent to prison for the crimes. Other cases were working their way through the legal process. At least that was what we thought the news stories had reported, so that was our frame of reference at the time.

After we had been at the party for some time, I walked over to Drew and quietly said, "Did you hear the news headline?"

"No, what?"

"Four missing San Jose bikers found in shallow grave near Sacramento."

"Yeah, well I hope the newspapers spell my fucking name right," he said.

Actually, we were treated quite hospitably that night. We all had a great time. There were some tense moments now and then. It was all part of our learning process. Drew and Dennis decided to leave and asked if I wanted to head back to Sac with them. Since I had missed the Bass Lake Run, I told them no way—I wasn't leaving this place early except on a stretcher. This was after many of the other club people left, so Drew and Dennis thought no one would care if they split.

They were wrong. Two San Jose *Angels*, Brad Loxley and Tom Damatto, went up to Dennis and Drew and told them they didn't think any San Jose people should be leaving. Brad and Tom didn't get right in our guys' faces and make a major deal out of it, but their message and intent was clear enough. This was one of those "flex the muscles" moments I mentioned earlier. Over the years, we would see firsthand how some *Angels* would have a problem if anyone wanted to leave their functions before the *Angels* thought they should. This was one of those times. Drew and Dennis stayed, which worked out good for all of us.

Later, as Lucas was throwing dice with a bunch of the *Angels* in the clubhouse, he found himself in a disagreement with one of the Nomads named Kendrick. It was kind of a Stagger Lee and Billy moment— but again, no big deal. Kendrick seemed to be one of those super intense guys who seemed to live right on the edge of things. One of his buddies from the Nomads chapter, a guy named Jester Joe, was just the opposite. Joe was free and easy and laughing all night. Kendrick and Jester Joe were the first *Angels* I had seen who looked to be of Pacific Islander background. They were some sort of Hawaiian, Samoan, or Polynesian, I guess.

The other un-fun moment, especially for Drew, came when he was asked his name by a couple of *HA*, and he replied, "Satan." Now, I know Drew liked his nickname, but I gently suggested to him that maybe he shouldn't play up the "Satan" handle too much around these guys. I mean they were the *Hells* Angels, after all. Here he was, calling himself *Satan*, the *ruler* of Hell. It just might happen that some of these guys might take exception to someone calling himself Satan at *their* party. Sure enough, someone didn't like it. His name was Franklin, and he was a Daly City member. He and a couple of other guys questioned Drew about his nickname.

"Do you know what the word 'Satan' means?" Franklin said.

"Uh, no, I guess not."

"It means 'adversary' in Hebrew. Are you our adversary?"

"Not that I know of," Drew said. "I don't consider you guys my adversaries. It's a nickname."

And so it went. Again, not a big deal, just more muscle flexing and testing by the *Angels*. It's their way of checking out the members of a club. I thought we handled ourselves pretty well, considering we were new to things . . . and outnumbered about 50 to 4. In addition, it turned out that Daly City Franklin was right. When Drew and I got home, we checked the encyclopedia. The word Satan comes to us from Old English, through Latin and Greek; and, before that, from the Hebrew language where it was "shatan", which meant . . . *adversary.*

I figured a wiseacre like me was bound to piss somebody off that night. With everyone drinking and getting high all night long, it seemed almost inevitable. However, as it turned out I got along with just about everyone. By everyone, I mean those who would talk with us. Some *Angels* just don't mix with *any* outsiders and keep exclusively to themselves.

One of the San Jose *Angels* and I hit it off well, right from the start. He was Brad Loxley, one of the guys who buttonholed Drew and Dennis that night. Loxley was a nonstop joke machine. He had a warped sense of humor and was always needling people, including other *Angels.* Loxley reminded me of Drew when I first met him at my friend Givens' place. Brad was about 27, with short blond hair and blue eyes. He was a stocky guy and looked a lot like my older cousin, Buddy, on my dad's side of the family.

Loxley was vastly amused that I liked his humor. I was amused that he liked mine. We became each other's best audience. It wasn't all about the fun, though. Brad could joke around and needle guys, and still have his radar on for any situation. I could see his mind working behind the smile. I learned a lot from Loxley that night. Hell, all of us learned a lot from all the *HA* we partied with at the clubhouse.

Late into the night, when not too many people were still around, I was sitting near the large campfire when Drew walked up.

"Hey, haven't seen you for a bit. Where you been?"

"Just walking around the property a little," he said.

"Anything interesting?"

"Not much, man. I did find a 55-gallon barrel . . . with your name on it."

"Good one. Oh, did they spell it right?"

Damn, that "adversary" dude could be one funny motherfucker.

Around daybreak, most of our guys were near the campfire when a Sacramento *Angel* named Scary Terry came up to me and said, "Who are you guys?" I told him we were the *Wheel Lords* from San Jose; just as we all said a dozen times or more to all the different guys we met throughout the night. "So where's all the other clubs at?" Terry said.

We all looked around and realized that there was no one else left—just some remaining *Angels* and us. What I didn't say, but what came to my mind when Terry asked where the other club guys were, was, "I don't know where they are. Have you checked your 55-gallon drums lately?" Drew would have laughed, but I doubt if anyone else present would find the gallows humor amusing.

Terry said, "Well thanks for staying." That was nice of him. As I said, we were treated well that night.

Just after sun-up, we fired up our bikes to head out. We were starving. The food was long gone, and most of the *Angels* left for breakfast or home already. We were headed for Yuba City, the next stop on our run, to see Les Clayton and John Cox and some other MMA friends in that area. As we rode out, we passed a group of *Angels* leaning against some cars. I didn't recognize them, but we all nodded to one another as we passed by. One of the *Angels* stuck in my memory. I hadn't met him the previous night, nor had I even seen him. However, for some reason I would remember him.

Drew and Lucas went to do some errand in Sac . . . I forget what it was. Dennis and I headed to Yuba City, although I missed a turn along the way and we ended up going the long way around to get there. We went up Highway 65 through the small town of Lincoln, which was fine with us. We needed some highway time and the country roads were preferable over the freeway.

We stopped at a burger joint in Lincoln. Dennis and I had a lot of laughs recounting to one another all the crazy and lively things we had seen and heard while at the all-night party. When we met up with Lucas and Drew in Yuba, there was but one question we both had for Drew. I gave Dennis the honors. As soon as we could, Dennis asked Drew, "So, bro, what does 'Satan' mean again?"

"Adversary, man," he laughed. "Fucking *adversary*."

That was my first experience at hanging out with a large number of *Hells Angels*. Over the next five years, the scene was repeated, but seldom with quite so many *HA* present. Overall, we had remarkably few problems with them. Being around those guys was a grow-up learning experience for young guys like us in a new club. We would be judged and tested by the *Angels*, but we knew that from the gate, so it wasn't anything that was unexpected. Besides, we were also judging them. Hey, nobody said we couldn't form our own opinions. I'm sure the *Angels* didn't care what we thought, but *we* certainly did.

Over the next couple of months, Loxley and I got to be good friends. We'd run into one another at some of the biker bars in town. One such place was The Cottage, in Saratoga, which was an upscale town on the West Side of Santa Clara Valley near my old stomping grounds of Los Gatos. The Cottage was right in the middle of downtown Saratoga, kind of an anomaly among the wine and brie crowd. The Cottage offered a fantastic deal on Sunday mornings. You could get a beer or cocktail, a rib-eye steak, beans, and garlic bread for $1.50. That was unheard of cheap—even in those days. The Cottage drew a good-sized crowd with that promotion, with lots of hung-over folks trying to recover from their Saturday night over-partying.

We held our one-year club anniversary at The Cottage. We invited all the San Jose clubs and covered the food and a few drinks for everyone. I wasn't too keen on that idea. I thought our limited treasury didn't need to be brought down to almost nothing just in an attempt to show the other clubs a good time. However, I lost that vote, so the party was on.

I had been going out with Marie for a few weeks by then. It turned out that Loxley was close friends with Marie's ex, the Daly City *Angel*. He knew Marie pretty well, too. Brad had seen Marie and me together, and I could tell that he thought highly of her.

Since my bike was down and my car was in the shop, Marie loaned me her car for the night. It was an orange-red Ford Pinto, which was somewhat embarrassing to drive; but, hey— it was kind of her to offer. We had a large turnout at The Cottage. Most of the *Unforgiven Sinners* were there, along with some San Jose *Angels*. As it happened, the Richmond *Hells Angels* were to have their anniversary party that weekend, so some *Angels* from various chapters were hitting a string of party events across the Bay Area that night. We had *Angels* from Oakland and Daly City stop by our party, too.

One of the guys who came by was Marie's ex. We didn't meet that night, but I saw who he was. He was the same large *Angel* whom I had noticed in the group that was leaning against the cars as we left the Sacramento clubhouse. That had been at least a month before I met Marie. His name was Davey Racer, and he kept walking around the bar that night saying, "Has anybody seen my gal?" I didn't know if he was pissed off, or auditioning for Mitch Miller.

Nothing happened that night, but as it turned out, he wasn't auditioning. He was pissed. Maybe seeing Marie's car in the parking lot set him off. She got a call from Davey a day or two later. He told her that he was going to stab me at The Cottage that night, but Loxley talked him out of it.

I saw Loxley shortly afterwards and he told me, "Hey Kid, Davey wanted to stab you that night, but I told him that you were a good guy and you treat Marie good, so he didn't. Don't get me wrong, Davey's one *hell* of a *Hells Angel,* and I'm not saying he was wrong. I just stepped in because I like you, and I like Marie."

"Excellent call, Brad . . . *really* good . . . thanks." I mean, what could I say? Loxley became one of my all-time favorite people . . . *obviously.*

I had to get this whole thing off the "un-comfortable" zone, so I decided to go and meet Davey. He worked at a bike shop in the Belmont area of San Mateo County that was owned by the Daly City President, Chicago Jed, so I rode up there to see Davey face to face. There was no confrontation or anything. He knew I was there just to break the ice, and I knew that he knew. I mean, nobody in our club had even heard of that shop, much less gone there before. We said a few words about bike parts and nothing much in particular and then I left.

Over time, once Davey came to know that Marie and I were for real, things were cool. In fact, Davey and I became friends. I soon came to find out that Loxley had been right. Davey Racer was one of the very best *Hells Angels* I ever came across.

❦

They wouldn't be *Hells Angels* without motorcycles. Some of the *Angels'* bikes were basic, some were high performance, and some were especially noteworthy to me.

A LACO member, whom I only saw once, was a guy named Harold. His bike was pink. I know, pink . . . I know. However, *this ride* was beautiful. A great light shade of pink with lots of new chrome; man, it was cool. I wanted to try painting mine pink too, but I didn't have the cash to "pretty up" all the necessary chrome to highlight that color scheme, or maybe I just didn't have the brass to do so. Regardless, it *was* pretty.

Several guys rode with ape-hangers for a retro look. These were extended handlebars that would be at eye level or higher. I ran ape-hangers (sometimes called monkey bars) on my Knucklehead for a time, too. The problem was they were illegal in California if the handle grips were above shoulder height . . . (to look *cool*, they *had* to be above shoulder height). The bigger problem was that every cop in the Bay Area seemed to know the ape-hanger law, and I was always being pulled over and receiving fix-it tickets for my handlebars. Eventually, I took them off and went back to my old ones. However, one *Hells Angel* managed to get around the shoulder height law. Franco Fuentes was a San Jose member who rode a Sportster. He had high ape-hangers, but he would leave the bolts loose on the handlebar brackets; so, he could lower the bars down when he saw a cop. After the cop would drive past, Franco would push the bars back up to the high position. I never knew of anyone else who did this, and I don't know how safe that was, but it seemed to work for Franco.

Davey Racer also rode a Sportster. He was known as "One Wheel Dave" because of his penchant for pulling wheelies. Davey was a stocky guy and the Sportster was lightweight, so it was easy for him to wheelie. Davey would wheelie through the gears and would even wheelie sometimes while riding in a pack of bikes—right down the middle between the parallel lines. That was awesome.

There was a Richmond *Hells Angel* named Roustabout. I didn't know him, but I saw him around quite a bit. He built a beautiful, clean, show-condition bike that he entered in the Concord Bike Show one year when we had an MMA booth there. The bike was cool, but the topper was the decal Roustabout affixed to the air cleaner. It was a round decal with lettering in the same style and colors as the *Hells Angel* patch. The decal read, "This bike belongs to a *Hells Angel*. Fuck with it . . . and find out."

In sum, through my observation, this is how I would describe the *Hells Angels* overall. I found that some *Angels* treated us with complete indifference (which was fine, nobody said we needed to be best buddies). A few I didn't care for, a handful I didn't like at all, a lot of them treated us with respect, and more than a few were some of the best people I have ever met.

However, my old friend Roy Givens— who, as far as I know— never actually met any *Hells Angel* in person, came up with the most succinct description of the *Angels* I ever heard.

Givens once said, "With the *Hells Angels,* two's company . . . and three's a mob."

Wish I'd thought of that.

☞ *Chapter Fourteen* ☜

"Sinners"

The other main outlaw club in San Jose during this time was the *Unforgiven Sinners*. The *Sinners* usually had around ten members, give or take, and they had been around for a few years before we formed the *Wheel Lords*. Two of our original members, Drew and Howie, had briefly been hang arounds for the *Sinners;* and, there was a lot of interaction between our two clubs. Everybody knew everyone else, and we all became pretty familiar with one another. That's not to say that everybody necessarily liked one another, of course. In general, we all got along okay.

The *Unforgiven* had a good-looking back patch. Naturally, every bike club believes their patch looks great. However, some of the club patches I have seen looked awful. Some were either badly designed, or poorly made; and, with some, you just couldn't tell what the patch was supposed to be.

However, the *Sinners'* colors were nice. They had a coiled rattlesnake wrapped around a swastika. They had *"Unforgiven"* as their top rocker and *"Sinners"* for the bottom rocker. Their club colors were blue and white (although the blue usually didn't stand out much. Most *Sinners* patches were on the dirty side, so oil and dirt muted the hues of blue and white. That was okay. Some clubs, or individual chapters, tended to have more worn-in patches than others did). Their patches were large and filled up the entire back of the vest. The *Sinners* didn't have a bunch of extra patches on their vests, either. Some clubs tended to sport all kinds of extra patches and pins on their colors. There would sometimes be 1%-er patches, or "13" patches, or FTW (Fuck the world) patches, and various other sayings or slogans attached to some club colors. Most of the Bay Area clubs we came in contact with tended not to have this stock car racer look.

The *Sinners* had a lot of big guys as members. They could be a physically imposing bunch to be around. Most clubs or chapters had at least some smaller guys; but, the smallest *Sinner* was Eddie, and he was about an average sized guy.

Fat Rodney was one of those large *Sinners* who left their club about the time that we started the *Wheel Lords*. I didn't really know him, but Drew said he was a fun guy. Rodney used to dress up as Santa Claus

165

and bring toys to children who were in the hospital during Christmas time. We took Rodney's idea one step further. We'd get Matt, or later on Bear, to dress up as Santa, and the rest of us would dress up as elves. We would decorate our bikes with deer antlers and streamers and the like. Then we would ride in a pack with Santa in the rear, so we looked as if we were reindeer-riding elves leading Santa and his sleigh. We would go to four or five San Jose hospitals and visit the kids who couldn't get home for the Holidays. Santa's elves would distribute candy canes to the children who could have sweets and to the nurses and staff that were on duty. Our friends Don Lundberg, John Robinson, and Planch would accompany us sometimes. Don had a red three-wheeler that he would let Bear ride. Then, he really looked like Santa Claus mounted on a sleigh with eight reindeer bikes in front.

We had a good time with the annual Christmas ride. Traffic would nearly come to a stop when we rode from hospital to hospital. It was unusual to see Santa and a bunch of elves riding motorcycles through town. Everybody had to tease one another about their elf outfits. Some of the guys wore those little elf ears—the kind that looked like Mr. Spock ears. It was nice feeling to see the kids' faces when Santa came around. Bear was an especially great Santa. He had the extroverted personality for the role, and he loved kids.

Our only difficulty was corralling some of our guys, like Drew and Fast Frank, when it was time to leave from the hospital. They would try to sweet talk the good-looking nurses during our visits. It was one of the few times that they could use that old line with impunity, "Candy, little girl?"

I thought most of the *Sinners* were good guys. A few I didn't much care for, some I liked a lot, one or two I genuinely disliked, and a few were just indifferent in my book. We learned a lot from the *Unforgiven,* and they treated us with respect. Nevertheless, sometimes they thought they could play mind games with us and would attempt to treat us as if we were their pupils or something.

Eddie Lezcano, their president for a few years, liked trying to play mind games on us. At least *I* thought so. Drew thought Eddie was great, and he could be at times. When my bike rested on its kickstand, it leaned at a crazy angle, which made it difficult to kick-start my bike. (I couldn't just straddle my bike and kick. Like a lot of small guys, I had to kick from one side with all my weight to get it started). Eddie had me come over to his house, where he had his welding equipment. He fixed the kickstand so that my Knucklehead stood at a straighter angle.

Problem solved. Eddie was kind of like our friend Planch. He could annoy you one minute, then be very generous the next.

Jacob Doles was the *Sinners* president after Eddie. Jacob was a real tall guy. He wasn't around when I first met the *Sinners* because he had been in a severe motorcycle wreck. Jacob spent more than a year in the hospital, I think. He had long hair and was older than us. Jacob liked to call himself a "shit disturber", and I wouldn't argue with that assessment. He enjoyed agitating things, and liked the mind games just as well as Eddie did. Jacob had done hard time years earlier for killing some guy out of state, if I remember correctly. He was a tough bird. Jacob's right leg was inches shorter than the left, due to his wreck. He had a boot with an extra thick sole to make up some of the height difference, but he still walked with a big cane and a noticeable limp. Jacob insisted on still riding a kick-start bike, and he would have to kick with his left leg from the right side of the bike to get it started. That was a very cumbersome process, and painful, too. When the bike didn't turn over or kicked back on him, he would often stumble hard on his bad leg and grimace.

Jacob once showed me his injured leg. This was years after his wreck, and it still looked terrible. Jacob wasn't my favorite guy in the *Sinners*, but he certainly had my respect.

My favorite *Sinner* in the early club years was a guy named Darren. He was one of the best people I ever met in the bike world. Darren was a real big guy, with fairly long black hair and beard. He looked a bit like that guy, Grizzly Adams, only darker and more menacing. Darren was just a straightforward, no-nonsense good dude. Everybody in our club thought well of him. Darren was easy to talk with and treated everyone with respect, and he liked to party and get high with you, too. Unfortunately, after a time, Darren left the *Sinners* and I never saw him again. That was too bad for the *Unforgiven*, and too bad for us, too.

My cake-fighting buddy, Slice, left the *Sinners* about that same time. Slice was a fun guy who usually had a bottle of something with him. He looked a lot like David Crosby of Crosby, Stills, Nash, and Young—only, again, darker and more menacing.

"Snake" was one of the *Sinners* whom I didn't much care for. He wasn't a bad guy, and I didn't dislike him, I just thought he was a windbag. Snake was a big guy (natch) and liked to talk a lot, mostly about himself. Snake's name, which he tried to keep on the low-down, was Francis McQueen. You could see why he preferred his nickname.

Gordy Nakatomi was known as "Zip". Gordy was Japanese, but he didn't get the nickname Zip as a reference to "zipper head," a derogatory term for Asians. Gordy became Zip because when he first came around the *Sinners,* he wore a leather jacket with about a dozen zippered pockets on it. The *Sinners* said that he looked like Eric Von Zipper, a caricature biker character in some of those cheesy teenage beach movies of the early 60's. Zip was a good kid. He was young but looked older. Gordy was one of the few clean-shaven guys we knew. He just couldn't grow facial hair at all. Gordy was another one of those *Sinners* that most everyone liked. He was low-key, but could get intense when it was necessary. Zip had a nice scooter, which he rode a lot.

Gordy's frequent riding buddy was Bear. Not the Bear in our club—the *Sinners* had their own Bear. His real name was Vincente Santiago, but nobody knew him as that. Bear was a mountain of a guy, with long black hair and beard. Zip and Bear were together often. If you found one, you usually found the other. Bear was a real extrovert, as was our Ben. Bear liked to laugh and, like our ex-member Keith, he would needle me about my size. I'd tease him back about his ancestors' rat packing all those guys at The Alamo, and shit like that. When both Bears got together, there was always lots of laughter.

Miguel Castro was another one of those *Sinners* that I didn't warm to. Lucas in our club thought Miguel was great, but I never saw it that way. Miguel seemed smart, and he wasn't a braggart. I just thought he looked down on us. He was one of those guys who wore sunglasses indoors—*all* the time. There were a few guys around like that. Maybe some of these guys had eye problems. Perhaps Miguel did, for all I knew. However, I doubt it. I think they just tried to look cool . . . and, they didn't. Miguel walked with a limp, but it seemed to come and go in severity. It seemed like another forced affectation to me. Miguel never seemed to talk to anyone in our club except Lucas. That's okay . . . he didn't have to. Just like I didn't have to talk to him, either . . . and I didn't.

One of the things I did respect about Miguel, though, was his, and Bear's views of Mexicans. Both of those guys called themselves Mexican—*not* Mexican-American—*Mexican.* They hated the word Chicano. They felt that referring to them as Chicano was like calling them nigger. Both Bear and Miguel mentioned that a few times. "Hey, no problem," we said, "If you guys want to be called Mexicans . . . great." Then we'd add, "So how come it took so many thousands of you *Mexicans* to take The Alamo, huh?"

The only *Sinner* I flat-out didn't like was a guy named Ross Dudley. He didn't like me at all, and the feeling was mutual, Omaha. Ross was a real tall guy with long blond hair and beard. I really can't remember exactly why I didn't like him, (other than the fact that he didn't like me) since I hardly gave him a thought.

As I said, the *Sinners* were fine overall. We felt lucky, especially after meeting other outlaw clubs over the years, to have had the *Sinners* in the same backyard. The *Unforgiven* was a first rate outlaw club and had a deserved reputation around California. They treated us well; even though at times, perhaps— a little grudgingly so.

Some of the San Jose *Hells Angels* seemed to like the *Sinners*, and some did not. Loxley and some of the other *Angels* referred to them as "Spinners" on occasion. That was pretty funny, and I couldn't help but laugh.

The only real issue that I thought the *Sinners* handled wrong was their demeanor around others. They would act one way when the *Angels* were around, and another way when they weren't. It's a common mistake. When the *Hells Angels* were around, the *Sinners* would be fairly quiet. When the *Angels* were not around, the *Sinners* were loud and full of bravado.

Everyone acts differently to some extent, of course. It's only natural to relax a little when the big boys aren't nearby. However, the *Sinners* would be noticeably different. We would notice. I'm sure others did, too. Word would filter back to the *Angels*. Remember those networks? They worked.

Once, at an all clubs meeting in town, some of the *Sinners* started talking about a fight they had been involved in at The Cottage, the bar in Saratoga with the great, Sunday morning meal deal. Not everyone there knew what they were referring to, and the *Sinners* were being somewhat coy about the details . . . letting out some sly and inside references to some brouhaha.

Loxley obviously heard all about the fight, though. He immediately chimed in. "Yeah I heard how it took two or three of you to beat up the old citizen guy with the crutch. Did you get his buddy in the iron lung, too?"

Silence . . .

Did Loxley have the all the real details? Probably not . . . was he exaggerating what he did know? Probably so . . . however, he seemed to have correctly captured the essence of the tale.

I always tried to act the same in public whether the *Angels* were around or not. The rest of the club followed suit. I'm not saying we were perfect at that, but we made a conscious effort to do so. That was one area in which I thought we were a little ahead of the *Sinners*.

One *Unforgiven Sinner* remains to be mentioned . . . Richard Pettigrew. Richard was the big, bad Sergeant At Arms who looked upon me so disapprovingly the night I first rode Shiloh and ran out of gas on the way to our club meeting when we received MMA approval for the *Wheel Lords* MC.

Long story short—Richard became my best friend in the *Sinners*. We weren't tight blood-brothers or anything, but we were friends. Richard reminded me of my older stepbrother Dave. He was an up front, straight-talking guy who was a sort of throwback to the 1950's. Richard would sometimes host a poker night at his house in south San Jose. We would have a great time. Richard was a dynamite host, and all the guys he invited left pretensions at the door. You could relax and have fun. Richard was easily one of the best people I've ever met anywhere.

I don't remember any one thing that happened that enabled us to become friends. I know that when we first met— back before I even had a bike—there was no way I thought I would ever be friends with Richard. We just seemed too different. However, I suppose I changed some over time. Maybe Richard did, too. It's just another example of how we got to know people who had a positive influence on shaping the lives of those of us in the club.

Around late 1978, the *Unforgiven Sinners* closed down as a club. Their numbers had been down, and the word on the street was that the *Angels* wanted them to fold and become prospects for the San Jose *Angels*. I guess that was true, because right away most of the *Sinners* sported *Hells Angels* prospect patches.

One of the few *Sinners* who did not prospect was Eddie. I didn't think he would. Eddie was a *Sinner* and only a *Sinner*. End of that story.

Just a few days after becoming a prospect, Richard had a serious bike accident. I went to see him in the hospital. He was depressed.

Richard wouldn't be riding again for a long time . . . if ever. You can't prospect from a hospital bed, so Richard never made the *Angels*.

Neither did any of the other ex-*Sinners*. Over the next several months, all of them dropped away. I think there was too much "Spinner" bias working against them, but I don't know for sure.

I do know that we had a lot of good times with the *Unforgiven Sinners* MC. We learned a great deal from being around them. To me, some of their members—notably Darren and Richard—were outstanding guys. All of us in the *Wheel Lords* missed seeing the *Sinners*, me included.

✑ *Chapter Fifteen* ✑

"Code"

C hopper motorcycle clubs are part of the counterculture. That may seem like an obvious statement; but sometimes, in modern society, we oversimplify and tend to label that which sticks out as the mainstream. Very often, that is *not* the case. In the 1960's most young people were not hippies. Yet, that tumultuous decade is probably best known for the hippie culture. True, many young folks were alienated and disenchanted with society back then; but, relatively few were actual hippies. Yet, we hear all the time how the 60's was the hippie decade.

As the 1970's rolled in, attitudes were changing; but, America was still a conservative place. The "Silent Majority" held power, Richard Nixon won a landslide election, and most people in the country were not opposed to the Vietnam War. Despite anti-war protests, the emerging drug culture, hippies and yippies, hard rock music, and the rise of alternative lifestyles— if you had long hair in the 70's, you were in the minority and on the outside edge of society.

For example, in 1969 the number one song in pop music—this during the time of the Beatles, the Stones, Zeppelin, Creedence, Blind Faith, Janis, Hendrix, and others—was . . . *Sugar, Sugar,* by the Archies. I mean . . . What the fuck?

Our bike club, to put things into context, was a part of the 1970's counterculture. We weren't an outlaw (sometimes called a 1%er) club but we had long hair, rode choppers, used drugs, and lived a lifestyle that set us apart from many of the norms of mainstream society.

As such, we developed a code of conduct and behavior. We didn't invent this code. We took parts of it from the other clubs we met, other elements came from people we knew who were independent riders, and a lot of it developed from the backgrounds and experiences of each individual who was in the club. All these elements combined to form the code as we knew it and as we lived it. We didn't refer to these "standards," if you will, as a code per se. We didn't use that term. There are no written rules or by-laws that could be pointed to. The code is simply a way to describe the mindset we had in the *Wheel Lords*— to explain what we believed in— and to define the conduct which we held others and ourselves accountable to.

First of all, it's not a motorcycle gang, it's called a club. Nobody . . . and I mean *nobody*, ever referred to a club as a gang. The term "gang", comes from newspaper reporters, Hollywood movies . . . and cops. Police love to use the term gang because it sounds sinister. To all of the people in the scooter world, gangs were either; a) inside the walls of prisons, or b) groups of urban toughs who committed street crimes. On the other hand, motorcycle clubs were made up of men who rode motorcycles.

Anyone who referred to a club biker as a gang member was inviting ridicule or fisticuffs.

Nicknames were common among the chopper crowd. I've mentioned quite a few nicknames previously. Most guys, and even some of the women, had a nickname. The best nicknames were given to a person by someone else. Those assigned nicknames were usually based on some physical feature or character trait that stuck out about the person.

A few people nicknamed themselves. This practice, however, was generally held in less regard. A person who self-nicknamed, tended to pick more flattering and self-serving names, and didn't really get to the essence of the person as well as a nickname that had been chosen by a second party.

In my case, I was "The Kid". Drew had named me that when we first met in 1970. I was not "The Kid" as in Cisco, Cincinnati, or Billy the . . . I was just . . . *The Kid*. That name stuck, in no small part, because I probably looked like a kid, especially compared to some of the guys. I tried to change my nickname once around 1976, but Lucas would have no part of it.

"I don't want to be 40 years old and still be called The Kid," I said. "I need another nickname."

"Bullshit, man," said Lucas, in one of his binary modes. "You're The Kid, and you always will be. That's it."

Drew sided with Lucas, so I knew my idea was a goner.

"Well, at least I can spell it differently. From now on, it's Kidd, with two D's. And that's it."

So . . . I became Kidd.

Women were a significant part of the code. Hey, one reason guys ride motorcycles is because it attracts women. In fact, some guys *only* ride motorcycles because doing so attracts women. Not too many of that type of biker make it in a club, however, because there are too many obligations in a club that could interfere with chasing women if that's all a guy's looking to do. For the guys whose primary concern was scoring with chicks, a club was usually too much bother.

In the *Wheel Lords*, like most clubs of the time, we had old ladies and we had sweeties. Old ladies were wives or steady girlfriends. Sweeties were casual girlfriends or women you had on the side. Not every member had sweeties on the side, but quite a few did.

All the other members treated old ladies with respect. Even if you didn't like a member's old lady, you treated her decently out of respect to that member. All old ladies were hands off to other members. You had to be able to trust your old lady around your brothers, and to trust your brothers around your old lady. Anything less was going to be a definite problem; so, mutual trust was a given and not to be broken.

Sweeties did not have the same status as old ladies. That doesn't mean they were treated badly. They just weren't accorded as much deference as someone's old lady. Many sweeties were here today and gone tomorrow. That's just how it worked. If another member took out someone else's ex-sweetie—that was okay. The first guy had to be cool with it. Hey, if you don't want her going out with others—make her your old lady.

Another custom concerning women and behavior needs to be mentioned. That is the axiom of no butt . . . no putt. That phrase was a standard in the 1970's and was generally adhered to by everyone we knew. If you saw a woman on the back of a guy's bike, it was a given that they were sexually involved. There were a few exceptions, of course. However, old ladies of other members or female family members aside, there was usually no such thing as a free ride. Most women we came across knew and understood this axiom . . . and were just fine with it.

MC doesn't just stand for motorcycle club. It also stands for man club. In our world, the man— not the woman, made the decisions; especially when it came to any decisions about the club. Now, to be sure, most couples make their critical decisions as a team, and that is cool. We all understood that every tight relationship has its own dynamic between the two partners. Just don't bring that dynamic into play around the club.

Around one another, as far as we were concerned, the guy decided everything. The opinion of an old lady, no matter how highly regarded she may have been, meant nothing when it came to any club business.

In addition, we never had any of the, "Property of _____", patches. This was a fairly rare custom that a few clubs adopted, whereby the old ladies would wear a small patch that identified them as belonging to a certain club member. A common property patch may read "Property of Pigpen" or whomever, from "So and So MC" or whatever was appropriate. These patches would usually be on a vest in the same color scheme as the club. We never liked that idea, and I can't remember any club in Nor Cal who had them; although, we would see them in bike magazine photos sometimes, so I guess some clubs favored them. We thought these property patches looked silly, and that only the men who were actually members of a club should wear the club name.

Most of these attitudes regarding women are probably considered examples of outdated male chauvinism. That could be true, I suppose, but that was who we were. We weren't looking to open a new chapter for the National Organization for Women. We were a bike club full of scooter tramps.

Drugs were everywhere in the world of chopped motorcycles. A few guys took no drugs whatsoever, but that was rare. Some guys took a vast quantity of drugs, but most bikers were somewhere in the middle— frequent users, but not every day. I hesitate to use the term "recreational drug user". To me, that sounds a little frivolous, a little too lightweight. Because, when most guys did take drugs—usually when partying, and frequently on weekends—there was nothing lightweight about it. There were high times, *big time.*

Very few guys did hard drugs. Of course, you must understand that what we considered hard drugs were heroin (or anything with a needle) or crack. Nothing else was thought of as hard drugs. Quaaludes, acid, hash, reds, cocaine, and methamphetamines were just the usual stuff to most guys. That doesn't mean that all of those drugs were always available and always being taken. It's just that they were considered the standard. (Marijuana didn't count. Weed was everywhere. It was a given, like liquor).

The most popular drugs in the scooter world were coke and crank. This is hardly a news flash, of course. To clarify, methamphetamine was always called crank. I heard that nickname came about because it made you cranky. Regardless, it was usually crank—not meth, not speed . . . *crank*. I can't recall anyone outside of the media talking about "methamphetamines".

How drugs fit into the code, was just this. You could take drugs; you could not take drugs. You could take a few drugs; you could take a lot of drugs. You could even sell a few drugs if you wanted. What you couldn't do, however, was to let drugs get in the way of club business. When the club needed you, it was time to perform. If drugs got in the way of that performance, you would soon have a big problem.

It was kind of like the old Johnny Carson skit with Art Fern and his "Tea Time Movies". Do you remember how Art was hawking used cars during the breaks in the televised "B" movies?

"Divorced? We don't care."

"No job? We don't care."

"Bad credit? We don't care."

"Not going to pay? *Then* we care!"

If a member allowed drugs to adversely affect his ability to function as a *Wheel Lord* . . . *then* we cared.

No one in the club was particularly fond of police officers. Most everyone had been arrested at one time or another, usually for some minor offense, so there was some prior history going on. Since we weren't an outlaw club, we didn't actually have an ongoing feud or any simmering animosity with the local authorities. In fact, most of them probably didn't know who we were. However, that didn't prevent some in the San Jose Police Department from hassling us.

San Jose PD had been having a running dust-up with the San Jose *Angels* for some time when we came along. About every year, there seemed to be a police bust of the San Jose chapter, usually for drugs, although not always. One year the *Angels* were accused of trying to explode a pipe bomb under the car of a Sergeant John Kracht. He was one of the main anti-biker guys in the San Jose PD.

Another time, three San Jose *Angels*— Lyle Grisham, Jack Elroy, and Duane Boitano, were arrested for beating up some guys in another local bike club. That other club was a kind of shadowy group that formed on their own, and didn't mingle with any of the other clubs around town.

They went to the cops and became informants against the *Angels*. We heard all about this episode later as the *Angels* got the word out to watch out for these guys. Drew knew their leader from his old days in the *Vi Kings* car club and didn't like him; but, none of the rest of us had ever heard of any of these squirrels.

Anyway, maybe the San Jose PD had something against us—or maybe they just didn't like anyone with long hair and a bike, because they started to hassle us. It wasn't anything substantial. It was certainly nothing like the spat between the cops and the *Angels*, but they would jerk us around from time to time. That was to be expected from San Jose PD from what I could tell. They had a poor reputation, at least among many young people.

One of the guys I worked with at McDonald's had once been a roommate of my friend Roy Givens. This guy, named Tony, thought he was hot shit. Tony was trying to get hired on at the San Jose PD. He soon made it, too. Less than a year later Tony was suspended for a few months when he and about four other off-duty San Jose cops beat up some hapless citizen one night in the parking lot of Cowtown, a large local country honky-tonk.

A few examples of why we came to dislike the San Jose cops. A SJPD officer stopped Matt once. The officer immediately challenged him to a one-on-one fight behind a nearby building. The cop said he would leave his gun in his car, and didn't mention anything about his secondary gun. That would be the one all SJPD cops were required to carry, and the one that he would certainly pull as soon as he got Matt alone and unarmed behind the building.

Another time, I was pulled over and given a safety check on my bike. That was standard stuff and not a big deal. The officer couldn't find a safety violation, and when I wouldn't tell him my destination, he declared my bike an "unsafe vehicle." That meant I had to take it immediately to a place of repair or have it towed. If he had seen me riding again, without somehow making my bike "safe", he would arrest me and tow the bike anyway. (Having your bike towed was always a concern. A tow usually meant the cops would drag it to impound, where it would somehow be misplaced while you were waiting to get bailed out. The cops always had the hammer over us on the towing tactic, especially if you were riding solo).

There were many more incidents, but you get the drift. Part of the regular biker code says that you don't talk to the cops, and the San Jose PD made it easy for us to fall in with that idea. We were just little fish around town. I know the *Angels* and *Sinners* had quite a few more problems than we did.

Other police agencies we didn't like were the Sacramento Sheriff, the Tuolumne County Sheriff in the Gold Country of the Sierras, and the City of Pomona in Los Angeles County—undeniably the worst group we ever came across.

On the other hand, we never had any problems with the Fresno County Sheriff, and we saw them many times. The San Francisco PD also treated us fairly. However, our favorite agency was the California Highway Patrol. The CHP had one charter—keep the California roads as safe as possible, and that's what they did. They didn't seem to have an axe to grind with anybody. Maybe it was because they didn't have city jurisdictions to worry about, I don't know. There were a few times when a CHP cruiser would pull up next to our pack as we were riding down the freeway at about 80 and over the loudspeaker, the officer would tell us to slow it down a little. Then he would speed off, and we would slow it down . . . for a few miles, anyway.

There were no black bikers in any of the clubs we knew. There were Hispanics and a few Asians, but no blacks. Racial mixing just didn't happen among bikers in the 1970's. It's not that everyone was prejudiced against blacks, but enough guys were so that there was no way a black biker, no matter how deserving he might be, would receive a unanimous vote for membership. It just wasn't going to happen.

There was a black bike club in San Jose during this time. They were called the *Funky Wheels*. They rode Honda 750's mostly, with some Sportsters, too. The *Funky Wheels* were good guys, and quite a few of them joined the MMA. They had a clubhouse off King Road, not too far from where Drew, Phil, Mitch, and I lived. The clubhouse was in an industrial area and had a large bar and cool lighting and pool tables and a jukebox and a dance floor. It was a hot set-up. We went to it a few times. Drew especially liked going to their clubhouse, since he was a fan of rhythm and blues, and the *Wheels* sometimes had soul bands perform there. The *Funky Wheels* did have one white guy in their club. His name was Nigger Charley. That was an exception, though. For the most part, whites had their clubs, and blacks had theirs.

178

Tattoos were not as popular in the 1970's as they are today. Most of the people who had a tattoo in the 70's were bikers, military, or convicts. There were a few people who had full-blown tattoo body art, but that was rare. Today, you can see more tattoos on the floor of any NBA game than we would see in a whole crowd of bikers in the 1970's. In fact, you could probably find more tattoos in any WNBA game, for that matter.

All of our members who made it past the first eight months or so got a club tattoo. Some guys had it on the arm, some on the chest. That was standard for the clubs we knew. Not every bike club had a club tattoo, but most did. For most of us, the club tattoo was the only one we had. A few guys did have multiple tattoos, but nobody was covered with them or anything. Dennis had a few tattoos. One said, "Born To Win." Drew had a tattoo that he had copied from a World War II pin he owned. It was a circular wreath with a sword and a swastika. It looked good and certainly was unique. Drew was into that Aryan stuff a little bit, but not overly rabid about it or anything. Mostly he just liked to shake people up with the look.

Our tattoo read *Wheel Lords* San Jose MC, along with the date you joined. If you were one of the original ten members, you had a "-10-" above the words San Jose. But only four of the original ten guys stayed in the club long enough to get the -10- tattoo.

If you left the club, an out date would be added to the tattoo. The whole tattoo would have an *X* drawn through it. Some clubs allow long-time members to keep their club tattoo with only an out date. That would only happen when they left, or retired in good standing. However, we weren't around long enough for that precedent to be established. That didn't stop each member who *did* leave the club with a tattoo to try to avoid the *X*, however. Every guy who left lobbied to keep his tattoo intact, but it never happened. They each had an *X* tattooed through the club name.

Many of the most vital parts of our code involved our machinery. A motorcycle was a must. If you sold yours, you needed to get another one quickly. We came across some clubs who were a little lax on this point, but not us.

Your bike had to be running, too. A winter re-build was no problem, and occasional downtime during the season was okay, if it was a temporary situation. Otherwise, your bike had to be on the road. We had mandatory runs every year, which each man and his machine had to be present for, or a fine was forthcoming. As I had the oldest bike, and was not a particularly experienced mechanic, I ran afoul of this rule a few times. I would bitch and plead my case, of course; but, each time the upshot was the same . . . *I paid* . . . my tough luck.

Your bike need not be pretty. We all appreciated nice looking bikes, but there were no points awarded for style. Lucas and Drew probably had the nicest looking scoots, Mitch and I had the most distressed looking, and everyone else was somewhere in between. We didn't have any fancy looking bikes. At least, not like the ones built by Arlen Ness in Hayward that were intended primarily for profiling down the Boulevard. Ness built beautiful machines for rich guys. Our bikes were set up for barhopping around town or hitting the open road for a run to the Sierras, and they looked it.

Another part of the unwritten code was that many chopper riders would kiss one another in public . . . and I don't mean a little peck on the cheek, either. We're talking, full, lip-to-lip, wet kiss. That didn't happen all the time; but, it was by no means a rare occurrence, either.

Usually when a couple of guys would embrace and kiss, they were two close friends who hadn't seen one another for some time. I must admit that the first time I saw this I was taken aback. I thought to myself that they must be *really tight*. Well, yeah . . . they were . . . and they didn't give a crap what anyone else thought.

Certainly part of the reason for the biker kiss was to shake up those in the general public. It worked, too. Regular citizens who would see a couple of badass looking bikers plant a wet one on one another, would freak out in amazement. However, it was much more than that. Many bikers are demonstrative guys, and it was a cool thing to see genuine emotion freely displayed. That was especially true in our society where men are only supposed to shake hands. However, bikers don't conform to that convention. They're frequently hugging or embracing their close friends; and yes, sometimes even kissing them, too.

I forget who gave me my first biker kiss; maybe it was Lucas or Drew or Loxley, I suppose. I had been used to only kissing women (when given the opportunity) with delicate, soft faces. It was quite a change to feel a beard against my skin. However, you get used to it.

And, for you wiseacres out there, I need to make one thing

clear . . . when two bikers *do* kiss . . . *no* tongue.

Some of our other club attitudes were pretty basic to club bikers. Club business was not conducted in public or even discussed with outsiders (and *everyone* else was an outsider). You stood beside your patch and your brothers no matter what. You didn't quit on your brothers. (Some guys seemed not to have gotten the memo on this one). You protected your patch and your bike at all costs. These were all elementary, albeit crucial, standards. No one was above these standards, and everyone had to adhere to them.

We were all trying to be "hard core" bikers. Hard core was a term we used quite often. That was our ideal, and we emulated those whom we thought were hard-core. At the other end of the spectrum was the term "sniveler." No one wanted to be thought of as a sniveler or a whiner.

Essentially, we believed, there were two types of guys in this world—the haves and the have-nots. The haves had chopped Harleys and were righteous bikers. Even if you didn't like certain guys who rode (and we didn't), at least they were some of the haves because they rode a bike.

The have-nots were everyone else. (Certain good friends who chose not to ride motorcycles and family members excepted.) The worst of the have-nots were the guys who said they were working to get a bike together and that "someday" they would be up and running. A guy would have a front end in his garage, or some engine parts in a box or something, and then would tell people that he was a biker. However, he didn't actually own a bike. Miguel of the *Unforgiven Sinners* was especially harsh on this type of guy.

Miguel would say, "How many years have someday been, huh? You've been getting this bike together for, how long now? Yeah, someday . . ."

If you were working on getting a bike up and on the road, you needed to maintain a low profile and just get things together before you tried to join the haves.

Another part of our belief system that people have misconstrued—the president of a motorcycle club is *not* the one guy in the club who can beat up everyone else in the club. The club president is chosen for leadership abilities, not for physical prowess. A club president *may* happen to be the toughest guy, but that is only coincidence. A president needs brains, heart, vision, and fortitude; but, mostly he has to have the ability to lead other men. Leadership skills are essential for any club or chapter president.

We were always leery of any club or chapter we met that had the same guy as its president year after year. What, no one else knows what to do? Nobody else can lead? There is no development of emerging talent? We saw the one-man rule as a weakness, not strength. Our club had Lucas as our president much of the time, but not always. The San Jose *Angels* had a number of different presidents, likewise the Daly City *Angels*, the *Sinners*, etc. A club was much more robust if it was continually developing potential leaders from its membership.

A final word about club presidents is the notion that the president sits back while his club does the work. Maybe those Clint Eastwood orangutan movies of the 1970's contributed to this lunacy, I don't know. Nevertheless, don't think for a minute that a club president is somehow above the rules or can skate by on any requirements that the rest of the club membership must adhere to. He can't. He must prove himself to his brothers on an ongoing basis. If, for instance, bikes are to be on the road, or dues to be paid, or some enemy to be faced, the president is expected to participate and not just sit around and direct traffic. Any president of a righteous bike club who would try that ploy would last about nine seconds before he would be knocked on his ass.

The code we followed was straightforward, but not simple. There were disagreements among us as there always are when there are expectations of behaviors. No one is right all the time and, despite what some may say, no one can be strong at every moment. When one of us needed help or guidance, we could turn to the one or two close friends in the group for assistance. That was fine, because you couldn't really turn to the club as a whole.

The club dealt with requirements, regulations, and respect. The club didn't deal with weakness, indecision, or sympathy. For those touchy-feely things that we all need, you had to get with your best partners individually.

As far as the club as a whole was concerned, if you were searching for sympathy, go look it up in the dictionary. You'll find it right between suppository and syphilis.

ᴄ⁄ᴏ *Chapter Sixteen* ᴏᴠ⁄ᴏ
"Old Ladies and Sweeties"

"Women . . . can't live with 'em . . . can't stuff 'em in a sack."

Larry, Darryl, and Darryl from "Newhart"

A good motorcycle club is a demanding mistress. She leaves little time for relationships with other women. But we tried real hard anyway.

I was sometimes amazed at the number of women who dated our members. Women had always been hard to come by for me (no pun intended) but such was not the case for many of my club brothers. From the first days of the club, there was an abundance of sweeties going out with many of the guys. Drew, Dennis, and Franky were especially adept at picking up chicks. Drew seemed to have multiple sweeties, often at the same time. How he juggled them all? The logistics was beyond me.

Some of the sweeties were familiar faces that we would see around town at the biker bars and such. Many of the others were not. There was a steady stream of new, and usually young, faces. The 1970's were known as a time of casual sex and that was certainly in evidence in the scooter scene. Most of the sweeties would come and go; but on occasion, one would stick with one of the guys. We even had one of our early members meet a future wife at the County Free Health Clinic. (That was a great place to pick up girls, by the way).

Some of these sweeties were very pretty, and some were, well . . . less pretty. There have been many jokes over the years disparaging "biker babes" as fat and ugly, and I suppose there is some truth to that (I will admit that some of those women were Granny Grusinia look-alikes); but, many biker chicks looked great, thank you very much. If a member did go out with a girl who was rather plain looking, it was a certainty that some of the other guys would rib him about it later. The usual response from the member would be to quote the oft repeated biker saying that defended taking any woman for a ride, "Hey, eight to eighty; blind, crippled, or crazy."

Many of the guys were generally on the lookout for the young, new-to-bikes sweeties. These chicks around 20 were usually stacked and anything but innocent. Guys who had one of those young, well-built dollies on the back of their bikes were generally high up on the peacock-strut scale. A few guys who chased sweeties said their motto was, "Find 'em, fuck 'em, forget 'em." I noticed that the last part of that statement didn't usually hold true. The guys would hang onto the sweeties' phone numbers for a rainy day, just like any guy would have done.

Not everyone chased sweeties. Some guys were perfectly happy with their wife or girlfriend. Other guys could never seem to keep a steady girl; and thus, had a succession of short-term girlfriends. A few others wanted nothing to do with a regular girlfriend and so were constantly on the prowl. Some guys had a wife or regular girl but wanted outside action, too. There were many different dynamics going on all the time.

Many of our boys were smooth operators, and many women evidently thought we had a bunch of good-looking guys in our club; which, I guess, was true. Some of the club's old ladies didn't like the smooth operator types because of their womanizing ways. Nevertheless, those old ladies reluctantly admitted that those guys were a handsome lot.

One member who wasn't much of a smooth talker was Matt. Matt was an average looking guy and usually had a sweetie, but he didn't have the suave charm and good looks of some of the other guys. Drew used to tease Matt about his not-too-subtle approach to picking up women. Drew would say, "Here's Matt's opening line to some broad he meets—'Hi, I'm Matt. Now gimme some head.'"

That was a large exaggeration, of course. There was a small element of truth to it, however. We all can't be "Jack Suede" like Drew, Dennis, and Franky were . . . *Goddammit*.

There was the group sex scene, too. That wasn't a regular occurrence, but it did happen on an infrequent basis. Most of the group scenes happened during the first year of the club, when we had more than a dozen or so members and prospects. Group sex wasn't called group sex. The term everyone used was turnout. They were rare enough events to be talked about at some length later, though. Again, some guys participated, and some did not. Before you ask, I was on the *not* side of things, so I don't really have many details to share about any orgy scenes. All right, I may have checked things out a few times—purely for educational purposes, you understand.

I had little interest in the group scene for two reasons. First, I was a little shy, I suppose, and had no real desire for any orgy action, although I soon found out that others didn't share that view. Second, I'm a little selfish. If I found a woman willing to go to bed with me, I had no interest in sharing the experience with someone else . . . brother or not. I wanted her all to myself.

Despite being the usual male chauvinist biker types, most of the guys treated their wives and girlfriends pretty well, I thought. Of course, my view is biased, and the old ladies may have disagreed with me on that. I mean, every couple had their arguments, along with the usual ups and downs of a relationship. From what I saw, however, while the man clearly dominated that relationship, there was respect, love, and compassion shown in most situations. The only exception I can remember was one of our early members, Howie. He sometimes treated his wife like crap. Howie would call her names in front of the rest of us. It was another of the reasons that I didn't cotton to Howie too well.

Very few of our guys had the same old lady throughout their time in the club. The lifestyle in the scooter world, combined with the usual wear and tear on a relationship, didn't lend itself to couples staying together forever. Toss in a spoonful or two of sweetie chasing for some of the guys, and the recipe for break-ups was easily served.

I got along great with some of the old ladies. On the other hand, I hardly knew some of them. I can't recall any of the guys' old ladies that I really disliked, and I don't know if any of them disliked me, although that was certainly possible.

Mitch's old lady was Connie, whom I mentioned earlier. Connie was cool and nice, but I hardly knew her. She tended to stay in the background on those occasions when she was around the guys. Connie seemed to like everyone well enough, and the guys liked her.

Greg was married to Sandi when he first came around the club. I hardly knew her, either. Sandi didn't seem to like Greg being in the club, and so she wasn't around us much. In fact, Rocky and Sandi were divorced not long after he made member, if memory serves. I don't think Sandi thought too highly of us, and that's okay. I'm not sure if the club was the cause of their breakup or not. Maybe they were headed for a split, regardless.

One couple that the club did help break up was Ben and Shirley. They had been together off and on for years when Bear came around. Shirley was very nice, but very conservative. She wasn't a biker chick like Connie, Sandi, and the other old ladies. Shirley just didn't understand the ways of club bikers; the whole lifestyle was foreign to her. Then she and Ben decided to marry when he was still a prospect . . . bad idea. Some of the guys—especially Drew, Matt, and Lucas— threatened to kidnap Bear on his wedding day to prevent the ceremony. They backed off that plan, but did follow the newlyweds to their honeymoon suite at the Dream Inn in Santa Cruz on their wedding night, where they jokingly harassed them for much of the night. Poor Shirley was out of her element with us. Although I barely knew her, I don't think that marriage ever had a chance. Ben and Shirley were divorced within a year. Both Greg and Sandi, and Ben and Shirley, had kids, so I know from experience that their breakups had to be tough on their children.

After going through quite a few sweeties, Fast Frank halfway settled down with a lady named Sally. She was pretty and tall and perhaps a little older than most of us. Sally seemed to be wise to things and was usually kind of quiet and in the background. I didn't know her too well either, but she appeared to be the kind of person who had everybody figured out but didn't pass judgments on them—at least publicly. Sally seemed to be a good partner for Franky. He could become a little moody and down sometimes (hey we all could, but Frank even more so) and Sally rather tempered that tendency. All the guys thought Sally was okay.

One of the old ladies I knew quite well was Drew's wife, Lisa. I knew her so well because I lived in the same house with her off and on for over two years. Drew and Lisa always put me up free of charge. Lisa was a great gal. She had to be to put up with some of Drew's antics . . . not to mention another club member living in her front bedroom half the time. Lisa came from a cool family. Her mom, Mrs. Martinez, would sometimes cook up great Mexican food for us. Lisa's brother, Dave was one of those guys involved in racing cars at the San Jose Speedway, and he was fun to party with. Lisa's sister Yvonne was really pretty, although already married when I first met her, dadgummit. Lisa was quiet most of the time, but when she would get around the club's old ladies, she would sometimes loosen up and could be quite funny.

Joann Kempton was Dennis's wife. Joann liked to party and could keep up with most of the guys in a drinking contest with no problem. Joann liked to tease and could instigate shit on her own very well. She was great fun to be around. Joann was smart, too. We would have great conversations on a wide range of subjects. Frequently, at parties, the guys would tend to gather to bullshit around, leaving the gals to themselves— at least part of the time, anyway. I would make a point to stop over and talk with Joann and the girls. They always had something funny or interesting going on. So let's see . . . Joann was pretty, smart, funny, a partier, and had a good figure. Yeah, Dennis had things pretty good, I'd say.

Lucas's new old lady was named Karen. They got together some time after Amanda, Lucas's earlier girlfriend, passed away. Karen was a cute, blonde-haired woman who was extremely thin. Karen had a daughter named Carla. She was about six and was cute and blonde like her mom. Karen was a real prankster and could instigate things just like Joann. When Bear joined the club, he nicknamed her Trixie. He gave her that handle because he playfully told her she should be turning tricks on a downtown street corner. Trixie was a partier like Joann, too. She also took very little crap from Lucas. She was feisty and stood up to him very well—especially considering that she only weighed about 100 pounds.

After Bear and Shirley divorced, he took up with a new girlfriend named Kate. She was a cousin of Joann's—Dennis's old lady. Kate was a real sweetheart. She was one of those people who was continually optimistic and in a good mood. Kate was kind of like our good club friend, Don Lundberg. Nobody ever had a cross word to say about either of them. Kate soon became devoted to Ben. She worshipped the ground that the 325-pound Bear stomped on.

My old buddy, Roy Givens became a manager at an electronics company in Silicon Valley, and he needed some dependable workers. He put in a good word for me and I got hired on as an assembler working for him. That worked out well as I had practically zero money for the first six months that Marie and I were together. She was finding occasional modeling work, mostly in San Francisco; but, sometimes in widely spread parts of the Bay Area. She was on the go a lot, and would come down to San Jose to see me as often as she could.

Ours was a pretty bare bones existence. We would eat at fast food places since we had almost no coin, and she generally bought. She practically supported me for the first few months that we were together. It was the typical low budget lifestyle for a couple of young, struggling kids. We would go on club and MMA runs, hang out in San Jose at Drew and Lisa's place where I roomed, or spend time with her parents at their house in Redwood City where she lived.

Marie's parents were great. Her dad was retired at a fairly young age and so was always around the house. He was an inquisitive guy who wanted to find out all he could about the opinions that were held by people like me. Her dad had grown up in France and was continually trying to figure out Americans and their culture. Then along comes this longhaired, biker guy who complicated his world even more.

Marie had only one sibling, a brother who was many years older. He was developmentally disabled and still lived at home, as he always would, I guess. As a result, all of her parents' hopes and dreams were centered on Marie. I'm sure her dad would have much preferred it if I had been a lawyer or a doctor or something. Who wouldn't have? However, he always treated me fair and square and made me feel welcome in his house. I got the feeling that Marie's previous biker old man, Davey, didn't come around the household very often. I got the impression that her dad didn't seem to mind having me about. He and I would have some great discussions about politics and culture. He spoke English very well, but if he got excited and started talking too quickly he would revert to French, so Marie would need to translate for me.

Sometimes, I went along with the family on their outings. There was a good-sized French community of seniors in that part of San Mateo County, and they did many activities together. The old men would play a lawn bowling game called petanque, similar to bocce ball, I guess. The men would gesture with their hands a lot and speak French rapidly over one another. It somewhat reminded me of those days back when I was a kid in Missouri when my dad and the Budget Pak route drivers would all bullshit with each other. Maybe those old French guys were really saying things like "That ole boy didn't know what to do then . . . *neeewww* . . . new sir." What did I know?

A couple of times, Marie's parents took us to the Pacific coast where they would gather sea urchins for us to eat on a family picnic. The urchins were inside purple spiny shells that her parents would cut open with big scissors that rather looked like tin snips. I tried the sea urchins, but I have to say that I was glad that Marie's mom brought along some ham and French bread and other good eats for the picnic.

Marie's mom was a super nice person, and a fabulous cook. I had never eaten food so good before. A regular dinner at the parents' house was usually a four-course meal with homemade soup, salad, main course, and dessert. Holiday time was another matter, as Marie's mom prepared the same four course meal, but would add a pasta course, a course of fruit and cheese and bread, and something extra special, too.

She would make things like squabs broiled over fresh french bread with the juices dripping down, or handmade ravioli, or chateaubriand in a savory garlic sauce. All this was normal for her. Marie's dad was spoiled by a lifetime of this cooking. Her mom would ask her dad "How is it?" He wouldn't look up from his plate as he said, "Bon."

During every meal, her mom would be up and down from the table like a jack-in-the-box, making sure that every course was served piping hot and fresh. She never really ate much herself because she spent so much time taking care of everyone else. Marie's mom would go to the grocery store nearly every day, like back in France, to ensure that she always used the freshest meats and vegetables and bought the latest-baked French bread for that day's meals. Cooking was her thing, and excellent food was the currency in her household. Whenever I showed up, I was well paid.

I had some great learning experiences being around Marie's folks. I was able to see and do some things I never would have been exposed to otherwise. But, well . . . you can keep the sea urchins. Thanks, anyway.

Marie and I, after saving for a few months, rented our own place in Mountain View. It was a little duplex on a quiet street but just a block from busy El Camino Real, so it was close to everything we needed. There was no garage, but there was a small utility room just inside a carport, so the bike had its new home, too. Mountain View was a perfect location for us. It was close to my workplace in Sunnyvale. It was a lot closer for her commute to San Francisco than my old place in East San Jose with Drew had been. It also wasn't far from her parents' house in Redwood City, and close enough to the rest of the club in San Jose for me. We fixed up our little place as best as we could with our meager funds.

Marie began to find more and better-paying jobs as a model. She did a lot of work at I Magnin, and Macy's in San Francisco. She worked in fashion shows for many of the famous designers who toured through *The City*. She also got some print work that paid even better than the ramp work at the shows. Some of Marie's friends from Frisco, in the modeling business, would question her as to why she would have a boyfriend who was a biker nobody, from lowly San Jose to boot. Good question . . . I never quite understood that myself.

Marie and I would spend some holidays with my family, too. My mom moved to the Gold Country of the Sierras, a relaxing place to go and get away from the city for a few days. My older sister, Embry was married by this time and my younger sister, Nancy was away at college in San Luis Obispo. Brother William was in the Navy, so everyone was pretty well spread out. Still, most of us would make it to Mom's and have a fun time. Marie got along well with my mother, and everyone else, for that matter. Sometimes my Aunt Helene and my cousins would come up, too. Then we would have loads of laughter and tales from everyone's recent experiences.

We stayed in Mountain View for over a year. While we were living there, my dad made one of his infrequent appearances. He had a fancy new Cadillac, too. I don't know how he managed that. Maybe it was from saving up the child support payments he didn't make to my mom all those years. Dad asked if he could stay with us for a few days. Knowing how it would turn out, I wanted to say no. Marie, however, wanted to be gracious, so she talked me into saying it was okay. Dad crashed on the day bed we had in the front room of our one-bedroom place.

That week was the first, and only time, I ever went drinking with my dad. I figured I wouldn't keep up with him, and I was right. Dad finished off two double, straight-shots, before I emptied my one small drink. Surprisingly, Dad didn't get thoroughly ripped that night, but he made up for it a day or two later.

Just like I thought, Dad went on a drinking spree and ended up passed out on the day bed for a couple of days. Marie had never seen anything like that so up close, even having been around the *Angels* for a couple of years. It was like old home week for me except I had to do my mom's old duty and get Dad down the road when he finally sobered up. I figured that would just about do it for Marie and me; but, nope, she hung in there with me, anyway. Dad wound up at my mom's place a few days later; another stop on his road tour of family destinations, I suppose.

Marie and I moved to a rental house in Santa Clara in 1976. It was in the Agnews section of town, an older area that was close to the Marriott's new theme park "Great America". We saw Bi-Centennial fireworks every night throughout the summer from our front porch. The house was an older style, two-bedroom with a claw foot bathtub and a large garage in back. It was in a terrific location on a wide street, and there was only one other house close by. We had a dynamite time at the Agnews place. It was a quiet, but convenient, neighborhood that had not been re-developed or yuppie-fied yet. Marie fixed up the interior with some of those neat, chick touches, so it didn't look like the typical biker pad. We spent two years at the Agnews house, and I loved nearly every minute of it.

At one time, I thought I might get to the point where I had women in general halfway figured out. Silly boy . . . I found that I enjoyed being around all the club's old ladies, but eventually I realized that I never *really* understood them. I think I might have McCarver Syndrome.

Bob Gibson, the superb Hall of Fame pitcher for the St. Louis Cardinals, used to wave off catcher Tim McCarver when McCarver would try to visit the mound during one of Gibson's rare times of inconsistency. McCarver was an outstanding player in his own right, but he wasn't the best hitter around.

A frustrated Gibson would dismiss McCarver's visit and say, "Get out of here. The only thing you know about pitching is that you can't hit it." McCarver would trudge back behind the plate.

It's kind of the same situation with females and me. Whenever I think I might have women dialed in to where I believe I just might know what's going on, they end up surprising me altogether. The only thing I actually know for certain about women is that I don't seem to understand them. That's my McCarver Syndrome.

Maybe Larry, Darryl, and Darryl were right after all.

✑ *Chapter Seventeen* ✑
"Lords Lingo"

We had our own way of speaking in the *Wheel Lords*. Some of the words and phrases we would use were common to bikers of that place and time, and some were our own unique lingo.

"When in doubt, knock 'em out" was a popular phrase of the time. We repeated that one, but really, it represented more of an attitude than an action.

"Hardcore" was a popular term with us. We all strived to be known as righteous, hardcore bikers. That was a common word, which we used all the time.

Another expression that we sometimes used was "Eee-quall Pass-quall", which meant that things were fair and equitable. For instance, say that you had a beef with another member, and you ended up settling things. Once the situation was back to square one, everything would be considered . . . Eee-quall Pass-quall. We're cool.

Other terms that we used as did everyone else, were words like, "incognito" and "copacetic". We loved those words. They sounded exotic and slightly dangerous at the same time. Sometimes the *Angels* would have a member who was on parole and couldn't wear his patch in public; so, when you saw him somewhere with no colors, he would say he was incognito. Soon we used incognito simply to mean that a guy wasn't wearing his patch at a certain time. You could be incognito if you went to the grocery store in your car, or if you went to your normal workplace—or anywhere, really. Incognito became shorthand for not dressing like a club biker.

Copacetic meant okay or all is well. Copacetic was used quite often simply because it was fun to say. Sometimes we would shorten it to cope, but then you would lose the fun of saying the entire word. Copacetic is just a hell of a fun word to say. Heck, it's also a fun word to write. Copacetic . . . *copacetic* . . . there, I think I've had my fix satisfied now. Wait . . . there's one more . . . *copacetic*. Okay, I'm good.

We had a number of sayings that were all our own. At least I think they were all our own, because I never heard them anywhere else.

"Until the wheels fall off" was one of those sayings. That came along during the first few months. The first person I remember saying it was Dennis, although I don't know who thought it up. *Until the wheels fall off* meant that you were in the club forever . . . through thick and thin. We also used that saying to bolster one another's spirits as in, "Are we gonna get this done?" The answer might be "You bet bro, *until the wheels fall off.*" In tough times, such as an all-night security watch on the third night of an MMA Run or something of the sort, someone might say, "Until the wheels fall off", as a kind of rallying cry to get everyone's spirits up. It always worked, too.

Keith, the hulking guy who was our first Sergeant at Arms, had a couple of sayings that none of us had ever heard before. Keith referred to lips as, "soup-coolers", and hands were, "crab-scratchers." If you were describing a fight you had been in it was "I knocked the guy right in the soup-coolers." Likewise, if some member were messing with your stack of poker chips you would say, "Keep your crab-scratchers to yourself."

Keith also liked to use the word "frap." Frap meant to smack somebody upside the head. "Give him a frap for me," for instance. Maybe other people used that term, I'm not sure. However, Keith said it frequently, and soon all of us were using it, too.

Since we were in San Jose, and mostly on the East Side, there was a strong Hispanic influence all around us. We adapted some of the standard Spanish greetings to fit our own usage. The phrase "Que paso?" quickly became "Quay El Paso?" for the *Wheel Lords*. I think Mitch started that one up. Then Quay El Paso was shortened to just "Quay?" as a way to say "Hey what's up?"

Likewise, "Adios" soon became, "Have a dose." That phrase quickly caught on when a lot of the guys had to go to the County Free Clinic to be treated for a dose of the clap. "Have a dose" morphed into a catch-all for what you said when you disagreed with something, but it was going to happen anyway. It was kind of a backhanded acknowledgement of some event. Like if someone said, "Hey man, we're heading out to the next bar." If you didn't want to leave, you would say, "Fine, *have a dose*. See you later."

One more Spanish based phrase came courtesy of Keith. He would twist muchas gracias into "mucus garcias." Soon we were all expressing our thanks to someone else with mucus garcias. Then we shortened it to just "mucus." When other people would hear us say that they probably thought we were diseased or something.

Another catch phrase was, "My nerves." I think Howie came up with it. "My nerves" was usually said with emphasis as in, "Oh my God!" or other such expressions. A guy would be telling a story and to emphasize a point he would say, "You should have seen this broad . . . *my nerves!* She was built." If something was *extra* special, you could double down, as in "My nerves! That was some killer of a hangover . . . oh, *my nerves!*"

Franky liked the word, "myself." "Myself," when used by *itself* meant, "I agree completely. Absolutely, pard . . . you got it." All that could be conveyed with the one, simple word, "myself." If you enthusiastically agreed with what was being said, you would accent the second syllable as in "my-*self*." People who didn't know our lingo would hear one of us say, "myself", and say to us, "Uh . . . *yourself,* what?" We would reply, "Just . . . *myself.*"

"Fertnick" was another saying we had. I think Drew or Howie came up with that one. *Fertnick* (sometimes modified to "vertnick" or even "footnick") was a multi-usage term. *Fertnick* could be a sound effect, used as emphasis. "We were riding along and all of a sudden— *fertnick*—something shot right past us." Just as easily, you could use *fertnick* as a noun, such as, "The little *fertnick* that hangs down behind the bar." You could even use it as a verb, like "Just kind of *fertnick* it in there with an Allen wrench." *Fertnick* had endless possibilities.

Another of our sayings was "liff up." That meant to pay attention, or get with the program. Drew might have come up with that term. *Liff up* meant it was time to deliver the goods and stop farting around. "Those guys need to *liff up* and get their shit together for this run," for instance.

One of our favorite sayings came from Matt, I believe. He borrowed it from an old cartoon series. There was a segment in each episode that featured this character named Tooter Turtle. He would get his friend Mr. Wizard to transport him somewhere in time, so Tooter could be in some great adventure. Have you ever seen that show? To free him from his predicament when he got himself into a real jam, Tooter would call on Mr. Wizard. Tooter would lament, "Help Mr. Wizard, I want to come home."

Once, we were stuck in some bullshit circumstance—I forget what— and we were all pretty down about things and just hanging on, waiting for everything to be over so we could head home. Matt suddenly said, "Help Mr. Wizard, I don't wanna be hardcore no more!" That cracked everybody up, broke us out of the doldrums, and got us re-energized. After that, we would use "Help Mr. Wizard" whenever we were in a tight spot or were facing some unpleasant duty, like providing security for a few hundred drunken bikers at an MMA event. Calling out for Mr. Wizard helped us to keep one another motivated.

Bear sometimes had his own unique terms. One he used quite often was "bearable". As Ben weighed in at well over 320, he couldn't just sit in any old piece of furniture. Ben would have to check out chairs to make sure that they were "bearable" before he could sit down. Bear broke quite a few campstools, picnic benches, and folding chairs over the years. He would get drunk and forget to apply his bearable scrutiny and—WHAM—instant kindling. Then we would have to gather around to get his fat butt up again. Soon we all began to refer to any item that didn't pass muster or measure up to our needs as not being bearable.

Lucas didn't invent any catch phrases that I can remember, but he had his own way of speaking nonetheless. Weasel would sometimes twist the pronunciation of certain words, kind of like the comic Norm Crosby did back then.

For instance, Lucas pronounced the word *tattoo* as, "tacktoo". The first time I heard that I did a double take. "Did I hear him right?" I thought. I asked him to repeat it. The second time it came out the same . . . *tacktoo*.

"Uh, Lucas, that word is pronounced 'tattoo', okay?"

"Right . . . that's what I said . . . tacktoo."

"Okay . . . *whatever*. Have a dose."

The *Hells Angels* had a chapter in San Bernardino, California. In fact, it was the first ever *Hells Angel* chapter. Almost everyone routinely refers to that city in the Southern California desert as "Berdoo." Everyone but Lucas, that is. Weasel called Berdoo, "Perdoo." Matt tried to correct him on that.

"Lucas, it's called Berdoo, with a B."

"Yeah, right . . . Perdoo."

I couldn't figure out if Lucas was talking about the university in Indiana or the town down south. Once, during the weekend of a car show in Riverside, Lucas was invited over to the *Angels* clubhouse in Berdoo. I thought that was the last we would ever see of Weasel. The *Angels* wouldn't take to him fracturing their town's name. They would probably toss him on a cactus or something for the offense. However, he made it back and told us how the guys in Perdoo—damn, I mean *Berdoo*—treated him great.

I tried to tell Lucas that while the *Angels* down there may very well *drink* boilermakers, I was pretty damn sure *none* of them actually *were* Purdue Boilermakers.

He just looked at me and said, "I never said those guys in Perdoo were drinking boilermakers."

"Right," I said resignedly. "I'm just out of my head today. Forget it, bro."

There was a Daly City *Angel* named Champ. He was a short, Mexican guy. I knew who he was (since becoming friends with Davey from Daly City I had gotten to know or at least recognize quite a few of the Daly City guys) but Champ was one of those *Angels* who didn't actually bother talking with any of us in the *Wheel Lords*. He seemed okay though. Anyway, one day Lucas said he had been somewhere and mentioned that he met a Daly City member named "Chump". Some of our guys said, "There's a *Hells Angel* with the nickname of, 'Chump'?"

"No," I said. "It's Champ. Maybe he's a boxer or something, I don't know how he got the nickname, but it is definitely not *Chump*. It's Champ. Lucas, next time you see him I would suggest you call him Champ, not *Chump*. Otherwise, we may have a problem, bro."

"Hey, no sweat man. I never called him a chump, or anything like that. I'll just call the man by his name. Chump."

Oh, good grief . . .

We needed Lucas to liff up and pronounce these words the same as everyone else did. But, that never happened. Those little quirks were what made each of us unique.

Maybe I was being paid back for fucking with Mitch's head when I messed with him, and his "Zelmo" tacktoo . . . crap, I mean *tattoo*.

One night, when Drew and I were hanging around and playing guitars and sampling some adult beverages, Drew suddenly announced, "Kidd, it shouldn't be, 'No butt . . . no putt. It should be, No *Smut* . . . No Putt.' We need to start our own saying, and smut is a better word."

"Why stop there? We can do better than just changing one word."

For the rest of the night, in between hacking around on our gitfiddles, Drew and I added our own twist to the biker's old credo that described rides for sweeties.

The ones I remember were, "No balling . . . No hauling," and "No lip . . . No trip." For our Western friends on the open range, we had "No hide . . . No ride." Need one for the holidays? Sure, "No lay . . . No sleigh."

Drew's favorite was a bit earthier, "No fuckin' . . . No truckin'." My preference was somewhat more lyrical than his was, "No perversion

. . . No excursion."

ᴄ⁄᷾ Chapter Eighteen ᷾᷾

"Business Bikers"

R on Roloff was the driving force behind the Modified Motorcycle Association. He was the lobbyist and the business manager for the association. Ron lived with his family in a nice north area suburb of Sacramento called North Highlands, which is near Roseville.

Roloff was constantly in motion. He would drive to Southern California to organize the reps in that part of the state, and the next day testify before a State Senate hearing at the Capitol in Sacramento. Ron ran every detail of the MMA. He was a superb organizer and knew how to budget his time to terrific effect. I don't know if Ron ever lobbied before his time with the MMA, but he certainly was effective in that role. He would meet with assemblymen, senators and their staffs, and then developed strong, working relationships with them.

Ron helped shape many of the transportation-related bills that worked their way through the legislature. Just as valuable, Ron was able to head off legislation that was contrary to the interests of the MMA. The biggest and most visible fight for the MMA was the mandatory helmet issue. Roloff was instrumental in keeping that law off the California books for 20 years. "Let Those Who Ride, Decide," was the slogan the MMA used. We'd sell bumper stickers and pins displaying that slogan.

The legislature tried to enact some laws that, while well intentioned, would have been disastrous if passed. Ron and other lobbyists like him across the country would run into legislators who had ideas like making seat belt use mandatory for motorcyclists, or requiring small dental type mirrors, which would have to be affixed to a rider's helmet, and other such nonsense.

One of the biggest success stories for Ron and the MMA was the passage of HR 3869 in 1975. A Connecticut Congressman named Stewart McKinney sponsored this bill, at the Federal level, in Washington D.C. Supported by all of the bikers' rights groups across the country, HR 3869 stopped the practice of withholding Federal Highway Funds from states that didn't pass transportation laws that conformed to federal policy. For example, if the Department of Transportation wanted states to establish a 55 mile per hour speed limit, then DOT would threaten to withhold highway improvement money from a state, which was reluctant to pass such a law. The DOT also used this tactic to pressure several states to enact mandatory helmet laws, even though those states had no desire to do so. HR 3869 ended this "blackmail" practice by the DOT. Roloff traveled to DC where he and other advocates spoke before Congressional Committees regarding this bill.

Every person who rode a bike in California in the 1970's and 80's owed Roloff a big debt of thanks. He worked for everyone, not just for those relative few who were a part of the MMA.

Roloff looked quite a bit like a young George Jones, the country singer. Like Jones, Roloff talked with a clenched jaw, so he seemed to be serious all the time. "SoCal Stan" Jennings, the *Hells Angels* President of the LACO chapter, referred to Ron as "Rolljaw" because of this affectation. When the work was done, however, Roloff could be the life of the party. He was a fun guy to hang with and he had great stories of the inner workings of the State Capitol.

Ron was highly driven, and had to be in complete charge of everything. He frequently said there was only one way to do things in the MMA—his way. Consequently, a lot of people—including those of us in the *Wheel Lords*—had an up and down relationship with Roloff. On a personal level, we got along well. On a business level, we sometimes had differences, but we always respected each other. You just couldn't help but like Rolljaw. He said many times that when he died he wanted but one song to be played at his funeral service. That song was *My Way* by Elvis Presley. It was to be played continuously throughout the entire service.

Part of our contribution to the MMA was the sale of Gold Cards. The Association sold high-end memberships to businesses and some individuals. The *Wheel Lords* MC, by each member renewing his Gold Card every year, added well over $5,000 dollars to the MMA. In addition, we sold quite a few Gold Cards as well as subsequent renewals, to cycle businesses. Soon, along with efforts of the MMA Reps, there were dozens of Gold Card businesses across the State.

Our vital task for the MMA in the winter months was the Car Show Circuit. Over six show seasons, we staffed the MMA booth (which we built) at 55 car and bike shows from Eureka to Reno, to San Diego and all points in between. If there was a car or bike show in California, we were there. For local shows in the Bay Area, everybody would pull a shift. If we went down south, we usually sent two guys for the weekend.

That meant leaving on Thursday—or perhaps Friday pre-dawn—for a drive to say, Anaheim, where the two guys would set up the booth on Friday afternoon.

Shows usually ran Friday night, all day Saturday and Saturday night, and Sunday afternoon until around 5:00. Then, the booth would be broken down and packed up for the long drive back to St. Joe. It was a long and often tedious duty, but it did spread the word about the MMA, and brought in some cash from membership sales, too.

Like most of our MMA duties, there was a bright side to the show circuit, and there was a down side, too. The down included the long drives, being away from home and the old lady, using up precious work vacation time, paying your own expenses, and dealing with the reluctant-to-get-involved general biking public.

The up side included being on the road (always a plus), spending a chunk of time with your club brothers, and meeting some good people at the shows. For instance, one year Frank and I met the actor James Garner (a great guy) at the LA show. Other guys had similar instances, not to mention all the local bike club people and independent riders we would meet while working the shows.

Creating the show work schedules usually fell to me, as I had the experience of mapping out the old kitchen duty workload back when I was a teenager, and there were 11 people in our family. I tried to make the schedule fair to everyone. We were helped out considerably when the *Highwaymen* MC came along as an MMA sanctioned club. They worked the show circuit alongside us and did almost as much traveling as we did.

One year, maybe 1976, the MMA really pushed the idea of voter registration. Registering to vote in those days was a much more cumbersome process than it is today. There was no Internet or any easily accessible computer databases. In Santa Clara County, they had Deputy Registrars who could register voters. I went down to the County Administration Building and attended a Registrar class, along with a bunch of other people—mostly housewives and hippie types.

Being a Deputy Registrar was fun. I carried around a hefty booklet that was full of multi-part enrollment forms, and I had an official stamp to use. When we had a Blood Run or a Helmet Rally, I would set up a table and register people. We had some lively political discussions at these events, and I registered a lot of folks. Some of the bikers I talked to couldn't register even if they wanted to, since more than a few were felons. Since we were in San Jose, and not Chicago, I didn't sign up any dead people, although some guys suggested it.

The *Wheel Lords* attended many local MMA Meetings. These meetings were usually headed up by local MMA Reps. We would stop by to help with the first couple of meetings and help the reps with the organization and logistics. The reps would learn quickly and would soon be running their own meetings. Then we'd back out. It was much better letting the local reps run things, rather than have some club come in from outside the area.

The down side to the rep meetings was the drive. Since these meetings were held during the week, usually at a pizza parlor or the like, we would have to leave after work and drive to the town on a weeknight. We'd unload the MMA supplies, help with the meeting, meet some people, and then drive home. We'd get back to San Jose late and have to get up early for work the next day. I remember Drew and me making the 300-mile round trip to the town of Hanford, near Fresno, a couple of times. Those were long nights.

The rep program was a terrific idea. The Reps did an outstanding job of organizing and involving the local bike communities. The Santa Cruz area had a lot of hard working reps. One of the reps from San Mateo County, by the name of George Everson, did all kinds of work for the MMA. He was a dedicated friend to us.

Even some of our former members became MMA reps. RollinandJason at some point split up. Jason Hood became a rep in San Jose, and Rollin Pickett moved to San Diego and became a rep there. Both of those guys always supported the MMA big time, and we'd see them at MMA functions and say hi.

The *Wheel Lords* averaged about three MMA Blood Runs per year. We'd host one Run in San Jose that was held at the Red Cross Blood Bank near downtown. Then we'd lead a pack of participants to a local campout, generally within an hour's ride of San Jose. It was an excellent way to get some of the local people together and replenish the MMA account of blood at the bank.

We usually made it to the Sacramento Blood Runs too, since so many of the MMA friends we knew would be there. The Sacramento people had all these great spots in the Sierras where they would have their campouts. We would be camped along some running, cold creek in say, Placer or Nevada County, where the scent of the pines would fill the clear mountain air.

The MMA sponsored regular Helmet Rallies. These were large events, designed to gain maximum media attention to the mandatory helmet issue. The first massive Helmet Rally was held in downtown San Francisco at the Federal Building on a Sunday. We organized a pack in San Jose that had hundreds of bikes. We rode up to Redwood City where we picked up hundreds more.

Lucas and I were in the lead row of that pack. When we entered the Frisco City Limits, just past Candlestick Park where Highway 101 climbs a hill, we looked back behind us. As far as we could see, about a mile back I'd say, were scooters by the hundreds. We couldn't see the end of the pack. It just disappeared into the fog. That was an awesome sight. We were the last large pack to arrive. When we got to the Federal Building, our pack just about doubled the number of bikes that were there.

After the rally, hundreds of people went to party in the Haight Ashbury District. This was long after the Summer of Love. The Haight was pretty much a rundown area of dive bars, junkie hangouts and weathered buildings. Most of the bikers crammed into a couple of neighborhood bars on Haight Street. For those of us too young to have experienced the real Haight Ashbury, it was a step-back in time . . . but only a little step.

We left the Haight after an hour or two. We got home to watch the news coverage of the Rally on television and saw more than we bargained for. As it turned out, some independent bikers, along with some local derelicts, started trashing the area. Whenever a large group gathers, there is usually a small group of folks bent on taking advantage of the situation. They think they can do whatever they want without any consequences, just as people sometimes do at sports celebrations that run amok.

The same thing happened that day in the Haight. The San Francisco Police closed the street and told people to clear out and go home, but some guys wouldn't listen. Later on, the SFPD came down the street in a phalanx and cracked the heads of anyone who resisted. No motorcycle clubs were involved; and, as far as we could tell, no MMA people either. Nevertheless, it did lend some adverse publicity to an otherwise successful event.

Later, we organized Helmet Rallies in San Jose. We would gather at Vasona Lake Park in Los Gatos and ride to the San Jose Civic Center for speeches by local politicians. There were hundreds of bikes at those rallies, too. The MMA also held additional Helmet Rallies in both Northern and Southern California, again with large attendance. These rallies kept the issue in the public eye and were terrific PR tools for Roloff to use in his lobbying efforts.

Another PR tool we employed was the Public Service Announcement. A "PSA" was a sixty-second spot broadcast on local television stations. Non-profit groups could use a PSA to spread the word of their organization, or to enlist donations, and the like. We wrote up some copy about proposed helmet legislation and the MMA, and I traveled to five or six TV stations throughout the San Francisco Bay Area to record our announcement. The spots helped spread the name of the MMA to more of the motorcycle riding community.

The MMA also was one of the first organizations to hold a Christmas Toy Run. At first, Roloff tried to gather toys to give to the Marine Corps for their Toys for Tots campaign; but, since the Marines wouldn't take the toys because they came from bikers, he decided to use the MMA to sponsor the Toy Run.

The big daddy of the Toy Runs was the one held in Pasadena, near Los Angeles. That Toy Run dwarfed the Frisco Helmet Rallies we had. Marie and I trucked my bike down one year, just to see this mega-event for ourselves. I don't know numbers, but there had to be over 10,000 bikes there. Nowadays there are large bike runs held every year, such as the Run to the Wall for veterans held each spring in DC. However, in the 1970's, it was a new thing, at least to us on the West Coast, to gather that many bikes in one place.

Another avenue for MMA revenue was to hold motorcycle drag races. These events were generally held in Sacramento, and guess who provided the security? You got it, the usual suspects of the *Wheel Lords* and *Highwaymen*. The good news with the Drag Race Events was that they were just one day in duration. The bad news was the working conditions. Summer days in Sac can get well over one hundred degrees, and even hotter on a drag strip than anywhere else. With the noise of revving engines and the smell of burning rubber in the mix, you've got yourself one *long day*, regardless of how well you like to see bikes racing down the track at high speeds.

We spent the night before one such racing event at our friend Marty Carpenter's house, which wasn't too far from the drag strip out near Mather Air Force Base. There were a few different people at Marty's that Saturday night, just hanging out and partying. Around three or four in the morning, when things had become quiet, I stretched out in a corner of Marty's front room to get a little shuteye.

One of the *Angels* there that night, a guy named Wayne Brooks from Daly City, announced something to the effect that, "Oh, here we go. Some guys need to go to sleep. They don't want to stay up all night with the rest of us."

I replied, "I've got a long day's work ahead of me, and I'll be out at the track early to start on it. So yeah, I'm going to rest up for a bit." I wasn't buying into someone else's idea of what was right for me.

Some of us got an hour or two of sleep. Then all of us in the club were up and out to the track at first light. When I was leaving Marty's house, I noticed Wayne from Daly City . . . he was fast asleep in Marty's recliner. He did make it out to see the drag races later that day—about noon, I guess it was. I must say that he looked to be in a lot better shape than I was. That was one, long . . . hot . . . noisy . . . headache-filled day. Even *with* the extra beauty sleep I had.

Roloff came up with another creative way to fund the MMA. He entered into a partnership with the chopper magazine, *Easyriders*. They agreed to sponsor some of the motorcycle swap meets. The MMA received a portion of the gate receipts in exchange for assisting with publicity and site security. Said security was to be provided by, well . . . who else?

The swap meets were not our favorites. For me, it was the worst MMA duty of all. There were two significant problems with swap meets.

First, most people who came to these meets couldn't care less about the MMA. At least at Blood Runs, local dances, or Statewide Runs, most of the people were there to support the MMA, and had a stake in making the event a success. With swap meets, all bets were off. Most of the people who showed up were just average chopper guys who hadn't joined the MMA and had no intention of doing so. They were at the swap meet, perhaps to buy a bike part or two, but mostly to watch the band and party, and maybe get into a fight. Most of these people didn't know or didn't care who the *Wheel Lords* were. Consequently, we were always running full bore at swap meets, trying to keep one-step ahead of any potential trouble.

At swap meets, we never had any serious problems. Instead, we had an unending series of minor crises to head off. The only time things got close to a significant problem was one day at the Vallejo swap meet. The *Hells Angels* got into a fight with another outlaw club called the *Misfits*, but it was over quickly. In fact, most of us didn't even see it. We heard about the fight only after it was over. Our problem was keeping the bystanders and other onlookers from becoming involved—which we did. There seemed to be no easy time at a swap meet. It was careful vigilance on our part all the time.

The other problem we ran into at swap meets was the people from *Easyriders*. They seemed to be working against us. The guys who were in control were some of the biggest instigators of problems for us. They would always seem to be at the center of any beef, and tried hard to stir up the crowd to get them just on the edge of being out of control. The magazine guys seemed to be at the swap meets to party and make money, and if any security problems came up—well, that wasn't their problem.

The *Easyriders* magazine was extremely popular back then; it probably still is. They pushed the outlaw chopper image with lots of photos of topless chicks draped on bikes, coarse humor jokes, and some fictional articles about the biker lifestyle. All that is well and good; but, we thought the guys who ran the swap meets from *Easyriders* were more interested in creating a storyline than developing a working partnership with the MMA.

Roloff must have had some doubts about *Easyriders* also. One time he sent Lucas (incognito) from our club out of state to count the attendees going through the front gate at a swap meet that the *Easyriders* magazine was sponsoring. I don't know if the MMA was involved with the set-up at this out-of-state meet, or the details even. I just know that Rolljaw had some suspicions about how the money was being split when it came to the MMA and *Easyriders*.

Our worst swap meet was one that was held at the Los Angeles County Fairgrounds in Pomona. The Pomoma Police Department decided they didn't like our looks, and they surrounded our Club as we were working security detail. We tried to tell them that we were the security guys—not causing trouble, but hopefully preventing it. It didn't matter to Pomoma PD. They ran checks on all of us; and, naturally, Drew had outstanding traffic warrants, so they hauled him off to jail. Then, they let the rest of us go. We weren't fond of L.A., cops, or swap meets in general; and now Pomona PD in particular. We bailed Drew from jail, and said to hell with the swap meet. We never saw the *Easyriders* people after the cops came around. For all we knew, Pomona PD could have arrested other bikers all day long at that event. We were just their first targets of opportunity.

Over the six years that the *Wheel Lords* existed, we participated in about 140 MMA events. These included dances, rallies, auto shows, bike shows, swap meets, blood runs, local runs, regional runs, helmet rallies, rep meetings, and toy runs. That averages out to about an event every two weeks. Not counting the local meetings we attended or organized, which numbered easily over a hundred.

I can't put a dollar figure on all the fundraising in which we assisted. I do know that we brought in about $13,000 from the car and bike show sales we had; and most of it from memberships sold at $5 each. We also sold memberships on our own (we even had a quota system early on for a time) on a day-to-day basis. Add in money we took in from our personal Gold Cards, the Dealer memberships, swap meets, local runs we put on, etc., and we probably contributed $30,000 or more to the MMA. All this was from a club that had less than ten members for most of its existence. All in all, we spent a considerable amount of our time functioning like business bikers.

However, the big dog for MMA funding came from the statewide runs. Those runs generated big bucks for the Association, and they required a lot of work on our part.

⚜ *Chapter Nineteen* ⚜

"MMA Runs"

After Roloff and the MMA Board realized how popular and profitable a statewide run could be, they scheduled more of them. Soon there were three statewide runs each year to the Fresno area: a spring run in late April or early May, a run in July to celebrate the MMA "Birthday", and an end of summer run around September.

Fresno was chosen purely for geographic purposes. It was accessible for both Nor Cal and So Cal riders without requiring a super long ride for anyone. There were many other potential run sites with much better scenery and more temperate weather than Fresno, but the San Joaquin Valley location was too valuable to ignore. The MMA couldn't hold a statewide run any further north than Fresno because they needed the Los Angeles bikers to show up.

L.A. is the massive motorcycle megaplex of the world. There are so many bikes in the L.A. area it's mind-boggling. That's mostly because of the great weather in L.A. and the fact that there are about ten gazillion people living there. The MMA needed a heavy turnout of L.A. bikers to make the big runs work financially.

Rolljaw found a few different county parks east of town that worked out well, but then he came across a site that fit perfectly for the MMA. The place was called Pierce's Park. It was a privately owned bar and honky-tonk with camping space on the property. Pierce's Park was right on Highway 180, the road to Kings Canyon National Park, about 20 miles east of Fresno proper. It was far enough out of town to be out in the country, yet not too far of a ride from Highway 99, the main north-south route through the San Joaquin. The terrain was flat with just the first hint of the rolling hills that lead to the Sierras.

We developed a routine for holding Fresno Runs at the Pierce's Park site. Some of us would take off work on the Friday of statewide runs and truck all our supplies down to our site. We'd set up sign-in tables, a front gate, establish our base camp and communication center, and take care of any tasks needed to get the site ready for the arrival of the thousand or so bikers we were expecting.

Lucas built a run box that stowed a lot of our gear. Lucas was an Okie packer supreme. He liked to tweak on finding just the right way to pack everything. He worked on the run box for weeks, making little cubbies for all our stuff. We had walkie-talkies, flashlights, cash boxes, cones, tools, all sizes of ropes, and dozens of other items packed "just so" in the run box. That box must have weighed a ton. We'd wrestle it into the club van, and then add our barricades, tents, sleeping bags, firewood, camp chairs, and all our other gear to the mix. One unlucky stiff had to drive the van. Usually the driver was whoever had a bike down for repairs, although sometimes one of the old ladies would drive. The rest of us rode our bikes.

We generally switched off on the set-up duty, so that the same guys wouldn't have to do that task every time. The rest of our Club would head to Fresno after work on Friday. That way, we could all be there when the crowds started pulling in late Friday night.

Riders would arrive at the run site beginning Friday afternoon and continue rolling into the site throughout the night. There would be a short break around four or five AM; then, at first light, the arrivals would start up again. Bikes would come in by twos and threes, or six or eight at a time, or sometimes in a pack of 10 to 20. We'd sign people in, take their entrance fee (usually around $5), answer their questions, and direct them to campsites. It was nonstop activity at the front gate from late afternoon Friday until dusk Saturday. By then, everyone arrived. We'd forward the entrance fee cash to Rolljaw every few hours for safekeeping.

We manned the front gate 24/7. People would want to go for rides through the countryside, or go to a café or bar, so we had a constant flow of bikes and other vehicles coming and going all the time. Even though there might be 600 to 1000 people at the campsite, we literally had *thousands* of vehicles go in and out over the whole weekend.

We established a work schedule for our security team. Preparing the schedule was usually my duty. Our team consisted of our club, the *Highwaymen*, and a few MMA reps and close friends who would pull a shift or two to help out. Besides the front gate, we would have roving security patrols of the perimeter, just to make sure we kept the locals and the bikers separated, and of the camping grounds, too. We kept the patrols up all night and day.

Walking the patrols as a team was a useful way to see what was going on with all the folks who were at the run site. It was also a means to let people know that there was a security presence around, too. The vast majority of the bikers at these big runs weren't a problem, of course. As usual in such situations, only a relative few caused any trouble. One of the benefits of having patrol duty was the free food, drinks, and smokes that were offered by many of the partiers. Plus, we would get to see a lot of old friends and make some new ones, too.

Pierce's Park wasn't the nicest of camping sites. It did have some advantages, however, since it sat directly on the Kings River. On a hot day, people could cool themselves off by jumping into the water. There wasn't an abundance of trees, but enough to make do. What Pierce's had going for it most was the site set-up. The river formed a natural border on two sides, the highway was elevated along the frontage, and the west end of the site was inaccessible, so everyone had to use the front gate. That allowed us to control party crashers or drunken campers who wanted to go out for a midnight ride. The MMA could hold the run and all the weekend activities in an enclosed environment, which was to everyone's benefit.

The other significant advantage was the bar set-up. Pierce's had an upper bar right on the highway that was for the normal day to day use and a large lower bar that was open on the weekends. The lower bar was capable of holding hundreds and had plenty of room for dancing, too. The buildings were old and smelly, but the whole place fairly screamed out "country honky-tonk".

There would be activities using the stage at the lower bar or the outside area. Rock bands would play for hours every Friday and Saturday night. During the day, there would be organized games and raffles. One of the biggest draws was the "Fewest Clothes Contest". This was essentially an organized amateur strip show . . . bikes, beer, and naked women? Of *course,* it was a popular event. The activities, especially the bands, required just about all of us on the security team to be on duty. There was always that small minority who would get over-medicated or over-amped and end up causing trouble. That's just what happens when you cram about a thousand people in a hot party place. We never had any serious incidents, but there were plenty of minor ones . . . every day and every night.

We'd have to break up fights or arguments. There would be beefs over women. Somebody would be falling down drunk and in need of an escort to his or her camp. Someone would fall and break an ankle. We even had a few folks try to have oral sex in broad daylight right in front of half the camp. The list of incidents we had to get involved with was endless. We felt like adult babysitters sometimes. It was a fun time for the participants, though. For them, everything was covered. They didn't have to do anything except party.

Some of the bikers, especially some of the ones from Southern Cal, weren't enthusiastic about having to follow the directions of a Northern California bike club when it came to security. We got a little blowback in that regard from some of them. That was understandable. We weren't too keen on having to shepherd around a bunch of L.A. independents, either. There has always been a little attitude between North and South in California, most of it coming from the Northerners. I have to admit those of us in the club thought that way, as well. We usually referred to somebody we didn't know who caused a problem as an, "L.A. asshole," whether they were actually from Los Angeles or not.

Some of the heavy duty partiers would arrive Friday night, get drunk, pass out, wake up Saturday, and then repeat the whole process. When Sunday morning rolled around, they would climb on their bikes and hit the road for home.

Most people weren't quite so overboard with the drinking. The runs undoubtedly were fun for everyone, and we got to enjoy ourselves, even though we worked 18 or 20 hours each day. Our club, the *Highwaymen*, and the MMA volunteers couldn't get high like everyone else. We were all there mostly to work.

There were some cool moments. One year Rolljaw got the idea to get a dunk tank and sell throws for a few bucks. He got a few volunteers to go in the tank, but there wasn't too much activity. We told Roloff that if he got in the tank the MMA would make a fortune, since everybody had been pissed off at Roloff at one time or another. He finally agreed with us and got in. Drew and I just smiled at one another. We had him now.

Most bikers are notoriously bad athletes, and that day was no exception. A lot of guys paid their money and threw, but Rolljaw only was dropped once or twice. Then, it was our turn. Drew dropped Roloff a few times, and then it was my chance. After a throw, or two, I was dialed in, and Roloff was splashed repeatedly. He finally was so worn out that he had to get out of the tank. I hated to see him go. I still had throws coming to me. No matter, though. It was money well spent.

Another time, we had an outstanding show put on by a quick-draw shooter. The Santa Cruz Reps had gotten to know a middle-aged guy from their area named Joe Barcelone. He was a quick-draw artist who, at one time, worked with actors like Charles Bronson and Clint

Eastwood. Joe wasn't a biker, but he agreed to put on his show at the Fresno Run to help draw in people.

Joe was a fun guy. He was exceedingly modest about his abilities, and when he wasn't scheduled to shoot, could usually be seen in the company of Jose Cuervo. Joe used a single action .44 caliber six-shooter, if memory serves correctly. Like all such exhibition shooters, Joe used plastic bullets to prevent ricochets.

Barcelone's exhibition was fantastic. He had impressive tricks . . . many that were performed while blindfolded. Every time he shot, he was prompted by a bell hooked up to a timer, so speed and accuracy measured his performance. It's difficult to appreciate the stunts unless you see them; but, I can relate a few things that will at least show a glimpse of Joe's amazing ability.

Joe needed to warm up his reflexes a little before the show. In this instance, he chose one of the security team—me—to be his foil. Joe had me take off my belt and fold it back on itself in half, flat. Next, I held each end in a fist at chest level, with my arms extended. Then, Joe had me move my arms slightly towards each other, to create a loop in the belt . . . *picture it?*

Then, all I was supposed to do was snap the belt closed in front of me the moment I saw Joe start to move and draw his pistol . . . simple, *right?* You've certainly done this before, just goofing around, right? One quick jerking motion with the arms and the belt is flat again . . . *easy!* I knew I could make one fast reflexive move before Joe could get to his gun, draw, and aim it . . . *no sweat.*

Joe went for his gun, and I snapped the belt closed. I was fast, too. One minor problem, though. The closed belt contained a .44 caliber revolver pointing directly at my heart.

Huh? Okay, let's try that again. I'll watch closer this time . . . I'll react quicker to that, too.

Any time, Joe . . . *snap!* I closed that loop very quickly that time.

Hmmm . . . there's that damn six-shooter again. Inside the belt and aimed right at my sternum.

I tried a few more times, but it was no use. Joe's draw was faster than a person's reflexes. Joe said he had been tested at Stanford University, along with people from other professions, to measure reflexes. Joe had beaten everyone there, even edging out the magicians with their sleight of hand abilities.

211

The gathered crowd grew in size as Joe continued his warm-ups. He put three 25-cent pieces on the back of his hand and held it at waist level. Then, he dropped his hand and caught the quarters in succession—one-two-three—before they hit the ground. Try it sometime.

For his last warm-up, Joe had me put a quarter in my open hand and hold it— palm up—at waist level. When I saw Joe start to move any portion of his body, I was simply to close my fingers back into my palm, securing the quarter. I had him now, I thought. I *know* I can close my hand before he can get to that quarter, no problem. I was getting a little tired of being shown up by a short, older guy who downed half a bottle of Cuervo less than a day ago.

Joe stood in front of me. Everybody got quiet. Joe made his move, and I quickly closed my hand. I felt Joe's fingers—ever so briefly—touch against mine. No worry, however. I could still feel the coin inside my hand. I started a sly smile. I had him, at least this once, I thought.

Joe told me to open my fingers. I did and looked at my palm . . . two dimes and a nickel . . . *damn! Son of a bitch!*

Joe put on his show and wowed the crowd with his skills. Then he did in Jose Cuervo again that night. Our only concern was that some of the bikers at the run would try some of Joe's tricks on their own later that night and end up shooting themselves. (We were never so naïve as to think that some people didn't bring along a few hidden firearms.) Nevertheless, the night passed quietly.

The statewide runs were three days of little sleep and hard work for us. Still, we had a good time. Another of our favorite times would come at the end of the run on Sunday afternoon.

Roloff would buy us drinks in the upper bar, and everybody would relate the funny or maddening incidents that we each had seen over the weekend. Rolljaw was always in an upbeat mood—for two reasons.

First, the MMA just received needed cash to keep the doors open. Second, nobody had been killed or caused any major trouble in the local area—always a plus for the "public image minded" Ron.

Our club was in an equally good mood as well. Besides putting another successful run behind us (Help Mr. Wizard, I don't wanna be hardcore no more!) we would now get to ride our bikes home as well. It was *hell* watching the other bikers come and go on their scooters over the weekend, when we were tied to gate or patrol duty. We wanted to ride and to get away from Pierce's Park.

Our adrenaline rush would wear off halfway home, though; and, by the time we got back to San Jose on Sunday night, we would be pretty burned out. The lack of sleep, the work, and the partying would catch up with us a bit. Then we had to go to work on Monday morning.

Matt and I once talked about the crash-down time on Sunday and Monday from the rigors of the statewide runs. We agreed that the real test on Monday was whether you rode your bike or not. Come Monday, it was a chore to get the bike out, unpack your gear, and clean off the San Joaquin dust for a ride when all you wanted was to rest in front of the TV for a spell.

Sometimes, we just wanted nothing to do with bikes for a few days. Monday evenings could tend to be a real "Help Mr. Wizard" time for us. Other times, we would drag our butts out on the road, if only for a short ride because, hey, we were the *Wheel Lords* Motorcycle *fucking* Club, man.

Pierce's Park was named for and dominated by one man: Otis Pierce. Otis was one of those unforgettable characters whom you meet and always remember. He was around 73 years old and always dressed the same each day with jean coveralls and a button down long-sleeved shirt. He topped the look off with a much-used straw cowboy hat, rolled and placed atop his head at a jaunty angle. For an older, more conservative country boy, Otis wore his thinning hair a little longer than others his age did.

Otis rented out his property to various groups. The MMA was just one of many organizations with which Otis did business. He even rented out his site to the Ku Klux Klan, who had a rally and cross burning a few weeks before one MMA Run.

Otis was a country singer of some local reputation. He looked as if he might have grown up around Jimmie Rodgers or Hank Williams or others from the early days of country music. Otis never did any work around the park; he would just walk around and supervise his employees. He ran the upper bar with a vigilant eye. Otis didn't like it when the local

Hispanics came into the bar and spoke Spanish, so he put up a sign that said, "Speak English or don't speak."

Every so often throughout the day and night, Otis would pull out his banjo, or sometimes a guitar, and sing a few tunes. The songs were usually of the "high lonesome" variety, such as those done by Ralph Stanley and others. Sometimes, Otis would sing an old traditional mountain or gospel tune. He sounded good, too. When Otis would feel especially frisky, he would pull out a Jew's harp and play an old jig.

Otis loved playing the part of a crusty old character. It was his world inside Pierce's Park, and he ran the show. All the Fresno Sheriff Deputies knew Otis, and we would see them stop by and check on things at the bar from time to time. The Deputies would banter back and forth with Otis, who we could tell didn't care much for agents of the law.

Otis carried a four shot, four-barrel derringer inside his coveralls pocket. Once, on a Friday night in the upper bar, before too many riders arrived, some local guy walked in the front door while Otis was playing the banjo. Otis quickly recognized him, stopped his tune, and shouted out, "I told you not to come back in here!" and drew his derringer and fired a shot over the guy's head. The bullet lodged in the wall above the front door. The guy high-tailed it out of there, and soon returned with a couple of deputies. They gave Otis a short lecture that went in one ear and out his hat. The deputies and the local guy left, and Otis was once again the boss of Pierce's Park.

There was always some kind of lively action around Otis and his bar. A bunch of Otis' family—nephews and nieces and such—worked there. We all got along well. One day, two or three of us from the club got into some beef with three or four of them—who knows why. One of our guys lost his patience and popped one of the Pierces for smarting off. It was one of the Pierce women, and she and the rest of them hit right back. We had a good little fracas going on for a few minutes, but then cooler heads prevailed. Five minutes later, we were all drinking and laughing together. Those Pierces were a great family to hang with.

Otis would provide running commentary during his impromptu concerts. During one such interlude, at the first statewide run held at Pierce's, Otis said, "I'm just an old country boy from Missouri."

"What part of Missouri, Otis?" I said.

"Ava, Missouri. In the Ozarks."

"Oh, I know Ava. I've been there. I grew up in Springfield." (I had, too. My parents' insurance agent and his wife, Lowell and Florence Snider, were from Ava. I'd been there with my folks on drives, and with my Dad on his business trips. Ava was deep in the Ozarks, maybe 50 miles from our place in Springfield).

"You're from Ava?" Otis asked.

"No. I've been to Ava."

"Well, what's your name?"

"Last name is Norman," I said.

"You related to Old Doc Norman?" Otis asked eagerly.

"Nope. No Doc Norman in my family."

Otis seemed disappointed.

At the next Fresno Run, a few months later, the same scenario unfolded. Otis announced once again how he was a poor old country boy from Missouri.

"I know you are," I said. "You're from Ava, right?"

"Damn right . . . how'd you know that? Are you from Ava?"

"No, I've just visited there."

"You've been to Ava? What's your name?" Otis was highly engaged now.

"Family name of Norman."

"Norman? You related to Old Doc Norman?"

I hesitated. This all seemed to be brand new to Otis. He didn't remember any of this conversation having taken place just a few months earlier. All eyes were on me. I felt like a relief pitcher on the mound in the ninth inning of a close game. I decided to go with my best pitch . . . the change-up.

"Doc Norman? From Ava, Missouri?" I asked.

"Yeah, Old Doc Norman. You related to him?"

"He's my uncle."

"Your uncle?"

"Absolutely."

"*Goddamn*, I *knew* it. Give this man a drink."

Otis played for a long time that night. He was in a good mood . . . and I raised a glass to Old Doc Norman, my long lost uncle.

Not all was laughter for our club, of course. One of our worst times came when we had to kick out one of our own members. Mitch got deeply involved with crank, and it began to affect his ability to function in the club. Hey, we all took crank from time to time, no big deal. However, Sleaze went way over the top. He got involved in running some deals, and began to let his club responsibilities slide.

Mitch did all the usual things that a person does when he goes over the falls on drug usage. He got a police scanner and always had it turned on, afraid the cops were going to bust him at any moment. He stopped riding his bike. He started carrying a sawed off shotgun everywhere he went. Club meetings and functions were missed. Assignments and duties were ignored. And so on, and so on.

The situation worsened. For one guy to go MIA for an extended period wouldn't have been so harmful if we'd been a large club. Maybe then we could have afforded it. However, we were small, and everyone had to pull his weight. We tried every corrective step we could think of—fines, suspension, and counseling from guys like Lucas and Dennis, who were closest to Mitch. Nothing worked.

Mitch was spending far more time with his connections and his drugs than he was with the club. Something had to change. No one wanted to take the ultimate step of expulsion. Mitch was one of the original ten. He had been an officer of the club from day one. Sleaze was there for everything we did, and was liked by everyone—both within the club and the MMA. Mitch was fun to be around, and stood his ground whenever we had trouble.

Finally, after months of problems, Mitch was brought up for his patch. He wasn't even at the meeting. There were only two votes to kick out; not many guys wanted to take the ultimate step. Lucas took the results of the vote to Sleaze to show him that he needed to change his ways or the rest of the guys would join the vote next time.

He didn't, and they did. A short time later Mitch was kicked out of the club. None of us felt happy about it. Nevertheless, that's the code. Like Art Fern would have said, "Not going to take care of club business? *Then* we care."

We felt bad for Mitch, but we weren't going to allow the club's standards to decline. Abuse of drugs robbed a good guy from carrying a lifelong honor with him. It was too bad . . . for all of us.

ᶜᵛᵖ *Chapter Twenty* ᵠᵛᵔ

"Club Runs"

Trail Boss Billy Green Bush: "You just like to travel."
Drover/Gun hand Luke Askew: "The best part is gettin' in to town
or gettin' out of town."

Western Film "The Culpepper Cattle Company"

The *Wheel Lords* averaged about six or seven club runs per year. That figure was in addition to all our MMA Runs, so we were on the road a lot. We traveled more than the other clubs in San Jose did. The *Sinners* and *Angels* and the other clubs in town went on their own runs, and sometimes we all ran together; but, the *Wheel Lords* were certainly on the highways more frequently than the other clubs were.

I loved being out on the road. That's what I had grown up with, and I loved being in a club with guys who felt the same. I never tired of pulling into a small town on Friday and Saturday nights and finding the great little cafés and bars. Then later, we'd head back to our campsite outside of town, where we could see the stars and be away from the big city and the crowds. A big campfire with your brothers and the old ladies, food, drink, music and games—man, it doesn't get much better.

Mariposa was just such a small town. Mariposa (Spanish for butterfly) is an old gold mining town that lies on one of the entry routes into Yosemite National Park. It's on Highway 49, the Golden Chain Highway that runs through about ten California counties. Most of the communities along 49 are around 1200-1500 feet elevation, which puts you above the fog, above the smog, and below the snow.

There were lots of activities to do in the area. If you wanted to go riding to the high country, the road east toward Yosemite climbed quickly. If you wanted to ride through the hills, there were plenty of back roads. Nearby reservoirs were outstanding for fishing or boating. On the other hand, if you wanted just to hang around the town, people were friendly. There were antique shops and general stores, as well as bars and restaurants to visit, too.

One year, we stayed in a small cabin outside of town that Rocky's parents bought as a vacation place. Some of us crashed inside, and others camped outside. Mariposa was about a four hour ride from San Jose, I guess. It was far enough to be a destination, but not so far that you spent all your weekend coming and going. There was an historic feel to the place, what with all the Gold Rush connections of the town.

Once we found a comfortable place that suited us, we tended to go back there almost every year. One such location was Bear River Reservoir, which was on Highway 88 below the Carson Pass in the high Sierra. Bear was around 6,000 feet. It was just past a more popular spot than Bear—Silver Lake. As a result, Bear didn't have too many folks camping there. We would reserve one of the group use areas, which were seldom used. Consequently, we had a lot of privacy at those runs. The Park Rangers were cool, too.

We did tend to have a minor ongoing controversy on runs, though. Some guys wanted to play music all night long, which was part of their way of partying. Lucas was the leader of that group. Others of us, like me, wanted a little more of an authentic camping experience. Lucas would play rock music tapes from one of the follow trucks we would bring along, or sometimes search the truck radio dial for an all-night rock station. Then he would hook up the radio to the extra set of heavy-duty speakers he had packed. You know, like the ones the Donner Party had.

Hey, I like rock and roll as much as anyone does, maybe more so, but I also like the sounds of nature. Hell, it's tough to get my John Muir groove on when I'm lying in the Sierras looking up at millions of stars, and Black Sabbath is making my ears bleed.

Sometimes my arguments held sway with the guys, and sometimes Lucas's did. I didn't mind losing out on the all-night radio question at Bear Reservoir one year. There was a hot FM station that we picked up. They were playing great tunes and the station came in crystal clear. The only problem, which rather bothered me, was the time. The station had the time wrong by one hour each and every time they announced it. They were one hour off, always. Maybe I had too much Early Times that night, but I thought I could at least still tell the correct time. Finally, the station announced the time and their call letters along with their city, which was Casper, Wyoming. It turned out that we were receiving a signal from Wyoming more clearly than ones from Reno or Sacramento. It was probably 1,000 miles to Casper, and maybe only 100 miles to Reno or Sac.

We had a bit bigger controversy over our so called "sweetie runs". A sweetie run was somebody's brainchild early on—perhaps Howie or Drew—I'm not sure. At any rate, the idea was for all the guys to bring their sweeties along and leave all the old ladies at home. Naturally, no run was officially called a sweetie run. The guys who had sweeties were constantly worried that the other members' old ladies would rat them out over their side chicks.

At most runs, if a guy brought along his sweetie, the old ladies— usually being friends with the guy's real old lady—would be put in a tough position. Do they tell the guy's old lady, or keep their silence? Well, they kept quiet, of course. Too many "un-good" things would happen in too many relationships if they didn't. That was unfair and unfortunate, but that was the reality.

A sweetie run was a convenient way around that difficulty—at least for the guys who were worried, that is. If they're all sweeties, then no old ladies have to lie, right? Plus, the guys would have no worries of being busted. To me, that logic can only be described as . . . peccable.

The debate back and forth went something like this.

My argument: "I have to leave my righteous old lady at home, so you can bring your new chickie along?"

Their argument: "Just bring a sweetie along."

Me: "I don't have a sweetie. Nor, do I want one."

Them: "Okay, so don't bring anybody, then."

Me: "But I have someone I do want to bring . . . my old lady."

Them: "But you can be with her any time."

Me: "Right, like this weekend on this run. That's when I have chosen to be with her. By the way, what are your old ladies going to be doing while you're away with your sweeties for the weekend, anyway? Needlepoint?"

So it went. Hey, I didn't care how many girls some of the guys had, but the logistics were their problem. If we wanted to make it a guys only run, fine. I just didn't like being told what I could and couldn't do with my old lady. I don't remember too many sweetie runs after the first year, so I guess I eventually won that argument. At any rate, once Marie and I were together, her schedule permitting, she was on my bike for most runs.

We were on a run to Lake Solano in the North Bay one weekend when Drew was involved in a bad accident. Marie had a job lined up later that day, and the two of us left camp for home early Sunday morning by ourselves.

Unknown to us, a few minutes later Drew tried to re-start the smoldering campfire by pouring a small pan of gasoline on it. The gasoline ignited and quickly engulfed his face and arms. Lucas tackled him to the dirt and put the fire out. Drew was pretty messed up. An ambulance came and took him to a Sacramento hospital.

Drew stayed in the hospital for nearly a week. His wife Lisa and Mitch both stayed with him the whole time. It was against hospital rules for them to stay. However, the staff allowed it anyway. They even brought in a recliner for them to sleep on. Drew recovered; and his face, which wasn't burned too badly, only had a few small scars. His hands and arms took longer to heal than the rest of him, but eventually everything was back to normal.

Our club made a run to Black Butte Reservoir every spring. The lake was near the small farm town of Orland, which was along Interstate 5 in the northern Sacramento Valley. It was usually our first good-sized club outing of the year.

Orland was a favorite for almost everyone. Black Butte was set in some rolling hills, which would be a beautiful green from the recent winter rains. The guys who liked to fish were in heaven with all the coves in the lake. We used the group use area, so no one else was nearby. Bear got most of the guys hooked on horseshoe throwing, so we had pits set up for that. Lucas and Bear were the leading barbecue boys. The old ladies would add their touches to the culinary mix, too. It was pretty much the typical camping scene.

The town of Orland was just the right size, with a few restaurants and bars for us to mingle with the locals. We would party in town Saturday night, and then head back to camp on a clear-your-head ten-mile ride. We never had any problems in Orland. Well, except for once, I guess.

Sleaze got a bit frisky one night after we left the bar. Some of us had gone to the late night café for a quick bite before heading back to camp. Mitch copped some kind of attitude. I don't know why he did (maybe he ate off somebody's plate, and he didn't like what he or she was eating) but the upshot was Mitch and the cook got into an argument. Mitch was dead drunk, and wouldn't let it go.

As the four of us were leaving (it was just Mitch and me with Connie and Marie at the café), the cook came outside to say some kind of parting shot. There was a small crowd of drunken locals looking on as Mitch walked up to the cook (who was a muscular guy with a grill scraper in his hand) and took his lit cigarette and put it out in the guy's cheek. The cook never even flinched. I was nearly as high as Mitch, and I remember thinking, "Gee, I've never seen that before. I guess we'll have to fight half the town now."

Surprisingly, the townsfolk intervened and calmed everyone down. There was no big fight or anything. We got ready to leave on our bikes. I had electrical problems with Shiloh at the time, so at night, I was running with no headlights and buddying up with one of the guys whenever I rode around the area. As we kicked on our bikes, I reminded Mitch that I had no lights. It didn't matter, though. Sleaze had forgotten about my electrical problems and took off for camp as soon as his motor started, leaving Marie and me to poke our way slowly through the moonless night back to our campsite. It seemed to take us forever to get there.

When we finally did make it to camp, I wanted to frap Mitch up side of the head for leaving me, but he was already passed out. I should have gotten him up anyway.

Sometimes the *Highwaymen* MC from Sonoma would join us on runs. Once, both clubs went to Bakersfield for a large run put on by some dresser riders. We usually didn't hang with the dresser crowd, but at this event, there were a lot of chopper people, too.

One of the risks of going on runs with the choppers is the breakdown factor. Since their owners modified most choppers, it wasn't uncommon to have mechanical breakdowns from time to time. Also, unlike the dresser crowd, most of our bikes were older and not maintained at Harley dealerships; so, despite the fact that some guys were solid mechanics, it wasn't unusual at all to have some problems on a run. We had our share, I suppose, but nothing like the troubles that the *Highwaymen* seemed to have on a routine basis. *Highwaymen* bikes were always breaking down. The Bakersfield run was the worst. It took us forever to get there.

Don, the *Highwaymen's* President, had a bike that looked like it was perpetually one step away from dying. On top of being ugly, it was held together by tie-wraps, bungee cords, and duct tape. Don kept breaking down on the ride to Bakersfield. At one point, he lost all his brake fluid. No sweat, Don said. He went to his saddlebags and took out a bottle of wine. Don poured the wine into his brake master cylinder, bled the lines, and was back on the road. None of us heard of that trick before, but it was old hat to Don. He insisted that Port wine worked best for brake fluid. We took his word on that.

We would frequently needle the *Highwaymen* for the seemingly endless breakdowns they experienced. In turn, they would tease us because they said we overused the term, "man". They laughed at us for ending every sentence with "man". We never noticed if we did overdo it with that expression. We thought we spoke pretty much the same as everyone else, but apparently, that wasn't so.

One year, at Bear Reservoir, we had another campfire problem. Matt arrived solo on Friday afternoon to pay the camping fee at the Ranger Station and to secure the site in advance of the arrival of the rest of the club. We got there after dark and found Matt's bike and a dying fire—however, there was no sign of Matt. Then some citizen campers from a nearby camp came up and told us that Matt had been accidentally burned at the campfire. The park rangers had taken him away for medical treatment.

We had visions of a scenario worse than what had happened to Drew at Lake Solano a few years before. Only this time, there was no Lucas around to have put out the fire. A couple of the guys went back to the Ranger Station, and soon returned with our missing member. The citizens had the basic facts right, but the situation wasn't nearly as serious as we had feared.

It seems that Matt tripped—or, as he claimed—was pushed into the campfire he was tending. The citizens heard a commotion and contacted the park rangers who took Matt to their station and applied some first aid to his face. No serious damage was done.

We were relieved. What was this about being pushed into the campfire? "Just who or what pushed you into the fire, Matt?" we asked.

"Uh, it might have been Bigfoot. Or it could have been these squirrels I saw running around here a while ago."

"*Really . . . squirrels?* You say squirrels came up behind you and pushed you into the fire? Those must be some *bad-ass* squirrels, Mattus."

"Well, it could have been Bigfoot, too. I'm not sure."

"Right . . . *Bigfoot*."

Then we found the empty bottle of Jack Daniels on the ground near the campfire.

Okay, riddle solved and case closed.

Matt never wavered, though. He admitted to sampling a bit of the whiskey perhaps, but stuck to his story that he didn't just stumble into the fire. Someone or something pushed him in.

Who were we to doubt a club brother? So I offer this safety tip to any who wish to camp among the beautiful lakes in the high country of the Sierras. Be wary of the local wildlife, especially two gray squirrels that may answer to the names Daniel and Jack. They can get downright testy . . . oh and, *happy camping*.

California never gets rain in the summer. From May to October, it is bone dry. That makes for a long and dry run season for motorcycles. Once in a while, there is an exception, however. Almost every summer, a tropical storm would run the length of the state from south to north, contrary to the usual flow of the jet stream. This warm storm dumps loads of water in Southern California before hitting the Sierras. We were caught in one such storm during one of our yearly runs to Bear Reservoir.

The rain started on Friday night and just wouldn't stop. We finally decided to have some of our guys take the one car we had and drive to the nearest city, South Lake Tahoe, and rent a U-Haul truck. It took forever to get to Tahoe, thanks to the storm damage to the roads along the way.

When we got there, we discovered everyone had similar ideas. All the campers—hikers, bikers, and boaters descended upon Tahoe from all directions to try to dry out. We got extremely lucky and found a rental truck. Then we went to Harrahs Hotel, which was our favorite casino, to secure some rooms. Everyone else had that idea, too. Fortunately, for us, the Harrahs people were generous and gave us one of the few remaining rooms to be had in the area.

All this took quite a few hours; and, by the time we arrived at camp back at Bear Reservoir, everyone there looked like the Donner

Party—wet, cold, and hungry. We loaded the bikes, the people, and the rain-soaked thousand-pound tents into the truck and headed for Tahoe.

We stopped at a laundromat before checking in at Harrahs. The citizens there were quite surprised when about 15 people came in and began stripping off their soaked and muddied clothes. We soon had the entire laundromat to ourselves. Once we all dried out, we went to Harrahs and took turns sharing the one room and bath. I'm sure the casino had some rule that limited the number of guests per room, but the staff turned a blind eye for us.

We spent the rest of the weekend gambling, then took the rental truck, and headed for home. The rain finally let up about halfway back to San Jose, and we pulled the bikes out and rode the rest of the way home.

The "Rain Run" turned out to be one of those weekends that you remember for a long time.

We made a couple of runs to California prisons. These were daytime events set up by the MMA to stage motorcycle shows inside prison walls.

Maybe 30 or 40 bikes came for the show at the two prisons we visited. I don't remember all the people who participated, but there were some *Hells Angels*, some independent riders, and our entire club present. Very few of the bikes were of show quality, but the point was to let the inmates see what real street bikes looked like.

We were told that prison officials were reluctant to allow the exhibitions and that security would be super tight. We had to submit names of all the participants to them in advance for a screening process by the prison authorities. We had one bike show at San Quentin and another one a few months later at Soledad.

Surprisingly, security was far tighter at Soledad, a medium security facility, than it was at the more famous high-security prison of San Quentin. At Quentin, we were told we couldn't wear denim jeans. Inmates wore denim, and visitors could not, to make identification of visitors easy. The "no jeans rule" caused a lot of guys in the group to scramble to find something else to wear. That was about the only requirement of any consequence, though. We had about 40 bikes roll into San Quentin's lower yard, and none of us were searched by any of the guards. They didn't search our bikes, either. We could have smuggled in just about anything in our saddlebags, had anyone been so inclined. We

225

stayed there for a few hours with inmates mingling freely around everyone. There were no problems, and I think a lot of the inmates enjoyed the afternoon, even those guys who weren't into bikes.

At Soledad, which is south of Salinas along Highway 101, security was tighter. All of us on bikes had to enter a sally port. Then, the gate behind us was closed. Armed guards patrolled the area from above. Our bikes were searched, and then we were searched. Then, the front gate of the sally port opened, and we rode inside the prison. Again, everything went well, and there were no problems. I don't know if that kind of event would be allowed inside today's prisons.

Marie went with me on a lot of our runs. She liked riding, and I liked having her along. She didn't make all the rides, but she was there most of the time. We spent a fair amount of time apart during the workweek, what with Marie commuting to Frisco on a regular basis. I was hired on at General Electric Nuclear in San Jose. It was the same large plant where Ben, Drew, and Lucas worked. I headed south in the morning, and Marie headed north. She spent quite a bit of time with her folks, and I had club meetings and obligations to perform during the week. When a run would come up, we would both be ready to do some traveling together.

The *Highwaymen's* old ladies sometimes teased Marie for bringing a change of clothes on runs. When we would end our ride for the day, she would disappear for ten minutes and re-emerge with clean clothes and fresh makeup. Hey, let them tease away, she looked terrific. Soon, the other *Wheel Lords* old ladies adopted similar routines. I dug that. It was a nice touch.

Unlike a few of the other couples we knew, Marie and I didn't argue much. Sometimes we would fight over something, but those were rare occurrences. About the only thing we disagreed on was her contention that one person in a relationship loves stronger than the other person does. She often said that she loved me more than I loved her. I told her she was crazy. I agreed that she certainly showed it more than I did, and I probably needed to work on that; but, there was no way she loved me more than I loved her.

Neither one of us could ever convince the other. Marie would say, "One lover loves more. And in our case, it's me."

I would simply answer, "No way."

226

At the start of one spring run season, the club got some unwelcome news. One of our best members suddenly quit. Fast Frank decided that he and his girlfriend, Sally needed to move away and change their life in a big way. I never did understand Frank's reasoning, and I certainly can't explain or remember it now, after all these years. Franky was always on the mercurial side, but then, hey—who wasn't?

Frank didn't sell off his bike and retire from motorcycling, as some guys do when they tire of the biker lifestyle. He wasn't interested in a leave of absence away from the club to try to work things out in his head. Frank just wanted to go.

We all hated to see Franky leave the club. He was a smart man, both in the world of scooters and in the world of everyday life. Frank was a main instigator at parties, and was a steady friend when we walked all-night patrols at statewide runs, or worked long weekend shifts at far away car shows. Frank left all that behind, though, and he and Sally moved out of state.

Maybe Frank needed to chase some demons in his head away, I don't know. We said goodbye to Frank and, "Have a dose." Then we got ourselves ready for our next run and got back to what we did, and what we were . . . *Wheel Lords* MC, on the road.

I grew weary of my bike frequently being down. I seriously needed to get a more dependable scooter. It wasn't that I didn't love my bike, but I longed for a newer, stronger, more reliable ride.

I set my sights on an early Shovelhead. I loved the way they looked, and that model was only produced for four years, from '66 to '69, so there was a nice rarity about them—at least in my mind. I knew I didn't want the FX model. Lots of guys had those—they were everywhere. I liked Panheads, but some guys in the club had them, as did quite a few people with whom we rode. However, *nobody* had an early Shovel, so, that's the bike I targeted.

Marie's dad was kind enough to loan me some cash so I could buy my new bike without having to sell my old one first. I found an early Shovel for sale in El Cerrito, near Berkeley. It was the Friday of a big club run, and my Knucklehead was down again, so I was the designated driver of the Club van for the weekend. I packed the van with all the run gear, hooked up the neat little motorcycle trailer the club had, and Marie and I headed up to El Cerrito. If things worked out, I might be able to bring a bike along on this run after all.

This was one of the few times when my well-drawn plans worked to perfection. The 1969 Shovelhead was running strong. We quickly closed the deal and loaded my new scoot on the trailer. The guys didn't know I had gone to buy the new bike. I told them I would meet them at the first rest stop with the van and the supplies. We were there waiting for them as they pulled in.

Drew was a bit ticked off that I hadn't consulted with him on my new purchase. He had been my original mentor in the world of choppers, and would always consider himself such. The thought of my being able to select a quality scoot on my own made Drew a little uncomfortable. He would have to get over that, though.

I started up the new bike. All the guys were impressed with the engine, even Drew, albeit a tad reluctantly. The Shovel was a Swingarm frame, which I hated, but I would have to live with that for the present. The bike needed other things too—the front forks needed work, the rear fender was awful, there was no kick-start—only electric, the carburetor wasn't the greatest; but, the basics were sound. I would have to change those things out as I could afford them.

We hit the road to our run site, the eastern slope of the Sierras. We camped along the Walker River, which was a great area with no crowds. Then we went to Bodie State Park, which is a well-preserved ghost town near the Nevada border. Bodie was a mining town that was abandoned when the metals ran out, and the State of California stepped in and preserved everything in an arrested state of decay. The road into the place was about 14 miles of washboard gravel, which was hell on my new bike's front forks. Johnny Appleseed had obviously never visited Bodie, because there wasn't a tree to be found anywhere.

When we returned to San Jose, I spent a lot of time and money getting my Knucklehead in top running condition. For a few months, I owned two bikes—something I never dreamed of. The difficulty was, all my time and energy was spent keeping them up and running. I sold the Knuckle to an MMA Rep from Frisco named Scott Marshall. He was a good dude who had quite a few plans to re-paint and customize the Knucklehead. Then I repaid Marie's dad.

However, to be clear, I didn't sell Shiloh. The name stayed with me. It moved from the Knucklehead to the Shovel. The '69 FLH Shovelhead became Shiloh when I bought it on July 22, 1977.

We have been together ever since. We may even have a vow renewal ceremony someday.

~ *Chapter Twenty-One* ~

"Parties"

The *Wheel Lords* had fun. Moreover, we were funny. We were easily the funniest club around. I'm biased, of course, but it wasn't even close. Loxley was a one-man riot of laughter, so I have to give credit to the San Jose *Angels*. However, nobody we came across had as many flat-out, crack-up guys as we did. Bear and Drew were probably the funniest; but Matt, Mitch, and Frank were hilarious, also. Consequently, we had great times whether it was at parties we attended, parties we hosted, or just general barhopping.

Speaking of barhopping . . . it gets cold at night, especially in San Jose during the winter. You would never know it by the actions of some guys, however. Husky guys, like Bear, would amaze me. We'd go out on our bikes in 40-degree weather, and I'd be bundled up tighter than Carrie's corset as we rode from bar to bar. Then, I would see Bear, and he would be riding with only a T-shirt and his colors. He wasn't cold at all. Matt was the same way. I got my revenge in the summer. Those guys would be dragging ass in the 100-degree heat in Fresno, while I would have no problem with it.

We always held a birthday party in October. Bear was born in October, as was Rocky, Drew, and yours truly. In addition, MMA President Marty Carpenter was born under an October sky, as well as ex-member Old Man Phil. Dennis's wife, Joann had the same birth date as Bear, so we had plenty of reasons to celebrate that month. Sometimes, we would have the October Party at one of our houses, or maybe at Matt's place, which we used as a clubhouse. Other times, we held the party at a bar like the Circus Room in the Almaden area of South San Jose.

One Circus Room October Party was a real blast. All our friends with October birthdays showed up. My brother, Bill had been discharged from the Navy, and was living with Marie and me for a few months; and he attended because, hey . . . he was born in October, too. Loxley was there, along with others from the San Jose *Angels*, along with Derrick Kershaw, the President of the Oakland *Hells Angels*. Loxley brought along a houseguest who was an *Angel* from Switzerland. Marty from Sacramento showed up with his ex-wife, whom I hadn't seen in years.

Brother Bill brought along the guys in his newly formed bluegrass band, one of whom was born in . . . you guessed it. We had people there that night from all over.

The club would always celebrate our anniversary in early November, which tended to coincide with Halloween parties. One year Marie was invited to a modeling friend's Halloween party in Frisco, but had to beg off because it conflicted with our club party. Her friend couldn't believe someone would forego The City for San Jose. "You're going to *San Jose* to party with a bunch of *bikers*?" she sniffed. "What are they going to do? Make one of their *runs* to the *Winchester Mystery House*?"

Good one . . .

We were a musical generation, so there were always plenty of tunes at our parties. Hard rock was popular, of course, but the new, "outlaw" country sound of Willie Nelson and Waylon Jennings had a growing audience. Bear knew all the country acts. He was a regular at the large, local, country honky-tonks featuring all the big names. A lot of us rock-n-rollers turned more towards country music during that time. That was especially true for the guys in the club who were musical. Drew played guitar and violin, and Bear played drums a little.

I was no musician, but I plunked around a bit, and I knew a little about music. My mom played piano every day. She is one of those people who know about 500 songs by heart. Brother William is a great musician. He can play any stringed instrument and sings well, too. I guess a little of that family knowledge rubbed off on me. At any rate, a lot of us weren't into the heavy metal or glam rock of the day and wanted a more traditional sound. We found it, too.

There was a newer alternative radio station in nearby Gilroy that had a growing following. KFAT radio called their audience "Fatheads". KFAT featured music from the worlds of rock, country, gospel, bluegrass, swing, folk, Cheech and Chong type comedy, and traditional mountain music, among others. Hell, KFAT probably had old recordings of Otis Pierce, for all I knew. KFAT, 94.5 on your FM dial, had as its logo the face of a fat, mustached cowboy wearing a big hat . . . who looked a lot like Bear.

Bear and some of his buddies started wearing those rolled straw cowboy hats, and soon many of us in the club had them too. We'd wear them at parties and such, although I don't think any of us knew straight up about a cow.

A few of our guys—Dennis and Drew, I think—wore earrings, as did quite a few bikers in general. Like tattoos, though, earrings weren't as widespread then as they are today. I've never had a desire for an earring. My reasoning is that I have spent a considerable amount of time and energy preventing people from piercing my body with sharpened objects. Why then, would I pay them to do so?

A lot of the bikers in those days played dominoes. The bones traveled well, and you could set them up at parties or runs with no problem. Plus, you could play as teams, which always increased the fun. Old Man Phil and Lucas introduced me to that game early in the club days. Phil was a great player, as was Don of the *Highwaymen*.

Any game that combined luck with skill, and which could be played with a drink and a smoke in your hand, would naturally attract the attention of Bear. As expected, "Barburger" as we sometimes called him, was excellent at dominoes. In fact, Bear had all kinds of cool party skills. He was a great dancer, even at well over 300 pounds. He'd shake his big butt and put a few moves on, and we'd call him The Great Dancing Root Bear.

Ben also could perform a nice little trick that he used to pull on unsuspecting ladies. He learned this gag during one of his frequent bartending jobs. Bear would engage in casual conversation with a woman (most often someone he knew fairly well, but not always) and while nodding his head as the woman talked, he would be wiping down a countertop or table with a small, damp towel—like the ones bartenders use all the time. He would be folding the towel as he wiped the counter. Folding and wiping . . . a nod of the head . . . folding and wiping . . . a quick comment . . . folding and wiping . . . and so on.

When Bear stopped his wiping motion and the woman eventually took notice of the towel right in front of her, she would invariably let out a yelp. Bear had quietly formed the towel into an erect, perfectly shaped, slightly curved eight-inch penis, complete with testicles. Every club old lady was tricked in this manner at least once.

Bear, after hearing the woman cry out, would just say "What . . . is there a problem, my dear? Something the matter?" That trick was a big hit with everyone, male and female. I never discovered the secret to Barburger's towel folding trick, but then, I didn't really want to know either. Some mysteries are better left unsolved. Know what I mean?

The most popular game at parties was poker. That's not surprising. Many of the guys were good players, and poker lends itself to a party atmosphere. The old ladies weren't crazy about the poker games, because some of the guys would play for hours and ignore their old ladies the whole time. I was guilty of that a time or two. Generally, though, I played cards a while then moved on to another activity. I couldn't sit in one place for hours on end like some guys.

I did make an exception one time. We were at Dennis's place, and he had just bought one of those fancy tables with a glass top that was perfect for card playing. Somebody organized a poker game, and one of the guys playing had a large quantity of high-grade cocaine. He'd gotten the coke cheap, but not cheaply enough to treat everyone, so everyone who wanted some chipped in and bought a share of the coke for the night's party. I threw in for my share. I guess that was the only time I ever bought drugs. Every other time, it was pretty much free.

All the guys took their stash of coke and spread it into little piles on the glass table near their stack of poker chips. As the night wore on, each guy would chop and re-chop their pile, playing with the powder as they snorted. It wasn't long until some of the guys were nearly out of coke . . . as I knew they would be. Each player's stack of poker chips, usually watched over so carefully by the player and scrutinized intently by his opponents, received almost no attention. What *was* being studiously observed was how much remained of each player's coke. That pile became the measuring stick of success and to hell with the poker chips.

Drew sat to one side of me, and Matt to the other. As their coke stack diminished, each began to look hungrily at mine. My stash was still plentiful, mainly because: a) I wasn't a glutton like certain *other* players at that table, and b) I purposely rationed my cut, because I knew that other guys would run out. Then, I would get my chance to fuck with them. The *Wheel Lords* always held needling and messing with the psyche of club brothers in high regard.

Sure enough, Matt and Drew soon ran out. To get me to give them some of *my* stash of coke, they began working on me. Bribes may have worked, but they were each nearly out of chips. They reverted to the bro approach.

"Hey man, be a bro and give me a line or two."

"Did you guys not get the same amount as me? You guys need to learn how to conserve your resources. I'm actually doing you a favor here. I'm teaching you how to be frugal," I said.

"Oh fuck that shit, man. Gimme a line already," said Drew.

I gave him my best Wicked Witch voice. "All in good time, my pretty . . . all in good time."

The boys kept on pleading.

"Okay, I will in five minutes. It's my turn to deal . . . after this hand, then." I wanted to string this out as long as I could.

Lucas chimed in. "Yeah, let's play. Do that crap later . . ."

You never saw two guys fold their hands so quickly.

I gave them each a line. Then we started the same dance all over again. I strung those guys along in this fashion for half the night.

Another game that we started playing at parties was darts. Some bikers had dartboards for years before we started playing; but, very few people ever played because the dartboards would invariably be used as targets for knives and tomahawks. The dartboards and surrounding walls would often be torn up from a steady stream of Bucks, Kabars, and Bowie Knives thrown at them. Bikers were like that.

However, we were different. We only threw darts at dartboards. I had gotten involved in a competitive dart league through my new workplace, an electronics company in Sunnyvale. Our mentor on the team was a hard drinking English engineer who used to be a "Teddy Boy," a kind of English street tough back in Birmingham, England in the early sixties. I got to be a decent player, not that I was an "A" class thrower like some of the Brits or anything.

Some of the other guys in the club got into darts, too. We would play straight up, with no knife and hatchet throwing allowed. We played teams, as we would in horseshoes or dominoes. Some of the old ladies played, also. I finally found one game where I could routinely whip Bear's butt. The Fat Kid usually beat me at dominoes, horseshoes, pool, and poker—but I nailed him at darts. In fact, Bear hung a new nickname on me—my favorite one, too. D'Artagnan.

Dennis liked to throw darts, he just wasn't very good. He always wanted to be on my team, and he usually was, to give the other team a chance. Dennis had a friend named Chaco, who was an independent biker. Chaco came to a lot of our parties. He was another one of those guys who wore sunglasses at night indoors. Chaco thought he was a good dart player. D'Artagnan showed him the error of his thought pattern. We played quite a few times, and we almost had a rivalry. I say *almost* because, to have a real rivalry like, say, the Yankees and Red Sox, doesn't one side need to win at least some of the time? See, Chaco was zero for his career against D'Artagnan. Maybe he needed a new prescription for the sunglasses.

Not every party I went to was a biker party. There were family functions to attend—weddings, holidays, and the like. I went with Marie to some of her family functions. A few of her girlfriends were married (not to bikers) and she was in the bridal parties. Those were fun events. There were parties thrown by people at my work, so I didn't spend all my free time in the world of choppers.

Marie and I would go to some of the parties thrown by her friends and contacts in the fashion industry. Most of these soirées were in San Francisco. The parties would be full of swanky people and beautiful models (and the women weren't bad looking either). Really, though, sometimes I felt that I was the only straight guy in attendance at some of these parties. It was certainly a different world than my scooter scene. I had no problem with it, however, and it was good to see Marie in her element.

One person who had completely stopped all "partying" was my dad. After Bob, Sr. left our place in Mountain View, he made a stop at my mom's house in the Sierras. Mom was living solo since my younger sister Nancy went away to college in San Luis Obispo.

A day or so after arriving, Dad suffered a major stroke. Local doctors were able to stabilize his vital signs, and he was then transferred to a Reno hospital. A short time later, my Uncles John and Maurice flew out and had Dad moved back to a facility near them in Missouri. Dad recovered somewhat, but had partial paralysis on one side, and his speech was severely limited.

His brothers and their wives cared for dad, just as my dad and others in the family had cared for my Uncle Sam when we were kids. I helped my Mom go through Dad's stuff that was left behind at her house.

There were perhaps ten bottles of prescription medicines; mostly tranquilizers and anti-depressants. Besides the alcohol, Bob had also been high on pills for years. However, Bob stopped drinking, smoking, and popping pills, *cold turkey*. The stroke saw to that.

There were about five bike clubs in San Jose during much of this time. Besides our Club, the *Angels*, and the *Sinners*, there was a club called the *East Side* MC, and another called the *West Side* MC . . . not exactly catchy names, to be sure. We didn't know the *West Side* guys, who were mostly white, too well. We knew the *East Side* club well, however, and most of them were Mexican. We partied with them quite a bit.

About once a month, there was an "all clubs" meeting held. The five clubs would get together, exchange ideas, BS, and hang around. There might be two to five members present from each club.

One month, the meeting was at Matt's house. His place doubled as our clubhouse. Brad Loxley was one of the *Angels* who showed up. Loxley was a regular smoker. I smoked too, but only about three to five cigarettes a day. If I were at an all-night party, or at a three day MMA Run, I would smoke more. However, I never exceeded more than half a pack in one day. Since I smoked so intermittently, I frequently had no smokes on me. That made me one of those pain-in-the-ass guys who would bum cigarettes. Loxley was one of those friends I was always bumming smokes from.

I bummed a cig from Loxley as the meeting began—no big deal. Just after I took my second drag,—BAM—the cigarette blew up in my face. For a second, I was shocked. Then I realized that Loxley put a load into my cigarette. I hadn't known that they still manufactured cigarette loads. I turned to look at Brad. I had never seen him display such self-control. If that had happened to someone else, by another's doing, Brad would have been cracking up. But, not this time. Loxley didn't laugh . . . hell, he didn't even smile. He just stared straight ahead, as nonchalantly as could be.

Nice touch, Lox . . . Goddammit.

I was the first guy in the Club to have his long hair cut. It was in December of 1977. I hadn't had a real haircut since late 1970, except to have the split-ends trimmed a couple of times.

I cut my hair for two reasons. First, it was a hassle to dry and to maintain. I was used to the hassle, but I was also a little weary of it. Secondly, I wanted to go for a throwback '50's look. I never really achieved that look, but what I did end up with wasn't too bad.

Within six months of my haircut, most of the guys in the club cut their long hair, too. Drew, Dennis, and Matt shortened up, although they were still on the longish side. Rocky kept his hair long, though.

One year, we decided to do something special for our November club anniversary meeting. We wanted to rent a house in Lake Tahoe and spend the weekend gambling. I took on the task of finding us a rental. I found a place at North Shore in Tahoe City that sounded good. The owners bought it as a vacation home, and they lived in San Jose. I worked the deal with a lady by the name of Barbara Lord, and paid the money and picked up the key.

When we got to Tahoe, I had a surprise for the guys. The house we rented was on Club Drive . . . *Club Drive!* That was perfect. Even better, on the front porch of the place was a bigger surprise. The owners had an engraved piece of redwood burl there with the words "House of Lords." I'd done good.

That house was great. It featured a 360-degree glass fireplace suspended from the ceiling in the family room. We had a super time that weekend. There was snow on the ground, and we had a snowball war. Drew had a good arm, but the top snowballer was Rocky. He had a cannon for an arm and he was very accurate with it; I was on the opposing team from him, and I can attest to that. Of course, I found out that Rocky was the type who put ice inside his snowballs, too . . . the big creep.

Every biker thought he could ride his bike no matter how wasted he became. That was just a given. We subscribed to that theory, too. Nobody would ever admit that he couldn't handle his bike, unless he was *forced* into reality.

We were partying at Dennis's one night, and things broke up around three of four in the morning. Drew and I were just about the last to leave. We were both hammered on crank, liquor, and whatever else.

Our old ladies weren't there that night. We knew we were polluted, so we decided to ride out together, at least until we would have to split up, in the belief that together we could form some semblance of a functioning unit. However, it didn't work out too well.

It was a very cold night. We got our bikes started, looked at each other, and took off. Even though there was no traffic out and Dennis lived in a quiet neighborhood, we made a point of stopping at the stop sign around the corner from Dennis's house. Perhaps it was just to prove to ourselves that we really had things dialed in.

We did stop, too. A full and complete stop, even when one wasn't needed. There was one small problem, however . . . neither one of us put our foot down when we stopped. Over we went . . . that happens once in a great while when a guy is really wasted, but two guys . . . at the *same time? Never* saw *that* before.

Fortunately, neither bike fell all the way over on its side. We each kind of half-caught our own bike against one leg at the same time. If they had gone all the way over, I'm not sure we would have been able to pick them up very easily. Once we got everything stabilized, we shot furtive glances around us to see if anyone had seen us do our pratfall. Silly boys, there's no one around at *four* in the morning.

We looked at each other. Drew said, "Maybe we should head back to Dennis's house."

"Good call, bro."

We stayed at Dennis's (after making our uneventful, full, and complete stops in his garage) until mid-morning—when the weather got warmer, and we got straighter. After that, we each rode to our own house. I was still wired, but I kept Shiloh upright the entire way home.

We had great fun at our parties. It wasn't as if everyone would be completely wasted all the time, though. It was rare for one of the guys or one of the old ladies to be totally out of it. I was generally in control of my personal shit, although in fairness, Lucas once claimed otherwise.

There was a party that Marie and I hosted at our place in Agnews, and at our next church meeting Lucas insisted that late that night I was so drunk that I was crawling around on all fours.

"Imposerous!" I said. "I have no recollection of that event, Senator." I thought Weasel was either full of crap, or hallucinogens. I asked everyone else if they had seen this alleged activity. No one had.

My conclusion was that Lucas was full of BS. In fact, I don't think I had been bullshitted that much since those surfer dudes Jan and Dean sang of, "two girls for every boy" in *Surf City*.

Marie was getting a lot of work modeling in San Francisco, but wanted to see if she could make it in the fashion center of Paris. Through some contacts, she managed to secure a place to stay and some intros at agencies in France. Needless to say, I wasn't thrilled with the thought of her going to Europe and spending some months among the "beautiful" people, but how could I hold her back? She had to try to be successful at the thing that drove her.

I thought that her stay in Paris would either make or break our future. If we could remain together and commit to each other after this separation, I figured, we would be a couple for a long time. She said I needn't worry. She knew the story of how a previous girlfriend and I had broken up after she moved, supposedly temporarily, to Los Angeles. She assured me that wouldn't happen to us. I wasn't as sure about it as she was. My history with long-distance relationships wasn't good. First it was L.A. with Sarah, then Washington with Veronica, and now Paris with Marie. Nevertheless, I reluctantly agreed that she needed to go, so I drove her to the airport.

Marie stayed in Paris for over three months, but never made the big breakthrough in the fashion scene there that she had been hoping for. We kept in steady contact while she was away. I could tell from the letters and phone calls towards the end of her stay that something had changed.

The day she came back from Paris, was the day she left me for some guy she had met in France. That was a dark day for me.

I know it sounds stupid, but the first thing I did upon hearing the news (well maybe the second thing, after bitching out Marie) was to go in my garage and figuratively speaking, hug my motorcycle. I guess there was some symbolism there for all the things that Shiloh represented to me. Maybe naming my bike after that song set in motion a self-fulfilling prophecy that was now coming true.

Marie and I lived together for more than three years, and we had a great ride, although it certainly didn't end well—at least from my perspective. I thought that Marie and I were just about perfect for one another. Then, however, my McCarver Syndrome kicked in—and once again—I realized that the only thing I knew about women with any certainty was that I couldn't figure them out.

Time for Kidd to roll on down the road . . . I reckoned another grace would have to save me.

I did come around to Marie's way of thinking on one matter, however. In the end, I had to agree with her that sometimes, indeed, one lover loves more.

✑ *Chapter Twenty-Two* ✑

"Special Angels"

The *Hells Angels* were a strong influence on both the *Wheel Lords* MC, and me personally. Each of us in the club had some friends or acquaintances within the *HA*. These are some of the *Angels* who made a lasting impression on me. I wouldn't say each of these *Angels* was a friend, but each of them showed some traits which I valued at the time, and which I continue to value.

Stan Jennings, aka "SoCal Stan", was overweight and didn't seem to be in terrific physical shape; and, when he attended Fresno MMA Runs, you could see that the heat affected him. Nevertheless, Stan would always lend his help to make the MMA a success. Stan was one of the prime reasons the MMA was so successful at generating interest in Southern Cal. He was extremely popular with the independent L.A. riders, and worked hard at attracting support throughout the region. SoCal Stan and Ron Roloff seemed to be close friends. It was Stan who hung the handle "Rolljaw" on Roloff. Stan had an unusual job. At the time, he was a radio engineer and worked for Dr. Gene Scott, a televangelist who had his own television and radio network throughout California. Scott was the kind of guy who went on the air and demanded that believers send him money. We wondered if he ever knew that he had a *Hells Angel* working for him.

Uncle Jace was an older guy from the Nomads chapter. I only saw him a few times. Early in the club years, on the way back from a Sacramento Blood Run, Jace invited the club to stop by his house. That was the first time I ever saw on display the wide array of banners, plaques, and other memorabilia that most of the *Angels* seemed to own. I guess when you've been a member for a lot of years you tend to collect a lot of stuff. Jace looked a little like one of our original members, John Howell. He had the same kind of 1950's look about him. Uncle Jace was gracious to us and treated us well; and over the years, quite a few of the other *Angels* I met spoke highly of him.

241

There were a number of *Angels* whom I met and liked; and, before I knew it, they would suddenly get sick and die. It wasn't unusual to hear of an *Angel* who was shot and killed, or died in a bike wreck, or died from some other violent end. Solo Steve, the Sacramento *Angels* chapter President, was killed in a powerboat race on a reservoir near my old stomping grounds of Los Gatos. To have so many of those guys die in a few short years from disease seemed weird. I don't remember the order in which they died, but I do recall the guys.

Scary Terry was a Sacramento *Angel* who was a real outgoing sort. He was a fun guy to party with. One run season I asked about him and some of his members told me he had gotten sick and died a few months back. That seemed to be a tough loss for the Sacramento chapter.

Cody Grant was a Richmond *Angel*. Cody was a soft-spoken guy, and one of the most intelligent people I'd met. He seemed to know a whole lot about a whole lot. Cody looked to be about 35 when I knew him; but, he got cancer—or maybe leukemia—and was dead within a few months. I definitely missed not being able to talk with Cody.

Righteous Russ of the Sonoma County *Hells Angels* also died of cancer. The first time I met Russ I didn't much care for him. Then, sometime later at a small MMA run near Calistoga in the Wine Country, Russ and a few other people drifted over to the area where I was on night security detail. The group of us talked awhile, and Russ ended up hanging around my area for hours. Righteous turned out to be a solid guy. It just shows that some guys take a while to get to know. Russ was kind of like my friend Richard from the *Unforgiven Sinners* in that regard. I hadn't liked Richard when I first met him, but later on, he became a true friend.

Another group of three *Angels* was related, only this time by blood. The Baxters, a father and his two sons, were in the Berdoo *Hells Angels*. The father was named TJ Baxter, and the sons were Henry and Beau. We never heard of two generations of a family belonging to a bike club. It seemed like a cool idea to us, although, few of us in the *Wheel Lords* could imagine being in a club with our own father. I suppose there are quite a few father and son combinations in various clubs today, but back in the 1970's, it was unusual.

TJ Baxter seemed like a good guy, and Beau, whom I knew a little, was exceptionally smart and well spoken. Beau was one of those people, like Dennis in our club, who generally spoke up only after careful consideration, which was a bit of a rarity for many bikers.

Joey Martin was a San Jose *Hells Angel* who was always on his bike. We'd run into Joey around town at the biker bars, or at our friend Planch's bike shop, and Joey was usually on his scoot. Joey was okay, although we weren't good friends or anything.

I thought it was a good thing to see *Angels* on their bikes. Some of the *Angels* didn't seem to ride too much and, as time went on, some of them rode even less. We would see *Angels* driving a new Pontiac Grand Prix, or a limited edition Corvette, or some other fancy ride, and we would think . . . *what the hell?* I mean, we drove cars around too, of course, but some of the *HA* seemed to spend most of their time in a nice ride and darned little time on a motorcycle.

Not Joey Martin. If you saw Joey, 90% of the time he was on his bike. Joey liked to do a little thing that a few of the *Angels* would sometimes do. Upon entering a bar, Joey would head to the jukebox and look to play the country song *Kiss an Angel Good Morning* by Charlie Pride. Recall that tune? Then he would go over to people who weren't in his club (like me), slap them on the back, get up close and sing along to the words "You've got to . . . Kiss an *Angel* good morning . . ."

Cute, Joey. I get it. Now go away.

Drew in our club had a favorite expression he used to say back in the days before either of us had a bike. This was in Drew's *wannabe biker* stage. Satan, just goofing around, would say, "I ain't bad, but the bad call me sir." That was funny at the time.

Joey Martin was joking around at a bar once and said to me, "Is it all right if I sit down at this bar stool, Mr. *Wheel Lord* Sir? I mean, if it wouldn't trouble you any. Is that okay Mr. *Wheel Lord,* Sir?"

I walked over to Drew and said, "See . . .? I ain't *bad*, but the *bad* call me . . . *Sir*."

"Filthy Gilbert" Edwards was a Sacramento *Hells Angel*. Gilbert was a good man—an up front and plain-talking sort. Gil had a sandy blond beard and hair. He looked an awful lot like the Western singer Michael Martin Murphey.

Filthy had a look all his own. Gil usually rode with a long scarf and a long coat that looked like a cowboy's duster from the 1800's.

Gilbert completed his look by wearing cowboy spurs on his boot heels. Damn, I wish I had thought of that. Filthy actually looked as if he were a modern-day cowboy riding his iron horse. Maybe Gil had horses of his own, I didn't know. Regardless, Filthy sure looked as if he were straight out of the Wild West.

Brian Helton was a San Jose *Hells Angel,* and was President of the chapter during part of the time the *Wheel Lords* were around. Brian owned a small bike shop in downtown San Jose. Brian was a burly guy who had short dark hair and a mustache. He had the rugged good looks of a Hollywood action hero in the vein of a Tom Selleck.

Brian made himself a hard guy to know. Nearly all the *Angels* around town had outside friends in the scooter world, but it seemed to me that Brian did not. When I would go to Brian's shop to buy something, he always seemed peeved that he had to stop what he was doing to make a sale. Brian seemed bored and put out that he had to deal with the general public, which struck me as odd since his business was dependent upon that public for its livelihood.

I can't say I actually liked Brian, but then I can't say I disliked him, either. In fact, it was hard to find anyone who seemed to know him well. Brian certainly had my respect. He must have had the respect of his chapter too, because they elected him as President.

I was President of our club during part of Brian's tenure and so we interacted from to time. Our conversations were always direct and cordial but never overly friendly or laced with any humor. That was fine. Brian was always up front with us, and I appreciated it.

One day I got home from work and turned on the local television news. The San Jose Police Department made a high-profile bust in town earlier that afternoon, and news cameras just happened to be along to record the event. The cameras showed the San Jose PD, the DEA, the ATF, and other Feds surrounding Brian's small house, and going up to the front door to batter it down and arrest any occupants.

There was just one minor problem. The cops could not gain entry into the house. The door was reinforced metal, and the windows were barred. As the cameras ran, the cops and agents were frantically trying to force their way into the house, to no avail. The authorities finally managed to enter the premises after a half-hour or so, and found no one home. A condensed version of the whole scene, including the failed door crashing attempts, ran on the newscast. I imagine the cops finally caught Brian some time later.

In this case, any *Wheel Lord* would have been glad to offer some advice had the San Jose cops ever asked us, although we never talked with them.

Brian Helton? Yeah, you'll find that guy's hard to get to know.

Going out of his way to be kind to me was the Oakland *Hells Angel,* Choctaw— he was the guy who once loaned me some much-needed gas tanks for my bike.

He was older than we were and spent time with our club as a kind of mentor and sounding board. He was involved with the MMA Board of Directors and had a good head for the procedural side of things. Choctaw seemed to be self-educated, and had an extensive book collection in his house. He loaned me some books a few times. Choctaw was an interesting guy to sit and around and BS with. He was the kind of guy who could give younger guys advice while not sounding as if he were preaching or talking down to them. Choctaw's real name was Chester Maggliocco, which was a mouthful—maybe that's why he was called Choctaw, I don't know. At any rate, Choctaw seemed like one of those elders of an Indian tribe, offering wise and sage advice to the younger people. I learned a lot from Choctaw, and I think a lot of our members would say the same.

Wolf was a *Hells Angel* from the Nomads charter. We met Wolf early in our first year in Sacramento at an MMA function. Wolf was tall, and had long blond hair. He looked as if he should be on stage as part of the Allman Brothers Band. Wolf was like SoCal Stan in that he did a lot of legwork for the MMA, and the independent bikers from his area of Contra Costa County all thought he was cool. I did, too. Wolf (I saw the guy off and on for six years and never did know his real name) treated everyone with respect and had no false pretensions. Like Joey Martin of San Jose, Wolf rode his bike a lot. He also had an understated wit that he would sometimes show.

Ron Roloff of the MMA also liked Wolf a lot. Roloff called him "Big Water" or "Tall Man" sometimes. One time when Wolf passed by me somewhere, I tried to address him like that, but the words just came out wrong. I jumbled up Roloff's two nicknames and I ended up saying "Hey there, Big Man." I immediately knew that didn't sound right, but it was out there. I mean, usually when you hear the words "Big Man" they are said sarcastically. I hadn't said it that way, but still, it could be a problem.

Wolf remained quite calm, though. He looked at me a second and then said, "Hey, what's up Kidd?"

The next time I met up with Wolf, I made a point to say his name.

"Hey Wolf, how are you doing?"

"Kidd, what's going on? . . . Big Man."

Touché . . . I thought.

Another time, on an early Sunday morning at a smaller MMA Run, I was eating bacon and eggs with a Coca-Cola chaser at a small café near the run site. (I never drink coffee *or* tea). Wolf and his old lady (whose name I forget, but she was nice) came in and sat down at the small table with me.

Wolf looked at what I was eating and drinking. Then he said, "I'm gonna tell your mother that you drink Coke for breakfast."

Now *that's* just *wrong*.

Lyle Grisham was President of the San Jose *Hells Angels* when we received our MMA sanction in 1973. Lyle always treated our Club with respect. Lyle exuded a quiet confidence, and seemed to have his act together—at least I thought so. He was one of those guys, like our friend Don Lundberg that I tried to emulate—with but limited success, I fear.

Lyle was perhaps five years older than I was, and had gone to high school not far from where I lived in Los Gatos, but seemed to have been around forever. Lyle was shown in the Rolling Stones movie *Gimme Shelter* that detailed the Stones' 1969 Altamont Concert. Lyle was one of the *Angels* on stage with a pool cue in hand.

I didn't know Lyle well, but he treated me fairly, and I liked the way he carried himself. Lyle just seemed to have a smooth way about him. Bear, in our club, knew Lyle better than I did. Bear worked as a part-time bartender at a local watering hole in the Cambrian area of San Jose called the Melody Lounge. It wasn't a biker hangout or anything.

Lyle used to go there in street clothes, and that's how Bear and he got to be friends.

It wasn't unusual for some of the outlaw club types to frequent local run of the gin-mill places without their colors. Sometimes they just wanted to go to some nearby place to relax and not draw attention to themselves.

Another guy in the San Jose chapter was not quite so laid back. Tom Damatto was an extroverted personality. Tom was a tall guy who was, like many in the San Jose chapter, into martial arts. Tom was President during part of our time as a club and had longish, wavy black hair.

Tom acted like a stereotypical New Yorker. He may have actually been from New York . . . I'm not sure. Tom liked to talk fast, which is cool because, on occasion, I liked to listen fast. Tom would also like to make his verbal points as a New Yorker does. However, he would take time to listen to your side, too. Conversation with Tom tended to be lawyer-like. Each side would present its argument, and then have to defend it. Talking with Tom was kind of like being in that movie that came out years later, *My Cousin Vinnie*.

Tom was also into needling and teasing people, big time, which was another reason why I liked him. One time Tom, Lucas from my Club, and I rode back to San Jose from a *Hells Angel* funeral in San Francisco. We took Highway 280 south from The City, which was, as usual, cold, windy, and foggy.

When we got to St. Joe, Tom gave me a hard time about the ride. "Kidd, every time I looked over, you had a death grip on your handlebars. It looked like you were going to go flying off your bike at any moment. You need to put on some weight, dude."

He had a point. Sometimes, when I was riding fast and it was windy, I kind of felt as if I were about to go horizontal. It reminded me a little of that tornado scene in the *Wizard of Oz* when everybody was being blown backwards through the storm.

Doug Jones was another San Jose *Hells Angel* who had an influence on me. Doug was an older guy who was extremely well liked by all of us in the *Wheel Lords*. Doug was similar to Choctaw from

Oakland and Richard from the *Sinners* in the way he would share his knowledge and experiences with me. Yet, you never felt as if you were being talked down to with Doug. He treated you as if you had value— and that you had real worth.

Now, to be sure, Doug never let you forget that he was the *Hells Angel* and you were not. In fact, all the *Angels* would do that, no matter how friendly they were. However, Doug didn't try to leverage any extra mileage off his status as a long-time *Hells Angel*. If Doug respected you, he treated you as an equal. Hanging around Doug Jones was a lot of fun.

Like many bikers of that time, Doug's bike, which he rode a lot, was all black. He had script painted on his gas tanks that read "Schwarz Wie Mein Herz" . . . German for, "Black Like My Heart."

That was funny, but from my view, inaccurate. I thought Doug Jones had a big heart, and . . . it wasn't black.

Davey Magruder was the Daly City *Hells Angel* who was with Marie before she and I got together. Davey was another one of those beefy guys who seemed to be everywhere in the local scooter world. He was barrel-chested and balding. Davey had poor eyesight and wore Buddy Holly-type eyeglasses. In fact, Davey looked a bit like Matt in our club, except that Matt was younger and had darker hair. Davey, frequently called "DR," was clearly *not* one of those *Angels* who rode around in a fancy Indy pace car. DR was into motorcycles and, like our Rocky, a car or truck was practically an afterthought. Davey rode his bike nearly all the time.

Daly City was something of a misnomer as far as a chapter location for the *Angels*. Daly City is just over the county line from San Francisco in San Mateo County. However, many of the *Angels* lived in mid-county, mostly in the Redwood City or San Mateo area. I doubt if any of the Daly City *Angels* actually lived in Daly City. Davey and a few others lived in Mountain View, which is actually in Santa Clara County. Confused? Me too. I think those guys liked it that way.

At any rate, whenever I spent time with Davey I enjoyed myself. DR was a full time, dedicated *Hells Angel*, but he was also a down to earth, up front man. After Marie and I split up, Davey had a few kind words to say to me, which I appreciated. He was easily one of the best people in the biker scene I ever met. Whenever it was that Davey was voted in as a member of the *Hells Angels*, the guys who voted him in . . . well . . . they had a good day.

Brad Loxley of the San Jose *Hells Angels* was one of the funniest people I have ever met. He ranked right up with Drew and Bear in our club as true masters of mirth. Loxley had a biting sense of humor. He would skewer anyone and everyone he came across, even other *Angels* on occasion, with his wit.

Brad had all kinds of sayings that were all his own. He would refer to people whom he thought of as stupid or arrogant as, "battling foot pegs", whatever that meant. He would call people "*Pop Tarts*", or "rumkins", or all sorts of other unique names.

One of Loxley's favorite sayings was a "slap in the mail". Lox was always saying he was going to send "so and so" a slap in the mail. I once asked him just what did that entail, really. How does one send a "slap" in the mail?

"Oh, you just write—

Dear Dickhead,

Enclosed, please find one slap.

As always,

Your friend, Lox."

Glad he cleared that up.

Brad had a steady stream of cutting comments for everyone he met. If anything looked slightly unusual or out of place, Loxley would jump right in with some remark.

"Kidd, did you see that guy's boots? They look like snowshoes. Did he come in on a dogsled? Is *Frosty the Snowman* out front? Are we in San Jose or Yodelville?" Brad went on and on with that kind of stuff all the time. I was glad Loxley would confide in me, but sometimes he seriously needed an editor, which I would often try to do— but then, hell—he hardly ever listened to me. He was too busy thinking up the next joke. The only way to slow Loxley down temporarily was to come up with a better joke, which I did sometimes, although that would prompt a new thread for Brad to attack.

Loxley once moved to a different house in south San Jose, near Foxworthy Avenue. It was on a street named Kilo. No *really*, it was called Kilo. For the next three months, Loxley beat the same joke into the ground to everyone he talked to. "Yeah, why don't you stop by my new place? Want the address? It's 2.2 Kilo Avenue . . . Got it?"

Nevertheless, most of the time, Brad was fresh and original. He would continually surprise me with his comments. Loxley and his chatter reminded me of when I first met Drew from our club when I was shooting pool at my friend Givens' place. Brad wasn't all about the jokes, though. He could be serious and menacing in an instant, just like all the *Angels*. Brad was constantly searching the room for some shit to instigate. It was a positive thing to have your "A" game handy when old Lox was around.

It turned out that Brad was from Neosho, Missouri, which wasn't that far from where I had grown up in Springfield. As I remember, though, Brad didn't know Old Doc Norman or Otis Pierce from the old country.

Unfortunately, Loxley had a severe case of, "jokeus interruptus", when the cops busted him for selling crank, and threw him in Soledad Prison. I went down and visited him a few times. The bad news was . . . he hated the place. The good news was . . . Ol' Lox had an entirely new captive audience to entertain.

✑ *Chapter Twenty-Three* ❧

"Wheels Fall Off"

We formed the *Wheel Lords* MC in 1973 with no thought given to making any money. Things held to plan quite well . . . we were always broke. We all worked at real jobs, but money was scarce all around for us. That was the way for nearly everyone we knew in the early 1970's. Everybody struggled financially, especially scooter tramps.

Things began to change late in that decade. California home prices began to take off. Silicon Valley was expanding significantly, and jobs were plentiful—even for guys like us. All of us in the club had regular jobs, at least most of the time. None of us in the club was flush or anything. Most of us still lived in rented houses. The only guy in the club who owned his own home was Matt.

It was becoming more expensive to live in California than it had been. Only a few years before, I had gone on weekend runs with as little as $10 in my pocket. All I needed was a few bucks for burgers and fries, a few more for some beers, and $1.50 to refill my gas tank, so I could make it home. Then recite a prayer or two that I wouldn't suffer a mechanical breakdown on the bike.

However, by the late '70's, everything was costing more; including gas prices that had gone up following the OPEC oil embargos. You could no longer live as cheaply as when I first moved out of my mom's house to the apartment I shared with Rick and Nate. Consequently, we all began to spend more energy making a living, and taking the financial side of life a little more seriously.

Some of the guys started families, too. Drew and Lisa had a daughter. Dennis and Joann had two children. Rocky and ex-wife Sandi had two sons. Bear and Kate had a daughter. We were starting to look like the original Club of '73, with half the guys having kids.

The culture around us in the San Jose scooter world was changing, too. As I said before, many of the bikers we knew, both in clubs and independents, were driving around in fancier cars and spending less time riding their bikes. Some guys, like Jacob in the *Sinners*, even bought boats and spent a lot of time with that crowd. Nobody in our club had those toys, but you could sense a change in the air.

Then, too, a lot of the local bike clubs folded. The *Unforgiven Sinners* closed down in 1978, and the *East Side* MC and the *West Side* MC disbanded around that same time, as well. We stopped holding the "All Clubs" meetings because there were so few clubs left. More clubs would soon emerge—that always happened. However, for a time, it was just the *Angels* and the *Wheel Lords*, at least as far as I can remember.

Our relations with the MMA changed, also. There were ongoing problems with Ron Roloff, due to differing opinions on some matters; most of them having to do with the role our club should perform. There was no singular main point of contention, just a series of disagreements and arguments.

Personally, I still liked Ron, but I didn't care for some of his attitudes and beliefs. Roloff was skilled at arguing—hey, he had to be; after all, he was a professional lobbyist. Some of us in the *Wheel Lords* were pretty versed in that skill, also. It made for some engaging conversations between us.

Essentially, we were tired of babysitting the drunks and loudmouths at statewide runs, and even more fed up with the bozos we had to oversee at the *Easyriders* swap meets. Roloff and some of the MMA Board saw those things a little differently, so that was the basis for quite a bit of our discord. There must have been some power struggles within the MMA Board because we were told that some of them were sympathetic to us. However, that supposed political intrigue didn't matter to us.

Roloff's autocratic rule of the MMA's direction was being challenged not just by some of the Board and, to a lesser extent, our club, but also by a number of the MMA reps, especially the ones in Southern California. They were engaged in their own beefs with Roloff. We got feedback from some of the MMA reps, and even from some of the board members, of ongoing proposals and counter proposals being tossed back and forth between those groups and Roloff. In retrospect, I guess Ron was having a tough time all around. It never affected our participation—or Roloff's either, for that matter—in any MMA events. We all continued to work together and had a drink afterwards, just as we always had. Still, everyone knew that things were changing.

The MMA as a whole was still quite effective. There was no helmet law in California, thanks in no small part to the two governors in office during the 1970's—Democrat Jerry Brown and, earlier, Republican Ronald Reagan. Those state executives were distant from one another politically, but each believed strongly in individual liberty.

The *Wheel Lords* biggest problem had nothing to do with politics or the MMA. It was keeping our member strength up. We had never been a large club, and that was okay, but we were slowly losing members, and not seeing them replaced. I maintained our biggest obstacle was the dual role we had. We were a club first and a support group for the MMA second. However, taking on two such heavy-duty responsibilities was too much for most guys who would come around and check us out. We never had a lot of guys who wanted to join the club. They would see how much real work was involved in supporting the MMA, and that the required effort would override the benefits of being part of our tight group. It took a special biker to commit to the requirements of a club and to take on all the duties we performed to benefit the MMA. Guys like Bear and Rocky, who *were* that special, were rare.

Matt quit the club some months before, much in the same way that Frank left a few years earlier. I don't recall his exact reasons, but I do remember that we were plenty pissed off at him. Matt had been the only member to leave the club and come back, and now he was pulling out again. That really hurt, since Matt was involved in just about everything and could always be counted on, whether it was for the fun times or for the hard work.

By the spring of 1979, some of us realized that Matt leaving the club a few months earlier had just been another symptom of the changing times. Each of us was changing, too. It would only be a matter of time until someone else left the club; and without any rush of new members, we would eventually fall apart.

I guess we were all becoming a little more mainstream than we had been. We had jobs and obligations, and quite a few of the guys now had families. It took a lot more cash to "get by" in the late '70's than it did earlier in that decade. All of us in the club had to deal with the realities of the world.

Then, too, I think we were growing a little tired of one another. We were together for extended periods of time nearly every weekend. Since there were only six of us, we probably got on one another's nerves a little. If we would have had 15 or so members, our time with one another would have been diluted somewhat, and we probably would have kept a fresher outlook on things. I'm not saying we were arguing all the time, or that we didn't like each other. It's just that the six of us knew each other—and each other's flaws—a little too well. When we had a chance to separate ourselves from each other and the MMA, no matter how briefly, we generally took it.

One example was when I moved out of the Agnew's house that Marie and I lived in. I had to move out because the landlord wanted to move his mother in. I found a small place in west San Jose that wasn't half-bad, but I couldn't get any of my club brothers to help me move. They all had something else to do that day. I wasn't as mad as I was disappointed. That would have never happened a few years earlier. The only guy who helped me move was our great friend Don Lundberg, who came down from the Frisco area on his day off with his truck and saved my butt.

Another sign of change was the break-ups between guys and their old ladies. I forget the order, and I'm not sure if some of these splits occurred before or after the club folded, but in pretty quick succession, a lot of guys were without an old lady. Lucas and Trixie broke up. Dennis and Joann divorced. Even Lisa finally had enough of Drew's ways, and she divorced him. Rocky and Sandi were divorced. Only Bear and Kate remained as a couple who had been together for any extended time. Most of the other guys soon found new old ladies; so it wasn't as if anybody were in a state of depression or anything. It was just one more aspect of our lifestyle that was in flux.

As for my personal situation during this period, it was kind of up and down. I had a decent job, and I could pay my bills. I'd had to move from the cool little house in Agnews, but those things happen. The real change for me was not having a steady girlfriend. All the time I had been in the club I lived with a girl—first, Veronica, and then, Marie. I had grown quite used to that luxury, and a little spoiled, I suppose. I was a solo act for the first time in five years.

I went out with a few of the women where I worked, and dated some girls around town from the biker scene. Heck, I even saw Marie a time or two. She returned from France, where things hadn't quite worked out for her. She made trips to Europe over the next year or so, with some modeling stints to L.A. and other places, too. We had some sporadic contact from time to time, mostly at her convenience. Those, "quickie blur, thank you sir", times just weren't working, though. We were never going to get back together, so finally we ceased all contact.

But, hey . . . we'll always have Paris.

The club talked at length in our weekly church meetings as to what our next step should be. There were some differences of opinions on things, but on one matter, there was complete agreement. We were determined not to continue to work the swap meets and statewide runs in the same way as before. We needed more input as to how things were run. We were devoting too much time, effort, and financial resources to the MMA, without the corresponding authority we thought we had earned.

We decided to draw up a proposal for the MMA Board to consider. It was our take on the situation between Roloff and our club, and some suggested solutions to get things back on a more even keel between us. We didn't think the MMA Board would necessarily adopt our changes, but we felt compelled to speak up nonetheless. I don't recall the details of our proposal, but it was a well thought out, proper presentation, at least it was in our estimation. A few of the MMA Board members who were sympathetic to us got the proposal on the agenda at the next meeting.

Over the next week or so, while we were awaiting feedback from our proposal, we had serious discussions among ourselves as to where everyone's heads were at as to our future as a viable club. We all agreed that we would not continue the status quo with the MMA unless some of our changes were made. Beyond that, though, we had some divergent views.

A few guys, including me, wanted to continue as the *Wheel Lords* and simply drop the MMA sanction. We could still support the MMA, but not devote so much time and resources to it. Instead, we could use our energies to build up our club, and drop the dual responsibilities that had worn us thin. I didn't care if we called ourselves an "outlaw" club or not. If we wanted to go that path, and guys were comfortable with it, fine. To my mind, we should just call ourselves a club and forget the labels. We could figure out those details later.

Some other members didn't see things that way. A few felt that they had joined an MMA club, and if their club were not going to be linked to the MMA, then their obligation was over. They might not want to continue as a club at that point. That stance surprised and disappointed me, but it was an honest one.

A couple of the other guys said they had no problem dropping the MMA connection, but if we did then they would have to rethink their commitment to the *Wheel Lords*. They weren't sure that they wanted to be in an outlaw type club with the current make-up of our membership.

Again, it was a view that I wasn't keen on, but it's what a few guys felt, so it was real. We had to be honest with one another.

I don't recall all the details of who thought what exactly, much less the reasons that were behind those thoughts. As usual, everyone was up front with things, and that was cool. The bottom line was that if things with the MMA didn't improve we were going to shut down the club. None of us wanted to continue with the status quo.

As I remember, the guy who thought most like me during this time was Rocky. We just wanted to continue the *Wheel Lords* MC and drop the MMA tag. To us, it was straightforward. We do our own thing—end of story. We even started thinking of new club colors. However, two guys don't make a club; so things weren't going to go in that direction.

We presented our proposal to the MMA Board, and then waited to hear feedback. None of us were optimistic that things would go our way. It seemed that the club was in the circumstances of the times as the 1970's began to give way to the 1980's. The combination of the waning of bike clubs in general, the changing economic times, the squabbles within the MMA, the low club membership, and the personal struggles and changing priorities of many of us seemed to all come together to force us to shut down the club.

We got the news we expected. The MMA Board, though split, was still backing Roloff and his way of doing things. That was fair enough, it was their call. We had a last club meeting or two, but no one had any enthusiasm for the upcoming run season; and, since we couldn't get more than a few guys to agree on any clear new direction for the club, we shut down the *Wheel Lords* MC in April 1979.

Our last club activity occurred a week or so before we folded. We held the local San Jose Blood Run, which we had always hosted. That year, after the usual blood donations at the San Jose Red Cross facility, we led the pack of assembled bikers to Frank Raines County Park. Raines was located deep in the Coastal Mountain Range east of San Jose. The most direct route to Raines was the most difficult—up the extremely windy road from San Jose that wound past the 4,000-foot elevation of Lick Observatory at Mt. Hamilton; and then along more twisting miles of narrow road over more ranges of mountains to San Antonio junction. From there, Del Puerto Canyon Road, with a six-mile stretch of gravel roadway, led down the eastern slope of the range towards Raines Park.

For safety's sake, we led the pack and the follow vehicles the long way around, over the Altamont Pass, and down Interstate 5 into Stanislaus County. Then, we rode the 17 miles up Del Puerto Canyon from the San Joaquin Valley. For being on the fringe of the San Francisco Bay Area, with millions of people living relatively nearby, it was hard to find a more isolated spot than Raines Park. Few people even knew it existed. It was a perfect place to hold a run. We had a band there that night, and the park rangers let us use the buildings on-site. We had about a hundred people all told at the run site, and we had the whole park to ourselves.

The next day, after everyone else left and the club finished packing, we got on our bikes and headed out on our last ride together as a club. We went the direct route—up the Canyon to San Antonio junction where there was a small bar and gas station. The place was called, "The Junction". It was kind of the gathering spot for the few locals who lived there year round. There was a large, open shooting range out behind "The Junction" where hunters could get in some last-minute practice. There were hawks soaring in the sky and all sorts of wildlife in the woods and hills surrounding it.

It was a terrific set-up, and the guy running the place—a burly, mountain man type—seemed determined to keep it that way. He eyed us warily as we entered. He saw club colors on us and thought the worst might happen to his family and his business. He probably had one hand on his shotgun below the bar the whole time we were there.

We sat around and had a beer or two. Bear played some country music on the jukebox. This was to be our last ride as a group, even though nothing was official yet. Nevertheless, everyone knew the end of the club was coming, and most of us were in a reflective mood.

Then came one of those times when everything seems to coalesce into one moment of utter clarity. Remember when that has happened to you? Some small event occurs, and it just stays with you forever. You can't shake it, even if you want to. For me, one of those moments came when the jukebox that day played the song *El Paso City,* by Marty Robbins. That tune, a tie-in to Robbins' earlier epic song *El Paso,* had been a country hit a few years before, although it hadn't been special to me. But on that day, in that setting, that song—which spoke of a modern traveler flying over the west Texas sand and believing he could have a supernatural link to the original ballad's tragic tale—seemed to bring everything into focus for me.

I never considered myself a spiritual person, and certainly not an overly religious one. I'm not saying that on that day, I immediately began to believe in reincarnation, or that fate controls our destiny. I just felt that hearing that song speaking to the cycle of life, the possibilities of time and space, and previous lives brought a calmness and sense of closure to the situation I found myself in. When I heard *El Paso City* that day, it seemed to have prompted an instant attitude adjustment. It got me to thinking about a lot of things.

It was soon time to go. We finished our beers, and the guys started to head outside. However, I couldn't leave just yet. I told the guys I wanted to linger at The Junction for a spell, and I would see them later back in San Jose.

I watched the boys start up their bikes and head out on San Antonio Valley Road. It was the last time I would see those patches together in a pack. They . . . looked . . . great.

I bought another beer and played *El Paso City* on the jukebox a couple more times. The mountain man storeowner finally relaxed a little.

My thoughts went back to when I had seen my first chopper at the McDonald's some nine years earlier. Had it been that long ago? It had been a spring day then, too. In many ways, I was in the same situation then as I was now. I was still living in west San Jose, and struggling to get by. I had no steady girlfriend. Hell, I was about *not* to be in a motorcycle club anymore, either.

What I did have was the confidence and determination that I could never have imagined having back in 1970. Being in the *Wheel Lords* gave me that. I wondered if the other guys felt the same about themselves. I guess they had to. How could they not?

I thought back to all the things I had seen—the good and bad times I had been through over the past decade. What a wondrous adventure—what a fabulous time.

I thought back on all the friends I met through the club. Don Lundberg, Marty, Ron Roloff, Planch, jeez . . . the list went on and on. I was lucky to have known them all.

I thought of the *Unforgiven Sinners*, and Darren, Richard, Zip and Bear, and all the others—even the ones I didn't like much. It was great to have been around them.

I thought of the *Hells Angels*. The ones I knew and the ones I just observed. A lot of those guys had been terrific to me. A few had acted like jerks, but those were more than offset by guys like Davey, Loxley, Wolf, Choctaw, and Doug. I'd had a learning experience that no college could ever match.

I thought back on the old ladies I'd been with over the last decade. Each had been so special to me, so full of life. Things hadn't worked out long term for me, but hey . . . I wasn't about to stop trying.

Lastly, I thought back on the guys who were in the *Wheel Lords* with me. I thought of the original guys like Keith, Howie, Old Man Phil, and John Howell. They had taken a chance on a skinny kid they had never met before who—*oh, and by the way*—had just bought his first actual motorcycle. I thought back to the guys in the club who had come and gone quickly. Why had I stayed and not them? Maybe that's just how things are. Who knows?

I thought back to Matt, Mitch the Sleaze and Fast Frank. They were once brothers to me in the *Wheel Lords,* which ranks them over almost everyone else in the world, but they didn't last to the end. And so, we were brothers no more.

Mostly, I thought of my true *Wheel Lord* Brothers . . . the ones who had lasted until the wheels fell off: Drew, Lucas, Dennis, Ben, and Greg. They overlooked my flaws and shortcomings, and accepted me fully for who I was. I had gotten from them so much more than I had given. I could never pay them back. I started to get a little down; but, then I realized that maybe going through life knowing you will always owe something to special people is a commendable thing. In an odd way, it rather sets the spirit free.

It was time to head down off the mountain and return to San Jose. I walked out of the bar and fired up my bike. Then, it died. That reminded me of the first night I rode my Harley. It was the same night that we became an official club. I couldn't help but smile as I remembered how I had kicked and kicked the newly rebuilt Knucklehead that night until—finally, it started . . . and then died. "No matter though. I had started my own Harley. My own *fucking* Harley! I did it once. I'll do it again."

Then I kicked the pedal through once more.

Shiloh started first try.

That's my girl.

I revved the engine. The bike made the difference, of course. The confidence, the determination, the experiences, the attitude—these things were the intangibles I now possessed. However, Shiloh . . . well, she was the tangible that brought everything together . . . for me and for everyone like me. Sure, the bike was just a symbol . . . but *oh, what a symbol* she was.

I shifted into first gear. I looked around at the serenity of the countryside. *Some day I'm going to move out of the city,* I thought. I lingered for a moment. This would be my last real ride as a *Wheel Lord*. I had come a far piece, but there were a lot of winding turns in the road yet traveled. For that matter, it was time to find a new, righteous old lady. "I did it once. I'll do it again."

I headed out the Canyon Road, down the hill to St. Joe. My heart felt heavy, but my soul seemed weightless. I was on the road once more . . . life is good.

I rolled Shiloh through the first of many curves. I did it once. I'll do it again. Hell, I could do almost anything now.

After all, I had once been a *Wheel Lord*.

"Stood alone on a mountaintop starin' out at the Great Divide
I could go east, I could go west, it was all up to me to decide
Just then I saw a young hawk flyin' and my soul began to rise
And pretty soon
My heart was singin'
Roll, roll me away, I'm gonna roll me away tonight
Gotta keep rolling, gotta keep riding,
Keep searchin' til I find what's right..."

Bob Seger, "Roll Me Away"

✑ *Chapter Twenty-Four* ✎

"My Density"

"Don't you draw the queen of diamonds, boy
She'll beat you if she's able
You know the queen of hearts
Is always your best bet."

The Eagles, "Desperado"

After the club folded, a few of the guys set out in new directions. I don't recall the exact time frame, but over the next couple of years, many of the guys began to scatter.

Bear started a janitorial business in San Mateo County. Not long after that, Bear's father-in-law moved his manufacturing company from the Bay Area to Chico, a small city in the Sacramento Valley. Bear took a job in the firm, and he and Kate and their daughter moved to Chico and a cozy set-up in a nice area of California.

Rocky went even further. He moved to a small town in Missouri to open a motorcycle shop with one of his old friends. It would be the first of many moves across the length of the country for Rocky.

To be near his kids, who were still living with his ex-wife, Joann, Dennis stayed in San Jose. He kept his same job and we saw each other regularly.

Lucas also remained in San Jose, although he first spent some time with his brother Jimmy and others of his family in the Pacific Northwest. We kept in touch quite a bit and did some riding together.

Drew took a different turn. He moved into a shared place with some people in south San Jose who knew nothing about the bike scene. I hadn't seen Drew around anybody but bikers for ten years, but suddenly he seemed to have little interest in scooters. His new passion became outrigger canoe racing. He joined a crew that worked out on Vasona Lake every weekend. Drew got into top-notch physical shape during this time, but we rarely saw one another. I was glad to see him get involved in something he enjoyed. It just seemed strange that he picked outrigger canoes.

Sometime later, Drew dropped the paddling and needed a place to live. I was only too happy to have him move into my duplex. I owed Drew and Lisa—big time— for letting me stay at their house for as long as they did. Drew lived at my place for a time, and then moved on to a different place in town.

Somewhere along the way, I don't recall when, Drew sold his bike. He said it was just a temporary move, and that he would soon buy another. I disagreed, and told him so. Guys like us—we just don't manage to wheel and deal and buy and sell bikes that often. The quick cash you would realize from the sale of your most cherished possession would soon be gone. Then you would be faced with the large task of replacing your bike—probably at a higher price. No, it was better if you found another method to get some bucks together than selling your scoot. I'd seen too many guys sell their bike to buy some "have to have" item, and then never own a motorcycle again. I hoped that wouldn't happen to Drew.

As for me, over the next few years, I kicked around the bike scene in San Jose a bit, but I didn't actually fit in too well with the independent biker crowd. I partied with some of our old friends from the club days, and that was fine. The spark and the drive weren't as strong as it had been in the days of the *Wheel Lords*. That wasn't a surprise. I expected as much.

I stopped at the MMA office whenever I passed through Sacramento, to say hello. Roloff and I still got along well, even though we'd had our differences over the years. Ron was still doing excellent work in the legislature and all of us from the club still supported the association. Roloff still had many entertaining stories about politics and politicians and other lobbyists.

Besides still riding my scoot, I developed some other interests. I continued with the competitive darts team we formed on my work site. My close friend, Larry Rowe made a dynamite partner for my alter ego D'Artagnan. Larry was a former college football lineman and was a super competitive guy. Larry exuded intensity from every pore. We pushed each other all the time to improve, and the teams we were on won our share of league titles. Larry was a fun guy to share beers with. He would have made a great biker . . . if only he'd had a passion for motorcycles, that is.

Two other guys who joined our darts team became close friends of mine. Ronny Duval and Terry Lewis had been best friends for years when they hired on at the company where I was working. Ronny was quiet, yet quick with his wit. Terry was the gregarious type who was sort of a Jimmy Buffet laid-back beach guy. They were about the same age as me and, although we had different backgrounds, we shared a lot of common ground and experiences.

My mom gave me an old set of golf clubs about that same time. The set originally belonged to my grandfather. I was one of those people who thought that football and baseball were the only real sports, and golf didn't measure up. I knew nothing about golf, although I caddied for my step dad, Clay a few times years before. He and his buddies would hit the links with a putter in one hand and a beer in the other. They were hackers, but they always had fun.

One day, I decided to give the old clubs a try. It turned out my old friend, Roy Givens got into golf at the same time as I did. There was a golf boom going on in the early 1980's, and Givens and I joined right in. We ended up playing a lot of golf over the next few years. Neither one of us was any good, though. I played a lot with Ronny Duval, too. Ronny was a decent player, and had the patience to put up with my game. I found that I genuinely liked being on a golf course. The problem was that I was a lousy player. For me, most trips to the golf course turned into a Bobby Fuller Day. I fought the ball . . . and the ball won.

Another friend I made through my work place was Rick George. Rick has the driest and most sarcastic humor I've ever seen. I'm cynical, but Rick makes me look like a motivational speaker. Rick and his young family moved away from Silicon Valley a few years after we first met, but they settled in the same town in the Sierras where my mom lived. That worked out well, as I would go to my mom's place a few times each year for family functions; and, while there, I would hang with Rick and we'd catch up on things.

The other close friend I met at work during this time was Steve Vogelsanger. Stevie is about my age and is one of the funniest people on the planet. He's also super smart, and an excellent blues guitarist. Stevie rivaled Loxley and Bear as the all-around biggest cut-up I've known. Stevie has been known to turn a beer mug or a wine glass upside down on a frequent basis.

Like most of my other friends at the time, Stevie had no interest in motorcycles. However, since I was into bikes, Steve would ask me all sorts of questions about the lifestyle, just so he was able to talk intelligently on the subject with a friend. In turn, I picked Steve's brain for his wide knowledge of the blues and rock guitarists of the day. Over the ensuing years, Stevie and I spent a lot of time hanging out and trading wisecracks. Stevie is also generous. He's the type of guy who would come over to help you move to a new place, and then take you out for dinner and drinks and pay for everything. He'd provide the comedy, too.

I had a few different girlfriends during that time, although nothing lasted for long. A few of the girls decided to stop seeing me, and a few I decided to stop seeing. The only relationship I had that was close to being serious was with Rocky's former sister-in-law. Diane was a tall, dark-haired, and attractive woman who treated me great. Unfortunately, I treated her *less* than great. We stopped seeing each other, which was my fault entirely.

I made a few trips back to Missouri to visit my dad during this time. Dad was in a care facility and recovered somewhat from his stroke. He could have improved a lot more, but he refused to participate in either speech or physical therapy. Dad's mind was still functioning well. My Uncle John would take us on drives around the area, just as my family had done 20 years earlier. Dad would point out familiar sights and make comments as best as he could. Still, Dad put no effort toward improving his situation. We all knew it was just a matter of time before his physical and mental condition would deteriorate. No one could convince him to go to any sort of therapy.

The good news, for me, was that I got to know my Uncle John well during those visits. He and my Aunt Mary were devoted to taking care of Dad. John was as religious and conservative as they come. However, he always accepted me—if not my lifestyle—completely. John and Mary had no children, and they would always do whatever they could for anyone in the family who needed their help. John was a terrific man and ranked right up there with my step dad Clay on the respect-o-meter.

I also got to know my Uncle Paul pretty well, too. He would drive me around and relate lots of stories from the old days when all of his brothers and sisters were growing up. I was lucky to be able to connect with some of the older generation of the Normans and learn some of the family history.

One day, in 1981, there was a new hire at the small electronics company in Sunnyvale, California where I worked. Her name was Sharon Wyatt, and she worked in the next office over from Steve Vogelsanger and me. Sharon was incredibly cute, outgoing, and had a dynamite figure. Once it was established that she was single, most of the guys in the company found some reason to stop by Sharon's office on some matter of great or trivial importance. I stopped by a few times myself—strictly on business, of course—and I ended up asking her out. Sharon turned me down, as she had done to any other guy at work who asked for a date. She thought she would get into trouble from her boss by being the new hire and dating guys from the office. I couldn't let small details like that stand in the way. I was too dazzled by this new woman in the next office.

Sharon and I became friends over the next few weeks, but I still had other plans. One day I saw an opportunity. Stevie had seen a floral arrangement delivered in the company lobby. It turned out to have been sent by Sharon's former boyfriend, a rich guy who lived in another town. I guess it was some kind of a "hope-for-a-makeup move", and it was a sweet idea, I suppose.

Stevie and I talked the receptionist into letting us deliver the flowers to Sharon's office. We made a detour on the way, and I whited out the dude's name on the card and substituted my own. Then we delivered the flowers to Sharon's office. I knew the little trick would be found out, but I thought that stunt just might prompt Sharon to agree to a date.

The delivered flowers were a huge hit, as was the ensuing discovery of my prank. Sharon then said she would consider going out with me, except that she never dated younger guys. Whoa, stop the presses! I told her I had her beat by years. She made me compare driver's licenses with her before she would believe that I was four years older than she was.

I finally got a "yes" to go out, although I have to say that I had never been carded for a date before. It also helped my cause when Sharon found out I rode a Harley. She wasn't a biker chick, but she may have been leaning that direction.

I had a few problems the night of our first date. My old friend Brad Loxley of the San Jose *Hells Angels* had just been released from prison that day. At the time, Brad was close to a girl who shared a rented house in San Jose with Lucas, my club brother from the *Wheel Lords.* Loxley was going to stop by Lucas's place, and we all agreed that I would come by, see Brad, and celebrate his return to town.

I stopped by Lucas's, and it was cool to see Loxley on the outside. We had a lot of laughs, some of which were at my expense. I'd gone out and purchased some fancy, black dress shoes for my date with Sharon. That was a leap for me, as all I usually wore were biker boots or sneakers. The trouble was that the style of the day was that disco crap— so the only shoes I could find had those platform type heels—which, as Johnny Cash sang about being named Sue, ". . . got a lot of laughs from a lot of folks."

The shoes weren't the only problem. I recently bought a three-piece suit. It wasn't a traditional suit, however. It was one of those light blue denim jobs, the kind that was popular in those days, with wide lapels and bell-bottoms. I looked like a refugee from the losing side in a Travolta dance-alike contest.

My next misstep was asking Lucas for advice on wine. I knew Sharon liked wine. I also knew I had zero knowledge on the subject. Weasel was only too happy to give me his recommendation.

"Oh, Kidd, you gotta get Mateus. It's great stuff."

"Mateus? Uhh . . . okay. I'll pick some up."

It took me a while to break away from Loxley and Lucas. I told them I had an important date, but they still gave me crap anyway (as I certainly would have done had I been in their position).

I arrived at Sharon's place about an hour late, but I hoped the wine might make up for it. It didn't. I could tell from the look on her face that my choice of Mateus was a washout. She put the bottle aside with some comment about how she might open it at "some later date." I didn't know then that Mateus was one small step up from Ripple.

Sharon asked why I was late, and wanting to get this new relationship off to an honest start, I told her the truth.

She considered my reply for a moment and then said, "Let me get this straight. You've been asking me out for weeks, and I finally say yes. Then you show up over an hour late, wearing disco clothes, and carrying a bottle of screw-top wine. Then, to top it off, the reason you are so late is that you had to first stop and see one of your friends—who just happens to be a *Hells Angel*— because he was only released from prison this very day. Is that about it?"

"Umm . . . well . . . actually . . . yes, you have the essential facts correct, I have to say. But, you know, when you put it that way, it sounds kind of funny, doesn't it?"

"Yeah, hilarious," she said.

Things weren't looking too promising for me. There was a minute of awkward silence.

At length Sharon said, "I have just one more question."

"Okay and that would be . . . what?"

"Where are we going? It's getting late."

We've been together since that night.

As it turned out, Sharon and I once lived near one another in East San Jose during the early club years. She lived on the other side of Story Road, perhaps a mile from where I lived in Drew and Lisa's house. We knew all the same stores, frequented many of the same eateries in that part of town—without ever having crossed paths.

It was probably a good thing that we hadn't met during those years. We both agreed after getting to know each other and comparing notes, that we almost certainly wouldn't have been compatible in those days. We decided that we met each other at just about the right time.

Once Sharon got to know my friends, she realized she had met Matt from our club back in the old days. Sharon had been at a friend's place when this big, bad biker guy came in with some other people. He was wearing a club patch and, when introduced to her, embraced Sharon and planted a big wet kiss on her mouth.

"Yep, sounds like Matt in one of his Jack Suede moments," I said.

Over time, Sharon got to know all the guys from the club days. Those of us still in the area continued to party together from time to time; and, although we were tamer than the club times, it was still a new experience for Sharon to be at biker parties.

We held a few club reunions on our anniversary date. Most of the guys who were anywhere nearby would try to make it. Once we were at Bear and Kate's place near Chico for an anniversary dinner. Drew noticed that Bear wasn't drinking.

Bear explained that he was clean and sober. He'd given up all booze and drugs. In fact, Ben said he was now a counselor, giving his time to mentoring young people with substance problems.

I rarely heard Drew laugh so long as he did then.

"What!" he said. "Barburger, who are you trying to bullshit?"

Bear insisted he was serious.

Drew remained unconvinced. "You're telling me that if an 18-year-old chickie lay down in front of you, naked, with a line of cocaine spread across her belly . . . that you would just sit there. And counsel her?"

"Yes."

"Bull-fucking-shit, Benny," laughed Drew.

We all had to laugh at that one.

One thing Sharon took to right away was riding on the bike. We'd go on rides through the mountains around San Jose, or sometimes head out with some friends on weekend runs. Some of us even hit our old run site at Black Butte Reservoir, near Orland, a few times.

One of our rides together stands out in my memory. We were going for a ride through the Santa Cruz Mountains one afternoon, and planned on stopping at various locations throughout the day. I picked Sharon up at her place. The Shovelhead was running smooth. However, when we started to leave, the bike just wouldn't start. I mean, would not start for *anything*.

I kicked and kicked. I tried all the tricks . . . nothing.

I cursed and threw my gloves. Then I kicked some more . . . nothing.

I cursed and threw my cap. Kicked some more . . . still nothing.

I must have tried for 15 minutes. I was *kicked out . . . exhausted.*

The whole time Sharon sat patiently nearby. She let me go on and on without offering a word of advice. This was a good thing, given my state of mind.

Finally, I calmed down. I got all my stuff back together, and motioned to Sharon to come over. My face was set in a look of complete resignation. Then I pumped the throttle and hit the button for the electric start.

Shiloh started right up.

Sharon looked at me for a minute, and then, over the engine noise said, "You mean there was an electric starter that you could have used this whole time?"

"Right . . ."

She didn't say anything as she got on the bike.

I think at that moment Sharon had a full and complete understanding of the biker's mindset.

Sharon and I were married in Carson City, Nevada, in 1984. It was a small ceremony, officiated by the Justice of the Peace. We just bought our first house a week before, so the wedding had to be a low-budget affair.

We had a blast that weekend. My brother, Bill and Sharon's best friend, Pat Cavanaugh stood up for us. Bill's wife Tonee and my sister Nancy were there from my side of the family. Some of the club guys lived too far away to make it, but Dennis, Bear, Matt, and Frank all showed up.

We bought a pair of simple gold wedding bands from a local pawnshop. Besides being poor, we selected that option because of the circle of life that the rings represented. Sharon believes in past lives, and I guess I do, too. It seemed fitting to use the band set that may not have worked out for another couple and make them our own. We thought those rings were waiting there just for us.

The judge held the ceremony in his courtroom. Most of our friends and family were in the jury box. I was in the defendant's chair . . . (just kidding). Sharon and I were each given a life sentence and, so far, she hasn't asked for any clemency. I'm not sure if that's a virtue or a fault.

We moved to our new house in a small town in the San Joaquin Valley. I had gotten to the country at last.

Sharon and I often refer to movie dialogues, especially when the lines sum up certain situations perfectly. One of those lines comes from the movie, *Back to the Future* which was popular shortly after we married. In that film, Marty McFly's dad, George, gets tongue-tied when he tries to sweet talk the girl he pines for . . . remember?

"Lorraine, I am your density . . . uhh, I mean . . . your destiny."

That's how it seems with Sharon and me. We complement each other well. The qualities I lack, she has in abundance. Those areas in which she comes up a bit short, I have covered. We laugh at the same things. We like the same music. We are each other's favorite person to talk with.

From the beginning, it has felt as if we were meant for one another. We are soul mates, and, most importantly, we haven't grown apart over the last three decades. She is mi amor . . . mi corazon.

I don't know if that's destiny or density . . . but she surely is a righteous old lady.

☙ *Chapter Twenty-Five* ☙

"After Lords"

"Now the years are rollin' by me, they are rockin' evenly
And I am older than I once was, but younger than I'll be
That's not unusual.
No it isn't strange, after changes upon changes
We are more or less the same
After changes, we are more or less the same."

Paul Simon, "The Boxer"

My father Bob Norman lived until 1992. He was in the care facility for 16 years before succumbing to a heart attack. Dad drank and smoked heavily for nearly five decades and still made it to age 76. I saw Dad for the last time about a year before his death. Nothing much had changed. He still refused any speech or physical therapy, and still didn't want to spend much time with me.

Dad was a smart and respected man who was derailed by alcohol. There was a lot to like about my dad, but he also came with a lot of flaws. Bear and I used to have discussions on alcoholism. Bear took the common medical approach that it is a disease, and people who are alcoholics can't help it. I held the more politically incorrect view that alcoholism is a weakness. Still do. Regardless, my dad died broke and alone, with no dreams. That is a sad thing.

My Uncles Paul, John, and Maurice all died within a few years of one another in the late 1990's. Fortunately, we had a large family reunion of the Normans in 1995 in the tiny town in southeastern Missouri where my dad and all his siblings grew up. There were relatives from all over the country at the reunion, and the brothers sincerely appreciated the turnout. I especially miss my Uncle John.

My mom Anne eventually married for a third time. His name was Frank Cole. He was from Wisconsin and was older than Mom was. Frank was a super guy, a champion trap shooter who had known and gone shooting with Gary Cooper and Clark Gable years before. Frank followed baseball all his life, and had seen all the famous players come through Chicago and Milwaukee, dating back to the 1920's. He had some wonderful stories.

Frank passed away some years back, and now Mom is back to living alone in the beautiful Gold Country of the California Sierras. Mom has five grandchildren and three great-grandchildren and still plays her piano every day. Not one of Mom's four kids has been divorced, or been to jail, or suffered a tragedy in their lives. Each child has graduated college and has made it to age 50, at least . . . not a bad record in this day and age.

My sister Embry married her college sweetheart, Craig. He's a civil engineer who builds gas pipelines and such and is a math whiz. They tend to move around a lot. Craig and Embry have two grown daughters, Erin and Megan, who are now married and have kids of their own. They were born during the club days, and I've watched them grow into beautiful young women.

Brother William married a woman named Tonee, and they have one son, Zachary. They live in Marin County, California, on a small horse ranch. Bill started out as an aircraft mechanic and later worked his way up into management. Bill has been an airline executive for many years. He is currently working in China for a few years running an aircraft maintenance company. Bill, Tonee, and Zach are all quite musical, and play and sing in various bands and jams throughout the Northern California region.

My sister Nancy lives and works in the Sacramento Valley. She ended up marrying a local guy from the town where she has lived for many years. Her husband, Steve, runs a car dealership and loves to golf. He and Nancy live quietly outside of town in a country place that is surrounded by kiwi and walnut orchards. They have no children. Nancy is one of those people who seemingly can do anything. She can run a computer system, re-shingle a house, create intricate needlepoint designs, and operate and rebuild a farm tractor.

The San Jose Police Department doesn't seem to have changed much from the old days. In 2005, the City of San Jose lost a lawsuit to the San Jose *Hells Angels*. The ordered judgment was nearly one million dollars.

The *Angels* filed the lawsuit against the San Jose PD for unlawful search and seizure during police raids in 1998. These were conducted at the *Angels'* San Jose Clubhouse and at some of the San Jose members' homes. The police confiscated and damaged truckloads of personal property and also shot and killed numerous dogs belonging to the *Angels*.

The *Hells Angels* sued and won their case in Circuit Court. The City of San Jose appealed all the way to the U.S. Supreme Court, but that body refused to hear the case, so the initial judgment stood. I'll bet the city officials weren't too thrilled about being forced to pay the *Hells Angels* a million bucks.

Then, in a Rodney King like moment, four San Jose officers were videotaped beating and tasering a San Jose State University student in his dorm room in 2009. I don't know the outcome of that incident, but I do know it would have been nice to have had cell phone cameras in the 1970's.

Ron Roloff continued to be the point man for the MMA's lobbying efforts for many years. In 1991, despite the best efforts of Ron and the entire MMA, California passed a mandatory helmet law, which exists to this day. In a further irony, many states that had mandatory helmet laws in the 1970's have since rolled back that requirement, at least partially.

A few months later, in a tragic turn of events, Ron was shot and killed in his home by his teen-aged son, in some sort of domestic dispute. It was difficult to imagine the red-haired toddler I first met years before growing up to gun down his dad in the family household. The boy was sentenced to 30 years' prison time for the crime.

I rode my bike from my home in Stanislaus County for Ron's funeral. I signed the register as representing all the former *Wheel Lords*. I saw a few familiar faces from the old days there, but I didn't mix too much. True to his word, Ron's close friends had one song looped for continuous play during the entire funeral service. It was *My Way* by Elvis Presley. Just like Ron would have wanted it.

Marty Carpenter, our friend and past MMA President, became one of my very best friends. Marty took up golf, and we played many rounds together. Marty suffered a serious back injury at his job site, which eventually curtailed his playing the game.

Unfortunately, Martin was a lifelong heavy smoker. In 2000, he was diagnosed with inoperable lung cancer, and was given no more than six months to live. Stubborn, like always, Marty lived until 2010. He even started his own small accounting business, which he ran until nearly the end of his life. Marty was a true friend, and a good-hearted man. I sure miss him.

Don Lundberg, our older biker friend who did so much for the MMA, later became MMA president. Don passed away from cancer in 1991.Don was a great friend and mentor to all of us in the *Wheel Lords*. I'll never forget him.

Scott Catton, Rocky's old friend, ended up as a prospect for the *Hells Angels*. He made member years ago; and, last I heard, he was president of one of the California chapters of the *Angels*.

Lyle Grisham and Tom Damatto of the San Jose *Angels* were named as some of the plaintiffs in the *Hells Angels* lawsuit against the City of San Jose a few years back. They at least made it into the new century.

I don't know what happened to some of my other favorite guys from the *Angels*—guys like Wolf and Filthy Gilbert, for instance. I hope they are still around and kicking—and riding.

Choctaw from the Oakland *Hells Angels* was tried and convicted of drug trafficking in the late 1980's, and was sentenced to a long prison term. He was one of the many *Angels* who were convicted from evidence gathered from a highly placed *Hells Angel*. The *Angel* turned FBI informant, while still a member in their club. This informant operated undercover for years. He later put out a book detailing his exploits. To think that the *Angels* used to lecture *us* about our club's security procedures. At any rate, I heard Choctaw is out of prison now, and I'm happy for him.

I saw Doug Jones of the San Jose *Red and White* a few times after our Club folded. We even played golf a couple of times, although I liked to play faster than Doug, so I was always trying to hurry him along. Hanging around with Doug was always fun and educational. Doug passed away in the early 1990's, from a heart attack, I think.

Davey Racer from the Daly City *Angels* was still around as of a few years ago, from what I've heard. If he is still riding a motorcycle today, I'll bet he hasn't stopped popping wheelies.

My buddy Brad Loxley of the San Jose *Angels* died some years ago, I was told. I don't know the circumstances or the time frame of his death. I do know that the world lost a sizeable chunk of its humor the day Loxley passed away.

I haven't seen or heard anything about many of the original ten *Wheel Lords* since back in the club days. I did run into Miller "Tank" Mahone in San Jose once, and we shared some laughs and memories. However, that was decades ago. I don't know what happened to John Howell Fowler or Bret "Angel" Hayes. I was told that Howie Heath eventually moved to the southwestern desert and joined another bike club.

Keith Wilcox, our giant-sized first Sergeant at Arms, died some years ago. I never heard any of the details of his death. Keith was a funny and unique character who invented a lot of his own vocabulary.

Phil "Old Man" Early moved away from San Jose and lived for many years in the Pacific Northwest near his old riding buddy Lucas from our club. Phil and Lucas were tight friends for four decades. I hadn't seen Phil in years, but we'd talk on the phone sometimes. Phil had some heart problems but lived into his sixties and still had his motorcycle. Phil, sometimes known as "Wrinkles", died from a heart attack in 2010.

As for the guys who were *Wheel Lords* only briefly, I don't know what happened to Jason Hood, Rollin Pickett, or Leo Hernandez. I understand that Jason and Rollin are still friends. Lenny "Snatch" McLaws was killed many years ago in a drug robbery in his home, in San Jose. Kenny Hampton died a few years ago in his native Texas. His riding buddy, Timmy Stuart, still lives there, from what I hear.

My knowledge is a little hit-and-miss for the guys who were solid club members but didn't stay in the *Wheel Lords* until the wheels fell off. "Fast" Frank Dinkins spent a long stretch in prison for committing a serious crime in the 1980's. He's on the outside now, and is doing well. It's been good to re-connect with Frank after all these years. I was told that Mitch "Sleaze" Moss passed away some years ago, but I don't know the circumstances. Sleaze was probably pulling outrageous stunts until the very end. I have been in contact with Matt Bartlett recently. He and Rocky talk sometimes. Matt is married and has kids. He runs a successful small business near Sacramento.

As to my *Wheel Lord* Brothers who stayed with me until the wheels fell off, a few have passed away, and the rest are spread out across the country.

"Doctor" Dennis Kempton married and divorced a couple of times over the years. Dennis kept up his martial arts, and for years had his own studio, where he and his son would train others in those skills. Dennis lived in the Philippines for some time, but last time we spoke, he was back in San Jose. I think both of Dennis's kids live close by. Dennis is still friends with some people from the old days who remained in the San Jose area. We talk on the phone now and then but haven't seen each other for years. Dennis remains the same even-keeled guy he always was.

Benjamin "Bear" Pender lived in the Chico area north of Sacramento until his death from heart failure in 2007. Bear and his wife, Kate split up after spending many years together. They had one daughter. Bear also had a son from his previous marriage to Shirley. Ben continued in the gambling tradition that he loved. He became a well-regarded poker player throughout the region. Bear had all kinds of varied interests until the end of his life, but I don't think riding a motorcycle was one of them. Bear was always the life of the party wherever he went . . . what a character.

Sometime after the *Wheel Lords* folded, Lucas "Weasel" Rodes became a prospect for the San Jose *Hells Angels*. Doug Jones was his sponsor, but Lucas didn't make it to full member. A few years later, Lucas moved to Oregon and became a farmer. He still rides the same scooter he had in the 1970's. Lucas is unmarried, but has a daughter who is in college now. Lucas and I talk on the phone now and then, and we met up at Rocky's place a few years ago. One of these days, I'll finally make the 3,000 mile trip to his place and enjoy the farm air.

Greg "Rocky" Gordon has lived all over the nation since the *Wheel Lords* days. Rocky has resided for some time now in North Carolina, where he works in an electronics company. Greg has been married and divorced a few times over the years. Besides two sons from his first marriage, Greg has a daughter and a stepson. Rocky is still a motorcycle man. He has three bikes now, including one he built up for his wife, Tara. Greg's dad retired from cycle riding and gave Rocky his full-dress Harley. Last time I was at Rocky's place, we went for a ride through the Carolina Piedmont—Rocky on the dresser and me riding his 90-inch screamer of a chopper. That was a bitchin' time. Rocky seems to know all the bikers in an area no matter where he lives. He gets around a lot. Rocky has even started up a memorial website to those *Wheel Lords* who have died.

Drew "Satan" Hilliard, my best friend in the club, had some tough times after Sharon and I moved away from San Jose. Drew stopped riding, stopped hanging out with bikers, and abandoned his go-fast lifestyle. Drew had always been driven to excel in the club days, but in later years, he seemed to have lost his edge. Drew started gaining weight, and eventually weighed over 350 pounds. Drew kept up his drug and alcohol intake, though, and his health began to fail. He had trouble keeping a good job, and he began to have financial problems.

I helped Drew get a job at the company where I worked, and he did okay there, but his lifestyle was still steadily deteriorating. It was hard to watch a guy who had been such an upbeat and hard-charging person only a decade earlier as he spiraled into a broken life. Drew didn't seem to want to improve his situation, and appeared resigned to a cruel fate. I last saw Drew when Sharon and I visited him in San Jose. He was living downtown in a simple rooming house. He had no car, or any visible means of support. Drew had recently re-connected with his daughter, and he was excited about that. He was drinking way too much, and not taking care of himself physically, but he wasn't about to change.

The Kris Kristofferson song *The Pilgrim* seemed to have been written to fit "Satan." Like that tune, Drew was "...a walking contradiction, partly truth and partly fiction." He seemed to have ". . . traded in tomorrow for today."

I found out later that Drew's health finally gave out in 2002. He was admitted to San Jose Hospital, dying there alone, only a few days later.

I prefer to remember Drew as he was when I first met him in 1970, and to recall all the fun times and great experiences we went through together in the *Wheel Lords*. Drew was one of those guys who was never meant to—and *never wanted* to—grow old.

As for my later years, it's been a quiet life. Sharon and I have two children. Rachel Elyse was born in 1989, and Ryland Clay in 1994. They are each healthy, smart, and funny—so we have been truly blessed.

Rae is going to college and holds down a good job, too. She probably takes after my personality a bit more than she does her mother. Rae is strikingly pretty and has the poise and charm to complement her outward beauty. Those qualities certainly did not come from me. Rachel is also quite comfortable being in the public eye.

Ry is in high school. His personality is more like that of Sharon. He is more extroverted, and more of a social networker than his sister. Ry has a cutting sense of humor, which can sometimes work to his advantage, and at other times can become a hindrance. Ryland is a talented athlete and likes computer games.

Like most parents in today's world, we try to give our kids many of the things we never had. Times were decidedly different for many of us growing up in the 1970's. When I grew up, all of the kids in the family moved out of the house shortly after high school. That was what our Mom expected of us. My sisters went away to college, my brother joined the Navy, and I moved out to an apartment in San Jose.

It was the same situation for all of the young guys in the *Wheel Lords*, and for Sharon too, for that matter. The social expectations for middle class or poor kids back then were that you moved out and struggled on your own. It's different today—not that it's better or worse—just different.

We have tried to instill in our children a sense of appreciation for the advantages that they have, and I think our kids do have that perspective. Parents have probably been saying that forever. I'm glad that our kids have things better than we did at their age. Still, there is something to be said for having to live out on your own first on the poor side of town.

My kids can't conceive of a world without the technological advances that are commonplace today. When Sharon and I tell the kids some of the stories of our early days together, they can't fathom how we managed to get through daily life in the "dark ages."

I asked them, "You mean, how did we survive without cell phones, computers, and voice mail . . . without e-mail, iPods, and iPads? What did we do before there was Facebook, MySpace, tweets, and Twitters? How did we get by with no texting, YouTube, or Google . . . with no Bluetooth or Blackberry, or no Skype, Garmins, or OnStar? How did we get along without VH1, ESPN, MTV, HDTV, PSP, or Xbox, or no flat screens, scanners, or transponders?"

How did we manage in life without all those things?

It was easy, really.

We did shit on time.

278

Our family moved to Florida in 1996 because of a job opportunity I had been offered. Parenting and family time, along with working for a living, have taken up the majority of my time over the last few decades.

I have had a few other interests, though. I did a lot of Civil War reenacting, on both the east and west coasts and other places in between, for quite a few years. That was big-time fun, and educational, too. I met loads of talented and dedicated people in the reenacting community. Before you ask which side I was on, let me just say . . . Southern rights at all hazards.

Over the years, I had come and gone from quite a few colleges. In fact, I claim an unofficial record of sorts. I attended college in five consecutive decades without obtaining a four-year degree. I finally put an end to that streak when I went back to college (my sixth one) and earned a Bachelor of Arts diploma in 2006. It was also cool to have a student discount card and an AARP discount card at the same time.

I still have my same motorcycle, although I ride infrequently. Nowadays I'm more like the "weekend warriors" that we used to make fun of back in the club days. I'm not much of a biker anymore, but the mindset stays with you always.

Now for the significant, "technical" stuff, that only some will care about. My bike, Shiloh, is "old style." She's still a 74-inch early Shovelhead, and *not* one of the large 90-inch plus bikes that are out today. In fact, I know little about any Harley Davidson motorcycle built after 1980.

My scoot has a rigid Paughco wishbone frame with three and a half gallon fat bob tanks. It's painted gray, with black and sky blue trim, with buckhorn style handlebars. It has a four-over wide glide front end with a single disc brake . . . belt drive primary with rear chain. I run a king and queen seat with a short sissy bar, and no speedo or turn signals. The motor has 30 over barrels with an H cam and an S and S carburetor . . . nothing fancy, just a throwback looking cruiser.

One concession I do make to old age . . . I use the electric starter most of the time.

Sharon and my daughter, Rachel, like to ride on the bike, but my son Ryland has not yet shown any interest in motorcycles. That's his choice. Perhaps someday he will change his mind and get into choppers, as I did out of the blue one day in 1970.

When I do ride my bike these days, I can't help but think back to the decade of the 70's and of all the people I knew back then.

One of my family's favorite films is Rob Reiner's *Stand by Me*, based upon a novella written by Stephen King. It is a coming of age story about four young boys in rural America, told through the narration of one of the boys—now fully grown.

At the end of the film, the narrator, seeing his own young son playing with his buddy, writes, "I never had any friends later on like the ones I had when I was twelve. Jesus, does anyone?"

I know exactly what the narrator of that story means. I've had tremendous friends in life, but I never had any friends quite like the brothers I had in the *Wheel Lords* Motorcycle Club.

Jeez . . . how could anyone?

"Well those drifter's days are past me now
I've got so much more to think about
Deadlines and commitments
What to leave in, what to leave out
Against the wind
I'm still runnin' against the wind
I'm older now but still runnin'
Against the wind."
Bob Seger,   "Against the Wind"

THE END

❧ Acknowledgments ❧

A number of people provided assistance to me in the production of this book. I would like to thank them for their efforts. Thank you to Bob Baggett, for his expertise in restoring old photographs. Thanks so much to Kim McPeek, Candace Westman, Cesar Lopez, and Susie Paul, for sharing their technical know-how.

A big thank you goes to Terry Mulligan, for all her invaluable help and hard work.

Thank you to Dr. Ruth Banes, a wonderful professor, for her enthusiasm and encouragement to prompt me to write.

Thanks also to Michael LaRocca, who provided valued feedback and incisive comments.

Many thanks to Don and Kathie McGuire at Brighton Publishing, for believing in me and in the story that I wanted to tell.

Special thanks to Mike Wilson, a writer and editor at the St. Petersburg Times, and to Pulitzer Prize winning journalist Lane DeGregory, also of the Times, for the help and guidance they have freely given to many aspiring writers in Florida.

Extra thanks to Nancy Rubie, for her hard work in reviewing the manuscript narrative. Without her, the story could have become redundant . . . and repetitive . . . and go on and on . . . . etcetera, etc.

Finally, to Sherry Two-Names, who for thirty years has been there to encourage, critique, and inspire . . . can't wait to work on the next chapter.

The Author and Shiloh

About the Author

Robert Clay Norman, a fourth generation Californian, traces his American ancestry back nearly four hundred years. Robert holds a Bachelor of Arts degree in American Studies from the University of South Florida. Robert has owned the same Harley Davidson motorcycle for over thirty years, and was a chopper rider in Northern California for much of that time. He likes classic cars of the 50's and 60's, classic cinema, old time rock n roll, and any movie featuring Lee Marvin. Robert has an affinity for U.S. military history in general, and Civil War soldiers in particular. Bob maintains a close devotion to homemade milkshakes, Southern biscuits and gravy, Asian cooking, and Mexican beer. His favorite color is plaid. Favorite authors include David McCullough, Joseph Ellis, and William Davis. Robert now lives and works in Tampa Bay, Florida, with his wife, daughter, and son. Other residents of the property include two cats, a dog, four feral cats, Blake the opossum, Magil the raccoon, and an armadillo named Barbarosa.

Visit the author at:
robertclaynorman.com or untilthewheelsfalloff.net

CPSIA information can be obtained at www.ICGtesting.com
Printed in the USA
LVOW071330290812

296490LV00003B/240/P